Baron Delvig's *Northern Flowers*
(1825-1832)

Baron Delvig's

Northern Flowers

1825-1832

LITERARY ALMANAC
of the
PUSHKIN PLEIAD

John Mersereau, Jr.

Carbondale and Edwardsville

SOUTHERN ILLINOIS UNIVERSITY PRESS

FEFFER & SIMONS, INC.

London and Amsterdam

PREFACE

This book was conceived several years ago at the time I began to devote myself to the study of Russian Romanticism. My research has been supported by several grants, including fellowships for summer research from the Horace H. Rackham School of Graduate Studies of the University of Michigan and the University of Michigan's Center for Russian Studies. I should also like to thank Professor Assya Humesky of the Department of Slavic Languages and Literatures of the University of Michigan for the careful reading she gave the chapter on poetry and for the suggestions and corrections she offered. I am particularly grateful to Mr. Vernon Sternberg and the Southern Illinois University Press for publishing this rather specialized work. My thanks and admiration go also to Elizabeth B. Kenyon of the Southern Illinois University Press for her prodigious efforts in scrutinizing the manuscript. Finally, I gratefully acknowledge the kind permission given by the publishers of *The Slavonic & East European Review* to reprint, with minor variations, material which had appeared in the June, 1965, issue of that journal in my essay "Orest Somov: An Introduction."

John Mersereau, Jr.

Ann Arbor, Michigan
December 1, 1966

CONTENTS

Baron Delvig's *Northern Flowers*
(1825-1832)

Chapter I

Introduction to the Period: 1825-1832

It would be difficult to insist that any eight-year period was more critical in the history of Russian literature than some other arbitrarily designated span of equivalent duration. Yet there is no question that the particular eight years which coincided with the publication of *Northern Flowers* (1825–32) witnessed unusual developments in Russian lettres. Some of these were conditioned by socio-political factors, others occurred as a result of literary determinism, and some were simply the inexplicable product of genius. But however one wishes to characterize or explain what happened during those eight years, his inevitable conclusion will be that this period lies right in the center of that very brief literary adolescence which links the derivative and imitative Russian literature of the eighteenth and early nineteenth centuries with the full maturity of the second half of the nineteenth century.

Political events of these eight years had a critical effect upon Russian lettres. The year 1825 saw the death of Alexander I and the rapid suppression of the December Revolution by his successor, Nicholas I. As a result of that abortive uprising, a number of important writers, including Alexander Bestuzhev (Marlinsky), Wilhelm Küchelbecker, and A. I. Odoevsky were exiled, and Kondraty Ryleev was permanently silenced. Unquestionably, memories of the December Revolution and its victims hung as a dark cloud over Russian life for the next quarter of a century. But its real effects can hardly be assessed, because of the total prohibition regarding reference to the event. Other political developments found a clearer reflection in the literature of the period, and often they had a direct effect upon the personal lives of Russian writers.

In 1826 the war with Persia was concluded with a treaty unacceptable to many of the vanquished, with the result that in 1829 a mob massacred the Russian mission in Teheran, among them Alexander Griboedov. The Russo-Turkish war of 1828–29 peripherally involved Pushkin, who took French leave to visit the front, subsequently chronicling his experiences in *A Journey to Erzerum*. The July Revolution in France had great significance for liberal circles in Russia, and, owing to the proscription against any mention of the event, it became the subject of their "literature of allusion"; it also sent to Russia George d'Anthès, who seven years later was to slay Pushkin. The Polish Insurrection of 1830–31 was richly reflected in Russian literature at the time and ultimately became one of its permanent themes. In 1832 the official doctrine of "Orthodoxy, Autocracy, and Nationality" was proclaimed, and it would not be too drastic to say that from that time until the Revolution of 1917 almost every major piece of Russian literature to some extent revealed a reaction to this doctrine. And it was this immediate post-Decembrist period that witnessed the birth of the intelligentsia within the various philosophical circles of Moscow, where, in the early thirties, a brain trust of young writers and thinkers gathered, including Nikolay Stankevich, Vissarion Belinsky, Alexander Herzen, Nikolay Ogaryov, Mikhail Bakunin, Vasily Botkin, Ivan Turgenev, and others.[1]

In the area of literary publications, the period 1825–32 was one of intense activity. In 1825 Polevoy started issuing his *Moscow Telegraph*, and Bulgarin initiated *Northern Bee*. In 1827 Pogodin founded the *Moscow Herald* and Voyeykov the *Slav*. Delvig's *Literary Gazette* appeared in 1830, Nadezhdin's *Telescope* was started in 1831, the same year that Voyeykov started publishing *Literary Supplement to the Rus-*

sian Invalid and Aladin initiated his short-lived *Saint Peters-burg Messenger*. In 1832 the *European*, edited by Ivan Kireevsky, was born—and died with its second number. And there were, as well, even other new literary ventures.

Literary almanacs flourished, despite the fact that 1825 marked the final issue of Ryleev's and Bestuzhev's *Polar Star* and Küchelbecker's and Odoevsky's *Mnemosyne*. The *Neva Almanac* appeared regularly throughout the period, which saw, at a conservative estimate, around ninety separate almanacs issued, most of the titles appearing only for one year.

In these particular eight years all of *Eugene Onegin* was published, not to mention many other of Pushkin's major works. But poetry was rapidly losing ground to prose, and after 1830 prose dominated the literary scene. In 1831 was composed a brief poem "The Angel," the work of the then unknown poet, Mikhail Lermontov, who within a decade was to create the first modern Russian novel of psychological realism. The same year another unknown, Nikolay Gogol, made his formal literary debut with *Evenings on a Farm Near Dikanka*. And concurrently appeared Pushkin's *Belkin Tales*, which, although ignored at the time, was to have a heavy influence upon later Russian authors.

But while new figures were appearing on the literary stage, old ones were leaving it. Vasily Narezhny, one of the very few significant figures in Russian prose from around 1810 until the mid-twenties, died in 1825. The following year Nikolay Karamzin died and Kondraty Ryleev was hanged. Griboedov perished in 1829, and in 1830 two poets of the older generation, Vasily Pushkin and Professor Alexey Merzlyakov, passed on. In 1831 Russian literature lost the fabulist Alexander Izmailov and Baron Delvig, editor of *Northern Flowers*. Two years later Orest Somov, a prose precursor of Gogol, critic, and Delvig's right-hand man on *Northern Flowers* and the *Literary Gazette*, died.

Literary criticism, too, may be said to have reached the threshold of maturity during this period. Systematic surveys of each year's literary product, which had been initiated in 1823 by Bestuzhev in *Polar Star*, were continued by Orest Somov in *Northern Flowers*. In 1830 Ivan Kireevsky, from the pages of *Dawn,* also contributed to the tradition. In the early twenties the provocative essays of Somov, Prince Vyazemsky, Küchelbecker, and Ryleev stimulated vigorous controversies regarding the quality of Russian literature and its proper future. Pushkin, too, contributed his own evaluations of the domestic literary product and provided additional interpretations of "true" Romanticism, Classicism, and *narodnost.*[2] The critic Nikolay Nadezhdin was also active, preparing the ground for his brilliant collaborator-to-be, Vissarion Belinsky, who was to make his grand entrance as a critic in 1834.

Literature and criticism in this period also had their dark sides: too frequently they were utilized for polemics which became little more than vicious personal attacks. Faddey Bulgarin, who had enjoyed a measure of respect in literary circles throughout most of the twenties, at the end of the decade defined himself as a particularly noxious opponent of the writer-aristocrats, who also felt the wrath of Polevoy and other so-called bourgeois authors. Periodicals were filled with epigrams, satirical epistles, lampoons, and heavily biased critical evaluations, some of which even led to complaints and denunciations to the authorities.

Thus, the years which saw the publication of *Northern Flowers* were ones of intense activity on the literary front. Russian literature was preparing itself for the enormous and rather incredible step forward which carried it within two decades from relative obscurity on the world literary scene to a position of full competition with the literatures of Western Europe. *Northern Flowers,* as the best almanac of its period, was at the center of this development. To study it is to gain a further insight into the developments of these critical years, for its pages of prose, poetry, and criticism represent a combination of the best of the old tradition with the seeds, shoots, and vigorous young growth which matured to the abundant literary harvest of the mid-century and later.

Chapter II

History of *Northern Flowers*

Establishment and Early Years

The literary almanac, an annual collection or anthology of belles-lettres, originated in France with the *Almanach des Muses*, published in Paris from 1765 to 1833. Immediately imitated, this almanac served as a model for the German *Musenalmanach*, first appearing in 1769. The history of Russian literary almanacs begins in 1787, in which year the students of the Gentry Pension (preparatory boarding school) attached to the University of Moscow published their *Blossoming Flower* [*Raspuskajuščijsja Cvetok*], primarily a collection of edifying compositions and translations, which was followed two years later by a similar almanac entitled *A Useful Exercise for Youth* [*Poleznoe Upražnenie Junošestva*]. In 1800 the same group resumed their publication efforts with *Dawn* [*Utrennjaja Zarja*], which for the next several years appeared annually under that title or *Useful Leisure* [*I Otdyx v Pol'zu*]. It was in *Dawn* that Vasily Zhukovsky made his debut in print.

The first strictly commercial almanacs were established by Nikolay Karamzin. His *Aglaya* [*Aglaja*], consisting largely of his own early sentimental works, appeared in 1794 and 1795 and was followed in 1796, 1797, and 1799 by *Aonides* [*Aonidy*], which included original Russian poetry of Kheraskov, Derzhavin, Kapnist, and others and also translations of Homer, Ossian, Gessner, La Fontaine, and Voltaire. In 1798

7

Karamzin presented his *Pantheon of Foreign Literature* [*Panteon Inostrannoj Slovenosti*], a collection of translated poetry and prose ranging from Saadi to Franklin.

Following the turn of the century, almost every year witnessed the appearance of at least one new almanac. From 1800 to 1822 several dozen important ones were published, but only three titles appeared in subsequent years. The contents and intended audiences varied considerably: some consisted exclusively of prose or poetry, while others combined them; some were intended for children or soldiers—others were aimed at the literate adult.

The year 1823 was marked by a significant development in the history of the Russian literary almanac. That year saw the establishment of *Polar Star* [*Poljarnaja Zvezda*], which in the next three years was widely imitated. In 1824 three important new almanacs appeared, including *Mnemosyne* [*Mnemozina*], and in 1825 eight were published, among them *Northern Flowers* [*Severnye Cvety*], *Moscow Almanac for the Fair Sex* [*Moskovskij Al'manax dlja Prekrasnogo Pola*] (1825–30), and *Neva Almanac* [*Nevskij Al'manax*], the last appearing yearly until 1833 and again in 1846–47. Firmly established as a popular type of publication by 1825, almanacs thenceforth appeared in increasing numbers: from 1829 through 1832 over fifteen appeared annually. After 1832 until the middle of the century around half a dozen new almanacs appeared yearly. Most almanacs were issued but once; the *Neva Almanac* and *Northern Flowers* were the exceptions, both appearing annually for far longer periods than their competitors.

Polar Star, which established the pattern for the "modern" literary almanac, was in reality a constellation of the very best contemporary authors, and its collaborators included Zhukovsky, Batyushkov, Vyazemsky, Baratynsky, Gnedich, Delvig, Kozlov, Somov, Griboedov, and Pushkin. Alexander Bestuzhev (Marlinsky) and Kondraty Ryleev, its editors, also contributed their own works, particularly Bestuzhev, who presented a number of prose tales and essays on Russian literature. Owing to the involvement of the editors in the December Revolution of 1825, a partially printed issue for 1826, which bore the modified title of *Little Star* [*Zvezdočka*] due to its reduced size, was confiscated and remained suppressed until 1861. The three issues of *Polar Star* which did appear established standards and patterns not only for that type of literary publication but also for literary journals in general. Bestuzhev's annual surveys of Russian literature, though weakened by the naïveté of his literary opinions, were nonetheless a significant attempt at a systematic critical approach to contemporary literature, and their author's constant plea for purification of Russian prose, coupled with his admonitions to authors who exhibited a careless style, doubtless had a beneficial effect upon the development of the literary language. Other almanacs, notably *Northern Flowers*, continued the tradition initiated by Bestuzhev's critical surveys, as did a number of literary journals. The quality of *Polar Star*'s prose, and more particularly that of its poetry, was unusually high, and very few later periodicals ever provided such a consistent array of first-class contributors.

Fifteen hundred copies of *Polar Star for 1824* were printed; these were sold out within three weeks. Paradoxically, it was this unprecedented success which was largely responsible for the establishment of the rival *Northern Flowers* and the subsequent difficulties of *Polar Star* itself. The first two issues of *Polar Star* had been published by the bookseller and publisher Ivan Slyonin, whose interests were primarily commercial. In projecting their third issue, Bestuzhev and Ryleev resolved to pay their contributors, a procedure which was at that time quite unusual. Slyonin was opposed to this, since it would reduce his profit. Accordingly, he determined to withdraw from the *Polar Star* venture and start a competing almanac whose contributors would not be paid, thus providing him a greater return on his investment. As editor of his projected publication he selected Baron Anton Delvig, a poet who enjoyed excellent relations with many of the foremost authors of the time. For a consideration of four thousand rubles, Delvig was to collect material and edit this new almanac.[1] Delvig immediately made known to Ryleev his intention to accept Slyonin's proposal, and, at least initially, Ryleev voiced no opposition.[2] However, Bestuzhev saw the implications of Slyonin's plan, and on March 23, 1824, he wrote to Ya. N. Tolstoy voicing his dissatisfaction.

> In 1825 Mr. Slyonin and Delvig will publish "Northern Flowers," exactly the same as our *Star*: this is a commercial speculation. They are envious that in three weeks we sold all fifteen hundred copies—their success remains to be seen.[3]

But Bestuzhev also believed that it was not Slyonin alone who was responsible for conceiving the idea of a rival almanac: he suspected that Alexander Voyeykov, editor of *Literary News* [*Novosti Literatury*] and *Russian Invalid* [*Russkij Invalid*], was also involved. Voyeykov was an unprincipled person and was, in fact, under an obligation to the editors of *Polar Star* for their earlier support of him at the time when Faddey Bulgarin and Nikolay Grech, both highly active and influential in literary circles, had conspired to deprive him of a livelihood in the publishing field. This controversy had taken place in September of 1823 when Voyeykov, because of a quarrel, had left Bulgarin's and Grech's periodical, *Son of the Fatherland* [*Syn Otečestva*], to become editor of the *Russian Invalid*, a government publication which was leased to private persons for operation. Bulgarin determined to force Voyeykov out of the *Russian Invalid*, to which end he offered the committee in charge of the journal double the compensation received from Voyeykov. Ryleev considered Bulgarin's action base and told him so,[4] as did Zhukovsky. The pressure of these two, plus the weight of general support from literary circles on Voyeykov's behalf, caused Bulgarin to desist. But Voyeykov, as it turned out, was not worthy of Ryleev's assistance. He had the bad habit, but one common enough in those times, of taking contributions from other periodicals without permission or compensation and reprinting them in his own publication.[5] Therefore, despite the patronage of Ryleev in the affair with Bulgarin, in July, 1824, Voyeykov pirated the beginning of Pushkin's *The Robber Brothers*, a selection which Ryleev and Bestuzhev had intended to publish in the 1825 issue of *Polar Star* and for which they had already received clearance from the censorship. On September 15,

Ryleev and Bestuzhev wrote to Voyeykov breaking off all relations.

> Sir:
>
> You heard from us ourselves that A. Pushkin had given us a poem for *Polar Star*—"The Robbers." In the same way you knew that it had been passed by the censor, and you had the baseness to misuse our confidence, forestalling us by printing the best part of it without the slightest right to do so. We have more than once suffered your thefts from *Polar Star*, but your present action, the result of some idle intrigue to which we have given cause neither by word nor by deed, exceeds the bounds of honor and patience. As a result of this, we respectfully request that you strike us both from your list of acquaintances. Of course, the loss of acquaintance with honorable persons is nothing important or new for you; on the other hand, it will be very profitable for us to become disacquainted with you. We consider it not without purpose to add that in case of a repetition on your part of a similar action we will not, as at present, be satisfied with merely despising you.
>
> 　　　　　　　　　　　Alexander Bestuzhev
> 　　　　　　　　　　　K. Ryleev[6]

Bestuzhev not only suspected Voyeykov of having encouraged Slyonin to start an almanac to compete with *Polar Star*, but he also believed that Voyeykov was seeking to undermine *Polar Star* by encouraging its regular contributors to withdraw their works or curtail their contributions. On September 20, 1824, he wrote to Prince Vyazemsky, enclosing in his letter a copy of the protest, quoted above, written five days previously to Voyeykov.

> Now I am writing to you to unburden my soul, saddened by human baseness, and, along with my complaint, to join my request for literary assistance. From the copy of our letter to Voyeykov you will see what sort of a person

he is; but if you knew the base motives causing him to act, then you would be even more astonished by such despicable envy and human avarice. The plan of "Northern Flowers" was devised by him and not without reason; he says this himself. There is trouble being made for us with Pushkin by means of Lev [Lev Pushkin, the poet's brother]. Verses by him and Kozlov, designated for [*Polar*] *Star*, are being reprinted, and Baratynsky, on the pretext that there had been some misunderstanding, has been instructed to withdraw his notebook [of poetry], which was sold to us long ago. In a word, they are making some sort of flea market out of literature. As a result of this we are, therefore, quite short of verses— rescue us, Prince, and ask Ivan Ivanovich [Kozlov] to do the same. Otherwise, we shall have to postpone publication [of *Polar Star*] until a time more favorable than the present, though we don't want to quit the field without a fight.[7]

That *Polar Star* was indeed losing its contributors to *Northern Flowers* is evident from Bestuzhev's subsequent letter to Vyazemsky of November 3. After thanking Vyazemsky for his concern on behalf of *Polar Star*, he continued,

Both last year and this year Zhukovsky acted differently [than Vyazemsky had acted] with us: he promised mountains and gave a mouse. He gave us "St. John's Eve" and then took it back. And now (to me, I admit, this is the most vexatious thing of all, since I had written to him so sincerely) at the same time that he refused [the request of] my letter, asserting that he had nothing [to contribute], he gave Delvig a new elegy.[8]

The correctness of Bestuzhev's remarks is indicated by the facts: Zhukovsky did contribute his prose "Excerpts from a Letter about Switzerland" to the 1825 edition of *Polar Star*, but he sent no verse. On the other hand, the initial issue of *Northern Flowers* contained four of his poems.

The serious effect on *Polar Star* of *Northern Flowers'* competition is reflected in the fact that the 1825 issue of

Polar Star came out in March, that is, several months later than originally scheduled. It has been stated in several sources that its tardy appearance was because some of the printed portions had been destroyed during the disastrous Petersburg flood of November 7, 1824.[9] This explanation seems unsupported, and, in fact, there appears to be definite indication that *Polar Star* did not suffer from the flood. Pushkin's epigrammatic poem on the occasion would suggest that *Polar Star* had fortuitously survived that catastrophe.

> *In vain did Europe gasp,*
> *Don't be dejected, all is well!*
> Polar Star *has been saved*
> *From the Petersburg flood.*
> *Bestuzhev, your ark is at the shore!*
> *The summits of Parnassus gleam;*
> *And in the beneficent ark*
> *Both people and cattle have been saved.*[10]

The writer and critic Orest Somov, who was involved in editorial work on *Polar Star*,[11] wrote to Ryleev on November 11 reporting the effects of the inundation, but he made no mention of damage to *Polar Star*. He did, however, comment humorously on the flood's damage to *Northern Flowers*. Having noted that the flowers would probably not soon be in bloom, as a consequence of having been soaked in the bulb, he added Bestuzhev's remark that whereas previously the flowers likely had been too dry, they are now too wet.[12] Nonetheless, Delvig's new publication, despite the destruction of some printed portions during the flood, did appear on schedule at the beginning of the year.

A more valid explanation for the tardy publication of *Polar Star* in 1825 was that the editors wished to avoid direct competition with *Northern Flowers* and hence delayed the issue of their almanac until initial interest in Delvig's publication had subsided. That this very procedure had been considered as early as September is indicated by Bestuzhev's letter to Vyazemsky quoted above. His subsequent letter to Vyazemsky, on January 12, 1825, already after the appearance of *Northern Flowers*, provides further evidence that it was not the flood which had caused the postponement of *Polar Star's* publication. In this letter, Bestuzhev again requested contributions from Vyazemsky, obviously having in mind the 1825 edition, and he also noted that the printing of the almanac had already begun.[13] It is unlikely that he would have still been requesting contributions for this issue had it already been in press as early as November of the previous year.

In this same letter Bestuzhev, among other things, questioned Vyazemsky regarding the reception of the first issue of *Northern Flowers*.

> How does *Northern Flowers* seem to you? Here [Petersburg] it is being purchased but not praised—what about where you are [Moscow]? I like Delvig's verses best of all. Zhukovsky has shot his bolt. Krylov now scribbles but doesn't write. Pushkin is not on the track, but the chief shortcoming of the booklet is the complete absence of humor. There is nothing to smile at. Except at the good nature of Pletnyev, who raises his paean of praise to Baratynsky and the like. However, don't think that envy is speaking here—I will say beforehand that our *Star* will not be much better than *Flowers*—we haven't had the cleverness, or the time, or the disposition to improve our almanac. However, what will be, will be, and that will be as God disposes.[14]

The competitive situation existing between the two almanacs is further reflected in the comments of the *Moscow Telegraph* [*Moskovskij Telegraf*] which appeared following the publication of *Northern Flowers for 1825*.

> From many people we have heard what seems to us a quite strange question: "Is *Northern Flowers* better or worse than *Polar Star?*" It is as if it were necessary to measure every literary almanac against *Polar Star* and then to pronounce in tones of a jury, "It is better!" or "It is worse." The real problem is whether it is good or not. It seems to us that *Polar Star* and *Northern Flowers* have their own particular merits, and readers can buy them without further inquiries.[15]

Unquestionably there was a strong rivalry between the two almanacs for contributions from the best writers and poets, and a reflection of this may even be found in the guest list of those who visited Pushkin in 1825 when he was in exile at Mikhailovskoe. In January, I. I. Pushchin, closely associated with Ryleev and Bestuzhev in the conspiratorial activities which led to the December Uprising, visited the poet, and in April Delvig made an appearance. Of course these visits may have been primarily social, since both Pushchin and Delvig had been close to Pushkin at the Tsarskoe Selo lyceum. Ryleev and Bestuzhev also intended such a trip, as is indicated by the former's statement in his letter of March 25, 1825, to Pushkin: "Bestuzhev and I intend to pay a call on you in the summer."[16] Their intentions, however, were not carried out.

Although Bestuzhev did cool somewhat toward Delvig owing to the competition between the two rival almanacs, apparently the friendship between Delvig and Ryleev was unaffected. Writing to Pushkin in April of 1825, Ryleev mentioned that he had heard rumors that Delvig had arrived at Mikhailovskoe, and at the end of his letter he asked Pushkin "to embrace Delvig" for him.[17] In May, Ryleev again wrote to Pushkin, mentioning that Delvig (on his return from Mikhailovskoe) had conveyed to him Pushkin's opinions about his (Ryleev's) "Meditations" and the fragment of the narrative poem *Voynarovsky* which had appeared in *Polar Star*.[18] In October Ryleev wrote a quite friendly letter to Delvig.[19]

By November of 1825 the editors of *Polar Star* had reached a decision to cease publication of their almanac with the issue for 1826. In a letter to Pushkin that month, Ryleev wrote,

> We are again getting up *Polar* [*Star*]. It will be the last, at least we have made that decision. We want to part on good terms with the public, and therefore we ask you to make us a gift of something like your latest gift to us.[20]

Pushkin, who had contributed seven poems to the 1824 edition and three to the one of 1825, obliged by sending one poem.

This pattern was repeated by several of *Polar Star*'s most illustrious contributors: Baratynsky, who had seven poems in
the 1825 almanac, gave but two, and Vyazemsky, despite the
pressure of Bestuzhev's requests, also sent only two works.
Fyodor Glinka and Peter Pletnyev, who had been mainstays
of the almanac, sent nothing. Whether it was that the editors
were too occupied with their professional or political activities[21] to solicit sufficient good material, or whether their
traditional contributors simply withheld their collaboration,
is difficult to say, but the paucity of material made it necessary
to reconsider their publication. The result was that the title
Polar Star was abandoned in favor of one more in keeping
with the limited content of the projected edition, *Little Star*.[22]
The almanac went to press with two prose works and twenty-
four poems, as opposed to the previous editions which had
not less than ten prose selections and an average of well over
fifty poems (fifty-four, sixty-eight, and forty-eight respectively for each of the three years). In scope *Little Star* was to
have been about one-third the size of *Polar Star*.

Little Star was not destined to rise. While it was in press
the December Uprising took place, the almanac's editors were
arrested, and that portion which had been printed was baled
up and stored by the government. In 1861 this printed material was burned, but two incomplete copies were preserved.
On the basis of these and an almost complete censor's manuscript, the almanac has been reconstructed.[23]

Once initiated and then fortuitously freed of the competition provided by *Polar Star, Northern Flowers* prospered.
Slyonin and Delvig continued as publisher and editor, respectively, for the second issue, but they then parted company
and Delvig became both editor and publisher for the third
number. However, the task proved too arduous for the
notoriously lazy poet, and therefore in 1827 he hired Orest
Somov to assist him in preparing *Northern Flowers for 1828*.
Once he had a collaborator, Delvig went to spend the summer
in Revel, leaving the entire project in Somov's hands. In a
letter to Vladimir Izmailov of August, 1827, Somov voiced
his concern at Delvig's insouciance.

> My Delvig went off to Revel and, as is evident, became
> lazy. It's been two months, and I've received only three
> letters from him and nothing at all for our collection.[24]

Somov had reason to be concerned, for the expenses of the
projected issue were unusually high: Pushkin was to be paid
six thousand rubles for *Count Nulin*, and the artist Kiprensky
was owed one thousand rubles for Pushkin's portrait, from
which an engraving was to be made for the forthcoming
volume.

Once Delvig was back in Petersburg, he conveniently
sprained his hand and was even unable to help correct proofs.
Thanks to Somov's efforts the issue was passed by the censor
on December 3, 1827, a month and a half earlier than the
previous issue had been cleared for publication. Writing to
Izmailov in January, 1828, Somov noted that

> everything was left to me, and without my efforts the
> business would have dragged on until Holy Week. Con-
> sequently, half the profit would have been lost, and any-
> one who has expended more than ten thousand on a
> small booklet should certainly give consideration to cover-
> ing this expense.[25]

Somov continued to expedite subsequent numbers of *Northern
Flowers*, all of which received censor's approval by early or
mid-December. This made it possible to have the almanac
with booksellers early enough to capitalize upon a market not
yet flooded with similar publications.

Somov's diligence and Delvig's prestige proved an excellent combination, and the two even found themselves with
sufficient material to publish another almanac for 1829, which
they called *Snowdrop* [*Podsnežnik*].[26] But *Northern Flowers*
retained its prime significance, and on its pages appeared the
best contributions of the era's most outstanding authors. The
issue for 1830 established a record for the longest consecutive
publication of any Russian almanac,[27] and it wasn't until after
the appearance of that number that difficulties were encountered. That year Faddey Bulgarin declared open war

upon Pushkin and Delvig, and this initiated a series of events which had serious consequences for *Northern Flowers*.

The Threat to the Almanac in 1830

It is perhaps paradoxical, but nonetheless true, that the publication of Bulgarin's historical novel, *Dmitry the Pretender*, had a definite effect upon the content of the 1831 edition of Delvig's almanac. The story is involved but of sufficient interest to justify a brief résumé here. When Bulgarin's novel appeared in 1830, Delvig wrote a very negative review which he placed unsigned in the March 7 issue of his *Literary Gazette* [*Literaturnaja Gazeta*]. The humiliated author ascribed the review to Pushkin, and, hoping to pay Pushkin with the same coin, wrote a scathing review of the recently published Chapter VII of *Eugene Onegin*. This review was so unjust that even the Tsar was scandalized, and he requested Benckendorff to prohibit Bulgarin from publishing any more literary criticism. Benckendorff carried out the order, but in his report regarding its fulfilment, he took Bulgarin's part, noting that the review of *Eugene Onegin* contained nothing personal against Pushkin and praising the legitimist tone of *Dmitry the Pretender*. To this Nicholas I replied that from what he had been able to read of Bulgarin's novel he thought the criticism of it which had appeared in *Literary Gazette* had been at least partially just. Then the Tsar, having stated a preference for Pushkin's "noble" works such as *Poltava* over "amusing forms" of literature such as *Onegin*, went on to threaten to proscribe criticism "everywhere" if it were continued in this manner, that is, in the manner of Bulgarin's criticism of *Onegin*.[28]

Meanwhile, Bulgarin had also published in the *Northern Bee* [*Severnaja Pčela*], on March 11, his "Anecdote," where he transparently likened Pushkin's attacks on him to those against Hoffmann by a xenophobic third-rate French poet turned critic. On April 6, Easter Sunday, Pushkin presented to Bulgarin an "Easter egg" in the form of an essay on the recently published volumes by the infamous head of the Paris detectives, François Eugène Vidocq, wherein Pushkin

sketched Bulgarin in Vidocq's portrait.[29] The quarrel continued, with Pushkin writing a scathing epigrammatic verse
against his antagonist

> *The trouble's not that you're a Pole:*
> *Kosciuszko was, Mickiewicz too;*
> *You could even be a Tatar,*
> *And I would see no shame in that,*
> *Or be a Jew—that's not the harm;*
> *The harm is you're Vidocq-Figlyarin.*[30]

Bulgarin was incensed. To lessen the effect of the epigram by
publicly playing the role of victim, and to get Pushkin in
trouble with the authorities for writing malicious personal
attacks, Bulgarin requested and received official approval to
print the poem. However, to make Pushkin's epigram seem
more vicious, he had changed "Vidocq-Figlyarin" to "Faddey
Bulgarin," and this amended version was printed in *Son of the
Fatherland* on April 20.[31] Meanwhile, Bulgarin also published
a snide note in the *Northern Bee* regarding the high price of
Eugene Onegin, which if purchased as the separate chapters
had appeared would have cost more than forty rubles.[32] On
August 7, Bulgarin launched his most poisonous arrow in the
form of his "Second Letter from Karlovo[33] to Kamenny Os-
trov," attacking the collaborators of the *Moscow Herald*
[*Moskovskij Vestnik*] and the *Literary Gazette,* and in
particular Pushkin. Herein was included an anecdote inferring
that Pushkin's Negro ancestor, Abraham Hannibal, far from
being of noble origin, had been purchased by a ship captain
for a bottle of rum. Pushkin responded from the pages of
the *Literary Gazette* on the ninth of August with an unsigned
note, "New Attacks against Our So-called Literary Aristocracy." The same issue contained a note stating that the previously published criticism of Bulgarin's *Dmitry the Pretender*
had not been written by Pushkin, and to this the following
comment was appended.

> It was proposed to A. S. Pushkin that he write a critique
> of the historical novel by Mr. Bulgarin. He refused, say-
> ing: "In order to criticize a book, it is necessary to read
> it, and I do not think I have the strength to do so."[34]

Pushkin subsequently supplemented his reply to Bulgarin's scurrilous allusion to his ancestry with the famous poem, "My Genealogy," which contained a special postcript for Bulgarin.

Meanwhile, "New Attacks against Our So-called Literary Aristocracy" had elicited an unfavorable reaction from Benckendorff, who found in the work, perhaps with Bulgarin's assistance, certain suspicious elements connected with the July Revolution in France. Delvig was called to account and told that he would be held strictly accountable for anything else displeasing to Benckendorff that might appear in the *Literary Gazette*. Two months later, on October 28, Delvig printed a poem by Delavigne about the July Revolution, for which he was rudely reprimanded by Benckendorff and forbidden to continue publishing his periodical. Benckendorff, in his rage, threatened to pack Delvig, Pushkin, and Prince Vyazemsky off to Siberia; he also indicated that Bulgarin had brought the matter to his attention.[35] Delvig wrote to Pushkin announcing the suspension of the *Literary Gazette* and expressing his dismay at the treatment he had received.

> The *Literary Gazette* has produced no profit and, moreover, it has been suppressed because new verses of Delavigne were printed in it. People truly attached to their emperor and who have clear consciences seek nothing and bow to no one, thinking that their truly loyal feelings and conscience will defend them in any case. It is not true. From covetousness wretches now go to the trouble of besmirching honorable people and profit from their vileness. Bulgarin is a true subject. For his libels, which are worthy of exemplary punishment, rewards are solicited for him, while I get the reputation of a Carbonari, I—a Russian, educated by the emperor, the father of a family who expects from the Tsar aid for my mother, my brothers, and sisters.[36]

The tone of this letter indicates the humiliation and chagrin which Delvig experienced. Disenchanted, he seems to have lost virtually all interest in his literary activities, leaving Somov to handle the affairs of *Northern Flowers*.[37] None of Delvig's poetry appeared in the almanac's 1831 edition, a fact which Pushkin, unaware that Delvig was at that moment on his deathbed, noted with irritation in a letter to Pletnyev on January 7, 1831.

> Now, down to business. My dear, I have seen the *Flowers*. A strange thing, an incomprehensible thing![38] Delvig didn't put a single line in it. He has acted with us like a land-owner with his peasants. We work while he sits on the chamber pot and abuses us. It's not right and not wise. . . . Poor Glinka works like a navvy but gets nothing out of it.[39]

Thus the strange circle of events: Bulgarin receives a bad review and lashes back, gets some more blows and becomes really vicious. The matter comes to the attention of the authorities, who are not pleased with the internecine struggle. Subsequently, Bulgarin sees a way to pay off his enemies by inciting Benckendorff against them, with the result that one periodical is suspended and its editor loses interest in his other venture, *Northern Flowers*.

Delvig, of course, was dead within a month of the publication of the 1831 edition of his almanac, which appeared on the twenty-fourth of December. Pushkin's personal conflict with Bulgarin continued until Pushkin published, in the September, 1831 issue of the *Telescope* [*Teleskop*], an outline for a work to be called "the *Real Vyzhigin*," the title alluding to Bulgarin's novel *Ivan Vyzhigin*. The chapter headings referred to certain very irregular episodes in Bulgarin's life which were not generally known to his Russian friends and which he could ill afford to have presented in detail.[40] Apparently Pushkin's threat to expand upon this outline unless Bulgarin ceased attacking him was enough to silence his unusually vociferous enemy, at least temporarily.

The Final Issue

If it is true that the 1831 issue of the almanac would not have appeared had it not been for Somov having assumed the burden of editorship from the apathetic Delvig, it is also certain that the 1832 edition would likely never have been published had it not been for the ceaseless effort of Pushkin. Although Somov carried out many of the editorial duties for the 1832 edition, it was Pushkin, with Pletnyev's assistance, who mustered support for the final issue and who, in Delvig's stead, provided the prestige needed to attract the best contributors.

Immediately upon hearing of Delvig's death in January, 1831, Pushkin wrote to Pletnyev

> Poor Delvig! We will remember him with *Northern Flowers*—but I would not want this to be a loss to Somov —he was sincerely attached to him—and our friend's death is almost a greater loss to him than anyone.[41]

Pletnyev answered on February 22, "You mentioned an edition of *Northern Flowers*. This must definitely be done, with a dedication to Delvig. From the proceeds it will be possible to pay Somov the same amount that was his share previously."[42] Pushkin responded in March: "Let's talk about the Almanac. I am not against editing a final *Northern Flowers* with you."[43] In early July, Pushkin again broached the subject to Pletnyev, this time mentioning an additional motivation for the project.

> What's happening with your plan for *Northern Flowers* on behalf of Delvig's brothers? I'll give *Mozart* [*and Salieri*] and several trifles. Zh[ukovsky] is giving his Hexameter tale ["Battle with a Serpent"]. Write Baratynsky; he will send us a treasure; he is in his village. We don't expect any poems from you. If you could make the effort, write something about Delvig! That would be good! In any case, we need prose. If you don't give anything, then it will run aground. No survey of literatrue is necessary; is our literature possessed by devils that we have to abuse Polevoy and Bulgarin? Is such a hallelujah proper on Delvig's tomb? Consider all of this very carefully and make arrangements—it's already time to publish, that is, to get ready to publish.[44]

Pletnyev, who had taken refuge from the cholera epidemic of 1831 in the country, answered immediately, accepting the responsibility of overseeing publication of the almanac but stating his inability to solicit contributions.

> *Northern Flowers* is being prepared, but don't give me any tasks. I am living in a village which is not on the post road. There is no one with whom to send letters and it's even less possible to receive them. And so you write yourself to Baratynsky, Yazykov, Vyazemsky and others. My job will be to watch over the publication in town.[45]

Meanwhile, Pushkin had written his lyceum comrade, Mikhail Yakovlyev, also a good friend of Delvig's, asking about *Northern Flowers* and expressing his willingness to assist,[46] to which Yakovlyev answered: "We must wait with *Northern Flowers*. However, on you alone depends the success of its publication."[47] The effect of this letter upon Pushkin is reflected in his next communication to Pletnyev, on August 3.

> What about the *Flowers?* My God, I don't know what to do. Yakovlyev writes that up to now it has been impossible to get on with it. Why? Certainly the presses haven't stopped? Surely there is paper? It can't be that Somov is ill or has refused to edit it?[48]

Pushkin continued to solicit contributions for the projected issue, and in a letter to Prince Vyazemsky in early September he mentioned the charitable motivation of the project.

> (Between us). Delvig left two penniless brothers on the hands of his widow, who has lost the major part of her small estate. This year we are publishing *Northern Flowers* on behalf of the two orphans—Send me poems and prose.[49]

In October Pushkin again alluded to the plight of Delvig's brothers, the older of whom was only twelve. Writing to P. Nashchokin, he noted: "By the way, I am publishing *Northern Flowers* for the sake of the brothers of our late

Delvig: make people pick them [the *Flowers*]. We'll do a good deed."[50]

Pushkin's efforts to get material for the almanac continued well into the fall of 1831, and the task wasn't easy, despite the generally favorable attitude of the foremost literary figures toward a final edition. Pushkin had to importune his friends to hasten with their contributions, and he was more than a little irritated at those who dallied. In mid-November he wrote thanking Yazykov for sending his several poems and asking for his help in expediting the contributions of others.

> Hurry up Vyazemsky—let him send me his prose and poems; he should be ashamed; and Baratynsky should be ashamed. We are preparing a lament for Delvig. And that's how they remember our own! And who? His friends! By God it's shameful![51]

Unbeknownst to the anxious editor, the dilatory Vyazemsky had already posted his poems on November 15 with a note of apology for the delay.[52] Meanwhile, Pushkin continued his quest, and as late as November 21 he wrote to Fyodor Glinka, previously one of *Northern Flowers'* active contributors, asking for material,[53] and very shortly he received Glinka's answer that he had already sent five verses and one piece in prose to Somov but was sending three more poems and a prose fragment. Apparently, this additional contribution was owing to Glinka's having learned for the first time from Pushkin's letter that the almanac was in memory of Delvig.[54]

Although *Northern Flowers for 1832* did not appear until December 24, 1831, mention of its imminent publication began to be made in the press in early October. On October 2, the *Northern Bee* announced that the almanac was being published by Pushkin, and later that month in the *Literary Supplement to the Russian Invalid* [*Literaturnoe Pribavlenie k Russkomu Invalidu*] appeared an elaborate "Literary Prophecy" outlining the most important prose and poetic contents of the anticipated issue. Here, again, Pushkin was named as the editor. In *Girlyanda* [*Girljanda*] both Somov and Pushkin were mentioned as the editors of the forthcoming publication.[55]

The hope that the almanac's final issue would provide financial relief for Delvig's widow and brothers was not realized. Although Pushkin apparently assumed final responsibility for the expenditures connected with the publication, he left the financial arrangements in the hands of Somov, despite the latter's wishes. Somov was very experienced and reliable in editorial matters, but he lacked a capacity for business affairs. Twelve hundred copies of the almanac were printed, of which a small number had to be given free to contributors, deposited with the censorship board, or otherwise could not be sold. However, at least eleven hundred copies could have been sold at the price of twelve rubles, thus realizing a total income of 13,200 rubles. The booksellers were to receive the usual 20 per cent commission (2,640 rubles), the publication costs were 2,270 rubles and Somov was probably to receive about 1,000 rubles for his services. The net profit should have been about 7,000 rubles. But owing to mismanagement, almost 500 copies did not even reach the booksellers. Even so, there should still have been a profit of over 3,000 rubles. This sum seems to have disappeared into Somov's pockets, if it ever indeed reached them. Pushkin, of course, was placed in a difficult position, for he had nothing to give the Delvigs. Somov admitted the debt, but he could not pay it. In a pathetic letter written in January, 1833, he authorized Pushkin to collect 1,000 rubles from Nikolay Grech, which represented Somov's annual salary for editorial work on Grech's publications, and he offered a personal note for the other 2,000. However, at the time he wrote the letter he was quite ill and thus probably not receiving any of his salary from Grech. Since Somov died in May, 1833, it is doubtful that Pushkin ever recovered any of the missing amount.[56]

Chapter III

Appearance and General Contents of the Eight Issues

1825

The initial issue of *Northern Flowers* was a pocket-sized volume about eight by twelve centimeters of three hundred and fifty-seven pages. The title page conveyed the following information: "*Northern Flowers for 1825,* gathered by Baron Delvig. Published by Ivan Slyonin. Sanktpeterburg. In the press of the Department of Public Education." The title vignette, an artistic inner title page typical of almanacs of the period, had the name and date enclosed by a flower-covered trellis rising from a garden of luxuriant blooms. The place of publication, St. Petersburg, was indicated below this garden and framed on the bottom by a garland stretching across the page. The contents were prefaced by a full-page reproduction of Bryulov's picture of Tasso's home in Sorrento, which a note explained was to accompany the prose selection of letters from Italy. The work was divided into prose and poetry sections, the former embracing the first two hundred and fifty pages. The print was large and the lines were widely spaced, so that each page of the prose section contained not more than one hundred and twenty-five words; the poetry was set in smaller type, but generous intervals between lines made it possible to carry but a maximum of twenty-seven lines per page.

The prose section featured a critical essay of almost eighty pages by Peter Pletnyev devoted to the thesis that

Russian poetry was not only more worthy of attention than its contemporary French counterpart but superior to it. No less than three travel accounts were included: Alexander Voyeykov's rather short "An Excursion in Kuskovo Village," "Mount Athos: An Excerpt from a Journey Through Greece," by an anonymous author, and a long epistolary account of travels in Italy. Yevgeny Baratynsky contributed a short satirical work, "The History of Coquetry," and Fyodor Glinka provided two brief pieces, one a reworked version of his sixth letter from *Letters of a Russian Officer*, here entitled "Ancient Castles," and an Eastern legend called "The Unknown Woman."

The poetry section was rich indeed and represented an anthology of the Golden Age. Alexander Pushkin alone had four pieces, including "The Lay of Wise Oleg," "The Demon," "Proserpine," and a short excerpt from *Eugene Onegin*, and Vasily Zhukovsky had an equivalent number, as did Baratynsky and Baron Delvig. Pletnyev and Ivan Kozlov each contributed five poems, and Prince Vyazemsky and Ivan Krylov six, five of the latter's being fables. Lesser lights, such as Glinka, F. Tumansky, K. Masalsky, N. Ostolopov, A. Vostokov, A. Izmailov, and some others also appeared.

The translations and adaptations, some by authors mentioned above, show a consistently Romantic orientation: Kozlov translated Byron's "Good Night," and Moore's "Irish Song," and Russian versions of Schiller's "Der Handschuh" and Goethe's "Der König von Thule" appeared. The Romantic interest in folk culture was manifested by Nikolay Gnedich's trio of translations of Greek popular songs, and A. Vostokov's three "Serbian Songs"; Delvig himself presented two "Russian Songs," original poems in the popular style.

1826

The 1826 edition of the almanac retained the format of the first issue, but the pagination for the poetry section began anew. The volume was considerably larger than in 1825, presenting two hundred and ninety-four pages of prose and one hundred and twenty-nine of poetry. The print and spacing remained the same. The title page was substantially the same as before, but the title vignette was new, revealing a path bordered by stands topped with flower-filled pots; a trellis at each side supported a leafy growth which inter-twined at the top of the page, thus framing the title, *Northern Flowers: 1826.* The place of publication was noted in a rectangular framework immediately under the picture. Five illustrations graced the edition, four of them in connection with the lead article, "On the State of Art in Russia," signed simply "V_____."[1] The last drawing, by Vorobiev, depicted the entrance to the temple of the Lord's tomb in Jerusalem and accompanied an essay, "Russian Pilgrims in Jerusalem," by an anonymous contributor.

The prose section, in addition to the aforementioned pieces, included an excerpt from a letter to Delvig from Pushkin, describing his journey through the Crimea, "The Inn Stairs," a travel account and character sketch by Nikolay Bestuzhev, Alexey Illichevsky's "A Journey from Saint Bernard," which presented interesting details of the Bernadine Order and their Alpine lifesaving monastery, three of Glinka's Eastern allegories, and a biographical legend of the Persian poet Firdausi by an anonymous author. The prose section con-cluded with D. Dashkov's refutation of an article in the *Moscow Telegraph* which had challenged information re-garding the Seral library presented in *Northern Flowers for 1825.*

As with the previous volume, there was hardly any real fiction, in the sense of structured narratives primarily written to amuse. Glinka's allegories were imaginative but hardly amusing, and Nikolay Bestuzhev's long selection, "The Inn Stairs," although obviously partly fictional, sought to give the impression that it was a true account of the author's experi-ence in Copenhagen.

Again, it was the poetry section of the almanac which, although much shorter than the prose one, represented the real literary value of the volume. Pushkin had excerpts from both *The Gypsies* and *Eugene Onegin,* in addition to "Imita-tions of the Koran" and "To Baratynsky." Delvig had no less than seven poems in the issue, Vyazemsky six, Kozlov five, and Baratynsky three. Several important names not present in the first volume now appeared: Nikolay Yazykov, Stepan Shevyrev, and Konstantin Batyushkov. Strangely, Gnedich, who was heavily represented in the first issue, appeared only once this year, and Krylov, who had six works in the 1825 edition, contributed nothing at all. Schiller and Byron were the only Romantic poets translated. An interest in folklore was manifested by Russian and Serbian songs, and Eastern themes seem to have become popular with the editor, as indicated by at least five poems. Gnedich presented a fragment of his translation of *The Iliad* and Ivan Kozlov a section of *Gerusalemme Liberata*.

1827

In 1827 the almanac returned to the consecutive pagination for both the prose and poetry section, and this year the former section was again larger than the latter, incorporating two hundred and fifteen pages as opposed to one hundred and twenty-seven pages of verse. The title vignette featured a pedestal bearing the date, 1827, and topped by a basket of flowers, behind which was an iron fence and trees to right and left. This view was framed on both sides and top by a heavy trellis covered with leafy vegetation, and across the middle of the top arched the title, *Northern Flowers*, in bold capitals. Below the pedestal a title base carried the inscription "S. Peterburg." The frontispiece was an engraving from a self-portrait by A. G. Varnik, one of the young artists mentioned in the lead article, a continuation of the essay initiated in the previous issue, "On the State of Art in Russia." This portion of the essay was devoted to a discussion of the activity of the Society for Encouragement of Artists, founded in 1820. Then followed Konstantin Batyushkov's "A Letter to S. from Gothenburg," an amusing travel account of his journey from London to Sweden in 1814. The indefatigable Fyodor Glinka favored the issue with two contributions, "The Miraculous Companion," a semi-allegory, and "Autumn Days," a vehicle for rather shallow philosophizing. Alexey Illichevsky's "A Remarkable Blind Man" reported on the unusual accomplishments of a blind village carpenter. The anonymous "Excerpts from Letters from Italy," presumably by the author of a similarly entitled selection in the 1825 almanac, described travels in Sicily. "The Almodavar Ruins," by Faddey Bulgarin, was ostensibly a first person account of an experience during the French invasion of Spain. Prince Vyazemsky contributed the brief "Excerpts from a Notebook," consisting of thirteen observations on various themes.

The 1827 issue differed considerably from the previous two numbers in the proportion of the prose devoted to fiction as such. "The Light Brown Tress: An Occurrence from Life," by Z———y, was a rather inane attempt at a light narrative about a man infatuated with a woman's hair. A much more ambitious and successful attempt at a fictional narrative was Orest Somov's "The Holy Fool: A Little Russian Tale," a suspenseful story of over fifty pages concerning the strange destinies of an officer and a holy man.

The poetry section was opened by "Tatyana's Letter to Onegin" and also closed by Pushkin's "October 19," celebrating the anniversary of the lyceum at Tsarskoe Selo. The same poet also contributed three other poems. Baratynsky and Delvig were represented six and four times respectively, and Vyazemsky and Kozlov twice each. A significant new contributor was Dmitry Venevitinov. The interest in Western poets was manifested by translations, imitations, or adaptations of Chateaubriand, Parny, Lamartine, Byron, and Schiller (twice). Müllner's *Die Schuld*, Act I, scene 2 was translated by P. Obodovsky, a poet represented in previous issues. There was slightly less emphasis on Eastern color than the previous year. Four of Alexander Vostokov's Serbian song adaptations were included, and, as a special feature, Gnedich's idyl "The Fisherman," significantly changed from its earlier publication in *Son of the Fatherland* in 1822, was presented accompanied by G. Vorobiev's illustration. For the first time all the poetry contributions were fully signed, with the exception of an epigram by E. B———y, easily identified as Baratynsky, and

two poems signed in an unusually cryptic manner "1——
8——."

1828

The issue for 1828 incorporated four hundred and
seventeen pages, three hundred and twelve for prose and
one hundred and five for poetry, each section was paginated
separately. The frontispiece was an engraving by N. Utkin
from O. Kiprensky's celebrated portrait of Pushkin painted
in 1827. There were no other illustrations. The title vignette
repeated the motif of the central bouquet, this time located
on a low base in an arbor formed by four pillars topped
with flower-filled urns. The pillars in the back supported
a flower-entwined arch bearing the almanac's name. A lyre
reclined against the central bouquet, and the date, 1828, was
indicated on the arbor's forward supporting edge. The title
page mentioned only the almanac's name, *Northern Flowers
for 1828,* which was separated by a horizontal line from
"Sanktpeterburg. In the press of the Department of Public
Education," below which was the date 1827. Neither the
editor nor the publisher were mentioned.

More than in any previous year, the almanac was devoted
to literary criticism and fiction. The lead offering was a
lengthy (eighty pages) "Survey of Russian Literature for
1827," by Orest Somov, the periodical's first systematic assessment of current literature. A historical tale by Bulgarin
called "The Fall of Venden," essentially a highly stylized
treatment of an episode from the reign of Ivan the Terrible,
followed. Glinka, always well represented, presented two
works: an allegory contrasting Classicism and Romanticism,
to the detriment of neither, entitled "Two Sisters, or: Whom
Should One Prefer?" and a short attempt at grandiloquence
titled "Sunrise on a Stormy Autumn Morning." Osip Senkovsky's "The Bedouin Girl: An Eastern Tale," a moralistic
story concerned with the duties of a monarch toward his
subjects, may have contained allegorical allusions to Nicholas
the First's Don Juanism. "On the Life and Works of Karam-

zin" was an anonymous contribution (by Nikolay Grech) noting the famous author's achievements and awards and stressing his significance in the development of Russian prose. Another anonymous contribution, the product of Pushkin's pen, was "Excerpts from Letters, Thoughts, and Remarks," a series of witty and sensible comments on a variety of subjects. Porfiry Baisky's (Orest Somov's) "The Rebel: An Excerpt from a Little Russian Tale" was a short piece, heavily saturated with elements of local color, concerned with the Ukrainian Robin Hood, Garkusha. Pletnyev's "On the Poems of Baratynsky" treated the subject with enthusiasm but was essentially a series of rather uninformative generalizations.

The poetry section, in keeping with previous years, opened with Pushkin, this time presenting his complete *Count Nulin*. Of other poets, Delvig and Illichevsky led in number of contributions, with eight and seven respectively, though most were quite short. Baratynsky presented two works, one a fragment of his *The Ball* and the other his celebrated "The Last Death." Vyazemsky, Pletnyev, and Glinka each contributed twice, but the standby Kozlov only had one poem, as did Batyushkov and Gnedich. Yazykov's single contribution was "To Nurse," an emotionally tinged tribute to Pushkin's celebrated nurse Irina Rodionovna.

At least four poems dealt with Eastern themes, to which must be added three translations by Illichevsky of Mickiewicz's *Crimean Sonnets*. For the first time there were no translations or imitations of Byron, and Schiller, too, was ignored. This year the folk element was considerably diminished.

1829

Larger than any of the previous editions of the almanac, the 1829 edition contained two hundred and fifty-four pages of prose and two hundred and five of poetry, separately paginated. The title vignette presented a perspective of two vine-covered arches, the one in the background framing a flower-filled urn standing on a railing joining the two sides of the arch. Before the front arch and between the two arches were pedestals supporting similar urns with flowers. The name *Northern Flowers* was incorporated across the top of the first arch, and the date, 1829, was on the second. No indication of place of publication was given. The exterior cover again made no mention of the editor or publisher, presenting simply the title, followed by "Sanktpeterburg, in the press of the Department of Public Education, 1828."

The prose section opened, as it had the previous year, with a critical article by Orest Somov, "Survey of Russian Literature for 1828." Among other things, this article contained some revelatory statements regarding the developing interest in prose and the generally deplorable state of epistolary, dramatic, and narrative prose styles. Although Somov was unquestionably basically correct, his argumentation was somewhat vitiated by the next contribution, the fourth chapter of Pushkin's "The Moor of Peter the Great," identified simply as "Chapter IV from a Historical Novel" and unsigned. Bulgarin's "Peter the Great in the Naval Expedition from Petersburg to Vyborg (1710)," detailing in hyperbolic terms the Emperor's personal achievements in this conflict, did, however, provide positive proof of the truth of Somov's assertions. Vladimir Titov's lengthy (over fifty pages) "An Isolated Little House on Vasiliev Island" was a rambling tale of demonic interference in the lives of simple people. Although the exposition was sufficiently clear and straightforward, the plot and characterization were too feeble to sustain interest. More engaging was Vyazemsky's contribution, "Excerpts from a Notebook," which, among other things, presented some amusing examples of Alexander Sumarokhov's incredible vanity . . . and lack of tact. The anonymous contribution, "About the Newly Constructed Church at the Obukhov City Hospital," was, in effect, a panegyric honoring the late Empress Marya Feodorovna for her charitable works, and its inclusion in a literary almanac seems hardly justified. The prose section closed with a short article by Vladimir Izmailov, entitled "On the New Periodical Criticism," taking to task those young critics who underestimated Karamzin's influence on Russian letters and, more particularly, his contrilution to Russian historical writing.

In connection with the poetry section, one interesting feature of this year's almanac was an index by authors of all the contributions, but there was no index of the prose selections.

The poetry section for this issue, about seventy pages longer than at any time previously, presented the usual rich anthology which readers of the almanac had come to expect. The sixteen works of Pushkin were by far the greatest number by any single author, but Baratynsky was represented six times, one contribution being a longer tale in verse entitled "The Transmigration of Souls." Vyazemsky also presented six poems, and Zhukovsky four, including the poetry section's lead work, "The Triumph of the Victors," from Schiller, and an excerpt from *The Iliad* of more than forty pages. Ivan Krylov contributed three fables and one poem, and Kozlov, two poems, one an adaptation of Mickiewicz. Delvig was represented three times and Yazykov twice, along with Illichevsky, Podolinsky, and A. Krylov. The "Testament" of the late Venevitinov also appeared. New contributors were Vasily Pushkin and Pavel Katenin. Zhukovsky's translation of Schiller was supplemented by Platon Obodovsky's translation of a fragment from *Don Carlos*, the same translator also presenting a scene from *Romeo and Juliet*. In general this issue was heavy with translations and adaptations, including, in addition to those mentioned, ones from Chenier, Parny, Byron, Villegas, Anacreon, and two from Moore. The interest in the East and in Slavic folksongs was scarcely manifest in this issue, though there was one "Imitation of Arabic" by Baron Rozen.

1830

The 1830 almanac presented two hundred and seventy-four pages of prose and one hundred and twenty-nine of poetry, separately paginated. The exterior cover was the same as the previous year, except for the obvious changes of the dates, but the vignette was quite unlike that of previous years; this time it depicted a path disappearing into a pine and birch forest. In the foreground light Gothic-style side pieces supported an arch, thus providing more or less of a frame for the view down the path. In the bottom foreground the date, 1830, was placed against a rectangular base. The title of the almanac did not appear on the vignette.

The prose section again opened with Somov's critical survey, this year entitled "Survey of Russian Literature for the First Half of 1829." The next selection, a nonfiction account by a nonprofessional author, Alexander Kryukov, of an attack upon his survey party by Kirghiz horsemen, was notable for its simplicity of style and underlying humor. Fyodor Glinka's "The Advance of the Main Active Army to the Position near Tarutino" was apparently written to glorify Kutuzov and inspire youthful students of Russian history. "Kikimora (A Tale of a Russian Peasant on the High-road)," by Somov, was a colorful story, in stylized peasant language, of a whimsical village Poltergeist, the kikimora. The next selection, "Excerpts from Travel Notes," by the patroness of letters, Princess Zinaida Volkonskaya, was an overly senti-mental and unexpectedly uninformative series of descriptions and impressions connected with her journey through Weimar, Bavaria, and the Tyrol. Alexander Pushkin's "An Excerpt from Literary Annals" commented with devastating irony on the literary pretensions of Mikhail Kachenovsky, editor of the *Messenger of Europe* [*Vestnik Evropy*]. Senkovsky's translation, "The Thief: An Arabian Tale," was a not very interesting short story laden with Arabic titles, words, and expressions, duly explained in footnotes.

The poetry contributors remained largely the same, again being listed by name with their works in a special index at the first of the almanac. There were, however, none of the long excerpts or selections which characterized the con-siderly larger poetry section of the previous year, with the exception of Katenin's "Elegy" and an unsigned "Scene from Shakespeare's Tragedy, *Romeo and Juliet*," probably by Obodovsky, who had translated part of the same work for the issue of 1829. Pushkin again led with number of con-tributions, presenting ten, including a part of Chapter VII of *Eugene Onegin*. Delvig had eight pieces and Baratynsky three. Kozlov presented two poems, and Vyazemsky only one. Alexander Izmailov provided two fables in verse. Other than the piece from Shakespeare, the only interest in Western authors was manifested by Kozlov's "free imitation" of *Don Juan*. The folk motif was evidenced by Russian and Little Russian songs by Delvig and Ivan Kotlyarevsky. A new contributor was A. Khomyakov. In general this issue was one of the least interesting yet published.

1831

The 1831 edition of the almanac was again a large one, with two hundred and eighty pages of prose and one hundred and twenty-two of poetry. A new innovation was the supplement of four pages of music by G. Niklevich to accompany the last piece of poetry, "A Rumelian Song" by V. Teplyakov. The title vignette was completely different again this year: a rectangular frame of small, roundish figures enclosed a shallow, stemmed vase filled with various fruits and leaves, the title of the almanac appearing above this vase in bold letters and "Sanktpeterburg, 1831" printed below. The exterior cover was the same as in previous years, with appropriate changes of dates. There was also a frontispiece, with cherubs at bottom right and left holding poles entwined with flowers which stretched out and grew together across the upper half of the page. *Northern Flowers* appeared in large letters above this leafy bridge, and the date, 1831, appeared below it. From the middle of the bridge of greenery was suspended a wreath of large blossoms holding a horn and pipes.

The back cover was bounded by a border of small figures, and in the center was a vase with flowers. Under the vase it stated: "Sold in bookstores: Slyonin's, Smirdin's and others' for 12 rubles, in other towns for 13 rubles."

Orest Somov's "Survey of Russian Literature for the Second Half of 1829 and the First of 1830" opened the prose section. His evaluation proceeded in much the same form as previously, but this year the element of personal antagonism, particularly directed at Nikolay Polevoy, was more pronounced than ever before. Above the unusual pseudonym "Soft-sign, hard-sign, short ee" appeared Vladimir Odoevsky's

"Beethoven's Last Quartet," followed by a very brief contribution of Princess Volkonskaya, "Excerpts from Travel Notes." Vladimir Titov's "The Monastery of Saint Bridget," a historical tale on the theme of the conflict between Lutherans and Catholics in Livonia, contained some interesting details about life in Revel in the early sixteenth century, but the story was no better than the usual examples of the genre. Victor Teplyakov's "Letter III from Turkey," described an excursion from Varna to the nearby monastery of Saint Constantine. Nikolay Gogol's "A Chapter from a Historical Novel," cryptically signed "o o o o," was an interesting effort, though far from representative of that author's real talent. Dmitry Struisky's "Excerpts from a Notebook" was primarily a sentimental reverie and much less interesting than material by Pushkin and Vyazemsky appearing in *Northern Flowers* under similar titles. Fyodor Glinka's "The New Assay Tent" dealt with a certain Eastern savant's ability to judge right from wrong, truth from falsehood, and so forth. Doubtless there was some allegorical significance to this short piece, but in general it was too dull to merit any concerted search for such additional meaning.

As usual, it was the poetry section which was particularly valuable, the poetic index displaying its expected gallaxy of leading writers. Pushkin's sonnet, "To the Poet," led the contributions, to which he added four other lyrics. Both Fyodor Glinka and Prince Vyazemsky presented seven pieces, the latter's "Parental Home" being a work of thirty-eight four-line stanzas. Baratynsky presented two excerpts from his novel in verse, *The Courtesan,* and Yazykov returned to the almanac with a seventy-two line "Elegy." Conspicuous by his absence was Delvig himself, and the usual emphasis on folk songs was also missing. There were altogether only a couple of translations from Western literature.

1832

The last issue of the almanac was the largest, presenting three hundred and four pages of prose and one hundred and ninety-six of poetry. As in years 1830 and 1831, there were alphabetical indices by authors of the prose and poetic contributions. The title page gave no indication that the editorship had changed with Delvig's death, reading simply *Northern Flowers for 1832*, and at the bottom of the page, "Sanktpeterburg, in the Press of the Department of External Trade, 1831." The vignette presented a large circular wreath of various leaves and blossoms, in the center of which was another wreath and a lyre. Above the central decoration curved the two words of the title, and below it was the date, 1832.

The prose section had twelve works of varying length, opening with Batyushkov's stylized legend from Vladimir's court, "Predslava and Dobrynya." Vladimir Odoevsky's "Opere del Cavaliere Giambattista Piranesi" followed, again signed only with the cryptic soft sign, hard sign, and short ee. (Actually it was signed hard sign, hard sign, short ee, but this was corrected in the errata.) A translation of part of a Chinese novel, called "An Excerpt from the Chinese Novel: *Hau-Tsu-Dzhuan*, that is, A Matchless Marriage," was next, detailing an amusing conflict between two Oriental noblemen. Ivan Lazhechnikov presented a fragment from his novel, *The Last Novik*, dealing with Old Believers' unusual preparations for doomsday. Two contributions, M. Maksimovich's "On the Life of Plants" and Mikhail Pogodin's "Something about Science," would have been more suited for the Miscellany section of a general periodical or for a journal of natural or popular science. The longest work was Somov's "Matchmaking," a racy account of the unsuccessful aspirations of a Ukrainian petty gentryman for the hand of his beloved. Somov also contributed the rather banal effort, "A Living Person in the Cloister of Eternal Bliss," a sentimental reverie in the style of Glinka. The latter was responsible for another of his allegories, "The Important Conflict," which concerned the contest between good and evil. Struisky's "Meditation: Dedicated to the Memory of Count Kapodistria" was occasional and literarily insignificant. Alexander Nikitenko's "An Excerpt from the Novel: *Leon or Idealism*," was a first person confession detailing the narrator's educational and family circumstances in a style reminiscent of the followers of Rousseau.

The poetry section presented more individual works (seventy-six) than any previous issue. The section opened with five poems, previously unpublished, found among the papers of the almanac's late editor, Baron Delvig. The source of these works was indicated in a brief introduction, perhaps written by Pushkin. Pushkin himself contributed seven pieces, one the famous "Poison Tree" and another his little tragedy *Mozart and Salieri*. Mikhail Delaryu led in number of contributions with eight, and Vyazemsky and Yazykov presented six. Zhukovsky's long ballad, "The Battle with a Serpent," closed the almanac. The latter also contributed to a poetic exchange of compliments with Ivan Dmitriev. Nikolay Stankevich, who had first appeared in the almanac the previous year with one poem, presented two this year. Among the new contributors was the well-known writer of comedies, Prince Alexander Shakhovskoy, whose work included a fable and two congratulatory lyrics honoring the sculptor I. P. Martos.

Chapter IV

Literary Criticism
in *Northern Flowers*

Northern Flowers first blossomed at a moment when vigorous, and at times vicious, controversies were raging across the Russian literary scene. The issues themselves were far from clear, and personal animosities often were more important in determining opinions than critical attitudes: there were those who were always ready to sacrifice consistency to contumely. Alliances were formed and broken to the accompaniment of unjustified tribute and uncalled-for objurgation. In such an environment, even the most discreet writers and critics found it impossible to maintain consistently a completely objective position.

Romanticism versus Classicism, "free" art versus didacticism, national identity [narodnost'] versus imitation, the ode versus "light poetry," Gallicisms versus Slavonicisms, prose versus poetry, mixed genres versus "pure" ones—these were just some of the issues, further complicated, of course, by the fact that the definition of Romanticism was itself a point of contention, *narodnost* was undefined, and there was considerable disagreement as to what constituted the literary language. Profit motives, political viewpoints, and class identification were significant, and even determining, factors in many of the conflicts.

Not one of the literary almanacs of the twenties and thirties, even if it had wanted to, could very well have maintained an Olympian detachment in the midst of the polemical hurricanes which swept across the literary scene. Since *Northern Flowers* was not intended to be a nonpartisan periodical, it naturally was deeply involved in various aspects of these controversies. But from the first it manifested an attempt to preserve a dignified tone and to treat issues as matters of literature rather than matters of personality or politics. In the course of years, however, this became increasingly difficult.

One cannot correctly speak of *the* critical position of *Northern Flowers*, because in the course of eight years its position was not static; secondly, the critical content of the almanac was the work of several contributors, each of whom expressed a somewhat personal viewpoint. And it must not be forgotten that its critical stance was not expressed only in its criticism but also reflected in the very character of its poetry and fiction, the relative space given to different authors and the frequency with which they appeared. However, it can be demonstrated that linking the individual numbers of the almanac were elements of consistency which, as it were, defined a reasonably consistent posture or attitude.

From the outset, *Northern Flowers* exhibited an editorial policy which reflected a desire to popularize domestic authors and further the prestige of Russian literature. The lead article in the first issue was Peter Pletnyev's "A Letter to Countess S. I. S. [Sofia Ivanovna Sollogub] about Russian Poets" ["Pis'mo k Grafine S. I. S. o russkix poètax"], in which the critic sought to prove to the Countess, a staunch partisan of Lamartine, that there were not only many Russian poets who satisfied discriminating literary tastes but most of them surpassed their French contemporaries. Noting that although Lamartine possessed captivating qualities of feeling, imagery and dreaminess—in imitation of English and German poets—Pletnyev asserted that he was nonetheless monotonous in comparison to other Romantics. His fame, and that of French poetry in general, in the critic's opinion, was simply owing to the fact that French was more widely known than Russian, a political circumstance rather than a literary one. Turning to the history of Russian poetry, Pletnyev remarked that it had acquired its basic character before French social mores had taken root in Russia, and therefore it was not affected by the "frigid rules and petty conditions of social politesse" which had negatively influenced French verse. He freely stated that for want of a domestic conversational language, Russia was poor in dramatic poetry, but he insisted that in those genres which depended less upon conversational language than dramatic poetry the Russians had achieved a great deal, even rivaling the achievements of classical antiquity.

The rest of his long essay was an enumeration of poets who he believed united "internal and external" perfection, beginning with the "most inspired, varied, and original" of all Russian poets, Derzhavin. In his list we encounter virtually all of those names we have come to consider the major figures of the late eighteenth and early nineteenth centuries. Pletnyev stressed their superiority to French counterparts: thus Derzhavin, Lomonosov and Petrov were better than J. B. Rousseau, Kapnist surpassed Lamartine, and Kheminitser, Dmitriev and Krylov equaled La Fontaine. Among those representing what Pletnyev called the "new period in our poetry," Zhukovsky and Batyushkov were lauded. The critic then made the important point that the apparent poverty of Russian poetry was because contemporary Russian poets generally appeared only in periodicals, their works not being published separately or in collections, as was done in France. Brief characterizations were provided for the best of these moderns, and Pletnyev's list included Pushkin, Gnedich, Davydov, Vyazemsky, Glinka, Ryleev, Delvig, Alexander Krylov, Baratynsky, Yazykov, Küchelbecker, as well as Mikhail Dmitriev, Alexander Pisarev, and Vasily Tumansky. The critic concluded on the sardonic note that more people wrote verses in Russian than read them.

Pletnyev's essay identifies him as a critic of the *Je ne sais quoi* school; that is, his criteria for evaluation are at best highly subjective and in the final analysis he makes his judgments on the basis of that certain "undefinable something" which is contained in a good poem. Thus he asserts that the special superiority which Russian poets enjoy over their French rivals is owing to their "deep and true feelings, bright and pure colors, new and powerful thoughts, a harmonious language. . . ." His remarks about Pushkin are equally wanting in definiteness or precision, but there is no lack of hyperbolic enthusiasm.

> In the course of the last four years Pushkin has enriched our modern literature with three poems [Pletnyev refers to the Southern Cycle] which would have gained him fame not only in France but even in England. I don't dare to compare him with any of the present French poets, for he is as much above them as Lomonosov was above all his literary contemporaries in Russia.[1]

Pushkin was unimpressed by Pletnyev's critical effort, despite its very positive attitude toward his own work. Writing to Prince Vyazemsky on January 25, 1825, he asked, "How do you find the article which our Pletnyev has written? What a jumble!"[2] And on March 15 he concluded his letter to Pletnyev himself: "Brother Pletnyev! Don't write *kind* criticism! Be sharp tongued and beware of excessive sweetness!"[3] Pushkin, as usual, was correct, but perhaps his reaction was too severe in view of the fact that Pletnyev was not, strictly speaking, presenting a critique of Russian poetry but simply seeking to advertise its virtues. He himself subsequently stated this to Pushkin.

> I wrote this letter to a lady who not uncharitably had said that for her there was nothing in Russian to take the place of Lamartine. You think it's funny, but it pained me to tears. Thus from chagrin I saw everything *chez nous* in a more favorable light than the situation merited.[4]

It is certainly clear from the content and tone of Pletnyev's essay that he was committed to the support of the new direction in Russian poetry exemplified by Batyushkov and Zhukovsky and which opposed the conservative strictures on genres and poetic language expressed by Admiral Shishkov and his partisans of Neo-Classicism. And in fact one of the common denominators of *Northern Flowers* throughout its eight years of existence, expressed not only directly in its literary criticism but indirectly by the orientation of its contributors and the nature of their works, was a satirical attitude toward Neo-Classicism and its disciples and, conversely, a very positive interest in and admiration for Western European Romantics and their Russian counterparts. Karamzin, whose reform of the literary language had been so productively extended through the practices of Batyushkov, Zhukovsky, and subsequently Pushkin, was clearly the spiritual godfather of the almanac. The deep admiration of Delvig, Pushkin, Orest Somov and other of the "principals" of *Northern Flowers* for Karamzin was, in fact, a major factor in determining that almanac's increasing hostility toward Nikolay Polevoy and his *Moscow Telegraph*, for though Polevoy's periodical was loosely allied with *Northern Flowers* in opposing Neo-Classicism, its editor was outspokenly antagonistic to Karamzin's interpretation of Russian history and thus, in the eyes of Delvig's camp, a heretic.

It has been asserted that Pletnyev's essay was a deliberately programatic refutation of ideas previously advanced by Alexander Bestuzhev in his critical surveys appearing in *Polar Star*.[5] Although it is true that Bestuzhev in his "A Look at Russian Literature in the Course of 1824 and the Beginning of 1825" asserted that Russia had as yet no literature, while Pletnyev insisted that Russian poets rivaled those of France, and that what Bestuzhev saw as deficiencies—for example, the dreaminess of Zhukovsky—Pletnyev interpreted as assets, the divergencies in their views arose naturally from differences in personal tastes and from different conceptions as to the function of literature rather than from any deliberate polemical intent on Pletnyev's part. Further, since both Bestuzhev and Pletnyev were highly subjective in their evaluations and prone to generalize without data, their opinions naturally differed in certain respects—but this does not imply intentional contradiction. Certainly Ryleev and Bestuzhev did use *Polar Star*, insofar as that was possible, for the promulgation of their revolutionary ideology, and it follows that those poets, or at least those poems, which reinforced that ideology would be particularly favored by them; Pletnyev, not being concerned with literature as a whetstone for the grinding of political axes, focused upon—or so he thought— the aesthetic qualities of Russian authors. But the two types of emphasis were not mutually exclusive, and if, in fact, *Northern Flowers'* stance was so opposed to that of *Polar Star*, how are we to explain that twenty of the twenty-three identifiable contributors to the first issue of Delvig's almanac had previously contributed to *Polar Star?* Further, thirteen of these twenty appeared in the 1825 issues of both *Polar Star* and *Northern Flowers*. Simply stated, Delvig wanted his almanac to function as a cultural force, not a political one, but his commitment to "free" art[6] does not imply a denial of the ideological principles governing the editorial policies or critical attitudes of *Polar Star*.

The "free" art stance of *Northern Flowers* is less indicated by direct statement than by the general content of its contributions, which span a wide gap from didactic fables and tendentious epigrams on one side to personal lyrics and stories *dulce* but far from *utile* on the other. Its list of contributors also would indicate that the steady collaborators of the almanac were political liberals (as mentioned, many of them had published in *Polar Star*) but not radicals, and hence less likely to harness art to the cart of tendency than, say, Decembrist poets. In 1829, Orest Somov addressed himself directly, if briefly, to this question of "free" art. Discussing the critical section of the newly established *St. Petersburg Observer* [*Sankt-Peterburgskij Zritel'*], he energetically took exception to the *Observer's* complaint that Byron's *Parasina* had no moral aim.

> In one line, he [the *Observer's* critic] condemned almost all famous artists who in the miraculous works of their chisels or brushes did not propose moral aims. Poetry also belongs to the fine arts: judging Byron, he judges also many extremely famous artists and sculptors, forgetting that all the fine arts are a goal in themselves.[7]

From the first *Northern Flowers* assumed an attitude of mirthful disdain towards militant Neo-Classicism and enthusiastic support of Romanticism—that is, Romanticism as understood by the almanac's chief contributors. Prince Vyazemsky was heavily committed in this matter, having in March of 1824 provided Pushkin's "The Fountain of

Bakchisaray" with an introduction which was a manifesto
of the movement. Entitled "A Conversation between a Publisher and a Classicist from the Vyborg Side or from Vasiliev
Island," this essay precipitated a violent polemic. The conflict subsequently involved attacks and counterattacks, and
other critics joined the fray. A note of personal antagonism
was soon sounded. Mikhail Dmitriev (called the "False
Dmitriev" to distinguish him from his more famous uncle),
who had praised Pushkin's poem but attacked Vyazemsky's
views, went so far as to compose a scurrilous epigram alluding to Vyazemsky's alleged political unreliability. Alexander
Pisarev, a talented composer of satirical vaudevilles and comedies, allied himself with Dmitriev, though his particular concern was to lampoon Vyazemsky for the authorship (with
Griboedov) of a vaudeville produced in January, 1824, *Who
Are Brother and Sister?* Vyazemsky replied in *Northern
Flowers* with "To the Journalistic Twins" ["K žurnal'nym
bliznecam"], an eight-line epigram which likened Pisarev and
Mikhail Dmitriev to petulant baby chicks trying to pass themselves off as roosters.[8] Although the poetic epigram said nothing about Romanticism, informed readers would have interpreted its presence as an indirect indication of the almanac's
Romantic orientation, since Vyazemsky was associated with
propagandizing the movement and Pisarev and Mikhail
Dmitriev, to some extent incorrectly, were regarded as literary
reactionaries.[9]

In 1826 there was no formal literary criticism in *Northern Flowers*, though the list of contributors and the types of
works would certainly have indicated the almanac's allegiance
to the principles and tastes implicit in Pletnyev's essay: support of the young, primarily gentry poets whose inspiration
was at the service of art. The following year the dart-throw-
ing at Neo-Classicists was renewed, with M. Yakovlyev's epigram on an unsuccessful tragedy—by one of the opposite
camp—and Prince Vyazemsky's "Excerpts from a Notebook,"
which chided the Neo-Classicists for rating adherence to the
precepts of Aristotle the most important criterion for literary
evaluation.

The anti-Classicist dart game continued in the 1828 issue

of the almanac, in which appeared an anonymous epigrammatic quatrain (by Prince Vyazemsky) entitled, "A Russian
Romantic to a Russian Classicist" ["Russkij romantik russkomu klassiku"]. In this piece the pro-Romantic lyric "I"
evinces unwillingness to take example from one who is like
a schoolboy trembling before his master's gaze, and he answers
the Classicist's charge that he is a schismatic with the epithet
"Old Believer."[10]

A conciliatory effort was represented by Fyodor Glinka's
"Two Sisters, or: Whom Should One Prefer?" [Dve sestry,
ili: kotoroj otdat' preimuščestvo?"], a hopelessly tedious allegory appearing in the prose section of the same issue. One
of *Northern Flowers'* most prolific contributors of both prose
and poetry—and also one of its consistently mediocre ones—
Glinka had been active in Russian letters since 1808, when
the first part of his extensive *Letters of a Russian Officer* appeared. In "Two Sisters" Glinka professes to be equally
enamored of Classicism and Romanticism, the "two sisters"
who are so different and yet so appealing.

> Both are charming, but each has her particular charms....
> One is radiant, in the fullness of her beauty, like a clear,
> clement day, manifesting all the picturesqueness of na-
> ture, all the luxuriance of nature. . . . Conversely, the
> *other* is kind, enticing, attractive, like a moonlit evening
> of the last days of summer. I love such evenings![11]

Delvig gave space to this saccharine bonbon for the same
reason that he accepted and printed so many other contributions of this author: Glinka was, at least at that time, appreciated for his "high" prose style, and his advocacy of a
peaceful coexistence of Classicism and Romanticism was not
essentially contrary to the almanac's pro-Romantic orientation. After all, Delvig's circle was not opposed to Classicism
as such but to Neo-Classicists who denied the legitimacy of
Romanticism. Good evidence for this can be found in many
issues of the almanac where high praise is given to competent
efforts of a Classical stamp. Thus in 1831 Nikolay Gnedich's
translation of *The Iliad* was termed "the most remarkable
poetic event" of the preceding half year, and in the same

review the almanac's critic enthusiastically greeted the appearance of the eight-volume edition of Ivan Krylov's fables. On the other side of the coin, not all manifestations of Romanticism received approval. In the essay mentioned above, not only was the translation of Alexander Dumas' (*père*) *Henry III* heavily criticized but the original itself was protested: "*Henry III* appertains to works of the new French Romanticism and to unsuccessful works."[12] It should be remembered that Pushkin, too, was unenthusiastic about "modern Romanticism," which he identified with contemporary manifestations in French literature, that he had a generally poor opinion of Hugo as a novelist and a dislike of Alfred de Vigny's prose, which he considered mannered and artificial.[13]

In 1828 *Northern Flowers* began featuring articles by Orest Somov which systematically surveyed recently published works. At the time of his collaboration with the almanac, Somov was already an established author and recognized critic. An avowed partisan of an independent Russian Romanticism, his literary credo, derived from Mme de Staël, stressed "national identity" [narodnost'] and "locality" [mestnost']; his ideas had been extensively developed in his long essay "On Romantic Poetry," which, appearing in 1823, was the first formal assessment of the potentials of Romanticism for Russian literature. Somov contributed to Delvig's almanac, in addition to several short stories, four annual critical surveys, and therefore he played an essential role in the definition of *Northern Flowers'* critical position.

As a theoretician of Romanticism and an author whose works were a practical demonstration of the possibilities of a national literature, Somov naturally continued the pro-Romantic line established in the first three issues of the almanac. His position on Romanticism is defined early in his first survey, where he reviews the newly formed *Athenaeum* [*Atenej*] edited by Professor Mikhail Pavlov. Somov expresses surprise at the journal's anti-romantic tendency: "When discussions on this matter have already been dropped even in the obdurately Classical countries of Europe, *Athenaeum* has decided positively to affirm the persecution of Romanticism."[14] Somov dismisses the threat, noting that if Classicism consists in writing in the style which characterizes most of the articles in *Athenaeum*, then no one needs it. The anti-Romantic stance of *Athenaeum* is even stranger, in his opinion, since the journal containes translations from Washington Irving, Cooper, Tieck, Guizot, and others.

Somov's surveys systematically assessed old and new periodicals, individually published works of poetry and collections of verses, short stories, novels, essays, and significant translations. Interspersed were remarks, often of some length, regarding the history of Russian literature, the qualities of individual authors, the development of the literary language, the deleterious effects of polemics, and the requisites of an independent Russian literature. His earlier surveys are notable for their restrained tone and their attempts at objectivity. Somov was obviously deeply concerned with fostering the growth and expanding the prestige of Russia's literature through stressing its achievements—admittedly limited—encouraging new talent, and establishing standards, particularly with respect to matters of style.

If there is one salient concern which Somov expresses throughout his series of essays it is for the development of a Russian prose language adequate to the service of fiction, essays, and technical exposition. He comments upon the style or language of almost every author he mentions, using both style [slog] and language [jazyk] more or less interchangeably to connote literary Russian. In 1828 he rebukes the *Slav* [*Slavjanin*], a new publication of Alexander Voyeykov, for using "some sort of unknown dialect of Slavic, but not Russian,"[15] while Pogodin's *Moscow Herald* is lauded for the "selection and style" of its translations.[16] At the conclusion of his first survey Somov analyses the problems facing the prose language and provides an explanation as to why the poetic language is more easily mastered.

> I will add that our Russian prose presents more difficulties [than poetry] and that these difficulties are greater than those which depend upon poetic meter, rhyme, harmony and so forth. The chief of these is that prose demands from us the most extensive and sound knowledge of the language, it demands greater exactness, greater precision

in those expressions which the writer almost constantly has to create himself, because we are still poor in models from which we might borrow. For verses we have already some sort of conventional language in which there are fixed locutions and even many expressions accepted as admissible or inadmissible by good taste.[17]

The following year he again expressed a belief that prose was still an unsuccessful rival of poetry, noting that in 1828 poetry had surpassed prose both quantitatively and qualitatively. To rectify this unequal situation, Somov urged young "candidates" in literature to cease producing faded imitations in verse and enter the service of prose.

> We don't yet have a narrative style for novels and long short stories [*povesti*], there is no conversational style for dramatic compositions in prose, and there is even no epistolary style. For this reason our young writers always advance gropingly and if, for want of a smooth and established road, they are fortunate enough to find themselves on a good trail, Glory to God! Not many, however, can boast even of this success: the majority either become lost in the rough plowland of antiquated Slavono-Russian or slip and fall over the heaps of foreign languages accumulated in the past (Gallicisms, Teutonisms, and the like) or sink in the low and marshy soil of a rude, uncultivated vernacular.[18]

He goes on to remark that examples of a good style which might serve to develop taste are wanting, and that if one studies the refinements of conversational language he will learn the subtleties of French rather than Russian. Somov finds an exception to the situation in the four stories of Anthony Pogorelsky (pseudonym of A. A. Perovsky) which appeared in 1827 and included "The Lafertov District Poppy-Seed Cake Seller." But these works are admired more for their pure style than for their narrative content, and Somov entirely misses the play with elements of Hoffmann. Incidentally, Pogorelsky remained in Somov's good graces, and the critic's essay for 1821 expresses unusual enthusiasm for "The Nun." He finds the style "vital, natural, and free, equally excellent in narration, description and dialogue,"[19] and for the critic the realistic impression of the heroine's letters is so strong that he almost seems to suspect the author had access to the actual correspondence of a nun.

Somov's final plea for the perfection of the prose language comes in his valedictory survey appearing in the 1831 issue of the almanac. Remarking with pleasure that more novels had appeared in the first half of 1830 alone than in the course of several preceding years, the critic nonetheless laments that Russian novelists are still less concerned with quality than quantity. He admonishes prose writers to be less hasty, reiterating the old complaint that the Russian prose language still lacks fixed formulae for literary expression and that this precludes rapid composition. He admonishes writers to be less impatient about presenting their works to the public.

> The public, moreover, has a right to be angry at an author's carelessness, which, as it were, is a sign of disrespect, just as guests rightly become angry at a host who dares to entertain in morning dress. The public demands that an author present himself with his work in formal attire.[20]

While Somov was calling upon Russian authors to demonstrate greater care in the composition of their works, especially those in prose, he nonetheless defended the accomplishments of Russian literature and, like Pletnyev before him, urged that the Russian reading public pay attention to the achievements of their own writers. He opens his "Survey of Russian Literature for 1827" ["Obzor rossijskoj slovesnosti za 1827 god"] with an admission that the number of works appearing in Russian is limited, but he puts the responsibility for this not on Russian authors but on the reading public which itself is poorly educated and prefers French to Russian works. Of those who condescend to read works in Russian and evaluate them, he continues, many feel that the domestic product is but a younger sister of French literature, and, "by virtue of this alleged kinship, such readers want the younger sister to dress, rouge, and bow exactly like the older one."[21]

In stressing the quality of Russian literature Somov was

merely formalizing a point of view implicit in the very character of Delvig's almanac, namely, that there were sufficient
good works by Russian authors to justify periodicals devoted
exclusively to literature and that the domestic literary product
deserved and demanded systematic evaluation. This conviction
was an obvious *raison d'être* of *Northern Flowers*. But Somov,
among others, was also aware that the public had to be treated
with respect if it were to replace its French tastes with Russian ones—thus his concern for the purity of the literary
language. He also was disturbed lest the carelessness and
cupidity of certain publishers negatively affect the reading
public, which was discriminating enough to know when a bad
product was being foisted upon it. He cautioned publishers
to respect even provincial readers, for "in regions most remote
from the capitals it is possible to find more than a few people
with truly European enlightenment and educated tastes."[22]

When Somov first initiated his surveys, he expressed a
deep anxiety about the violent polemics which dominated
almost all aspects of criticism. Concerned more with personalities than issues, repetitious and undignified, these polemics were, in Somov's opinion, not only pointless but harm-
ful to the image of Russian letters. It is perhaps paradoxical
that Somov's initial pleas for a critcism governed by impartiality and restraint were made on behalf of Faddey Bulgarin, for it was Bulgarin's subsequent actions which were to
strain Somov's forbearance to the breaking point. In his first
survey Somov pointedly noted that in view of the previous
year's paucity of worthwhile prose it was surprising Bulgarin's
Works had been completely ignored by Moscow journals.[23]
Having commented upon the deliberateness of this slight, the
critic went on to discuss the deplorably personal nature of the
journalistic wars.

> Often not the journalists alone but their friends and even
> their literary acquaintances are subjected to persecution,
> innuendos, and nagging from the opposite side. Impar-
> tiality is seldom the slogan in this war. Cavils are sought,
> not the truth. . . . Thus works which deserve no re-
> proach are attacked in one journal simply because pre-
> viously they had been praised in another. Therefore, all

receive the same desserts, both the righteous and the
guilty. . . . Our boring polemics include anticriticism, re-
criticism, and re-anticriticism, which often drag along in
a continuous chain of new *re-* and *re-anti-* critiques.[24]

Somov further suggests, in the interests of promoting variety,
that once a critic has expressed his opinion, he be done with it:
"It seems to me that a critic, having printed an evaluation of
a work, has already expressed his opinion; repetitions are in
no way necessary, and answers to abusive anticriticism even
less so."[25]

Of course, Somov's remarks were not only addressed to
the Moscow journals which had greeted Bulgarin's collection
with eloquent silence; the principal addressee of this admonition was Bulgarin himself, who was constantly attacking
other writers, critics, and publishers from the pages of *Northern Bee, Northern Archive [Severnyj Arxiv]*, and *Son of the
Fatherland*. Bulgarin had already defined himself as an una-
bashed intriguer and merciless competitor, but at the time of
Somov's first survey his unconscionable aggression against
Pushkin was still to come and, moreover, he was still a contributor to *Northern Flowers* (his pieces appeared in the three
issues from 1827 to 1829). Further, Somov was also employed
part time by him on *Northern Bee*. But that Somov's well-
intentioned appeal for restraint and reason fell on deaf ears
is quite clear from the opening paragraph of his "Survey of
Russian Literature for 1828" [Obzor rossijskoj slovesnosti za
1828 god"]. Here he sardonically recounts an anecdote about a
preacher whose congregation so stubbornly behaved exactly
contrary to his exhortations that he even considered supporting
sin so his flock would act virtuously.

The "Survey of Russian Literature for the First Half of
1829" ["Obozrenie rossijskoj slovesnosti za pervuju polovinu
1829 goda"] marks another step in the Somov-Bulgarin relationship. In this survey Somov sought to present an objective
assessment of Bulgarin's recently published *Ivan Vyzhigin, A
Moral-Satirical Novel*, which had already been extravagantly
praised by Bulgarin's allies and unjustly scorned by others.
Somov first rejected the contention that with *Vyzhigin*
Bulgarin had created the first original Russian novel, since

the right to that claim belonged to Vasily Narezhny, whose *Two Ivans, The Seminary Student,* and *A Russian Gil Blas*— to which Bulgarin's works bore resemblance—had been written much earlier. But at the same time he characterized as unjust those critics who found no merit in the novel, which he felt had value as an anecdotal picture of contemporary times. The critic went on to remark that the success of Bulgarin's work had been indicated by its large number of readers from all classes, which also had accounted for the variety of opinions regarding it. Having praised *Vyzhigin,* albeit faintly, Somov then proceeded to discuss its artistic deficiencies. The hero, as well as some of the secondary characters, he found interesting but lacking in consistency, and the author's use of tag names was, in his opinion, boring and out of place in a novel. He hypothesized that an awareness of the plot's improbability had led to Bulgarin's attempt to reinforce his work with unusual adventures in exotic settings. Regarding this the critic said,

> Such novelistic means were already worn out at the time of l'Abbé Prévost's novels, and when descriptions and mores of distant countries include nothing new, or do not present national qualities [narodnost'] and local color vividly and sensitively, then such means greatly weaken the attractiveness of the whole and too clearly reveal that the author was straining his imagination.[26]

But what probably hurt Bulgarin the most was Somov's assertion that the author of *Vyzhigin* consistently revealed a lack of knowledge about the life of the Moscow and Petersburg *haut monde,* a fact which the critic demonstrated by noting a number of the novel's unrealistic social situations. Bulgarin, who was unusually sensitive about the social position and prestige of the "author-aristocrats" associated with Delvig and Pushkin, could not but have been chagrined by the implications of Somov's observation. Perhaps it was to soften the effect of these and other remarks that the critic concluded by noting that the first volume, which dealt with Vyzhigin's youth, was well done and that the anecdotal material was unusually engaging.

The complete deterioration of Somov's once neutral attitude toward Bulgarin is chronicled by the critic's last long essay, "Survey of Russian Literature for the Second Half of 1829 and the First of 1830" ["Obozrenie rossijskoj slovesnosti za vtoruju polovinu 1829 i pervuju 1830 goda"]. This contribution, of course, appeared in *Northern Flowers for 1831*, which means that it was probably written during the last months of 1830—and a great deal had happened in the course of the previous twelve months which had directly affected Somov's personal attitude toward Bulgarin. Among his list of grievances were Bulgarin's rude dismissal of him from his position on *Northern Bee* owing to his intention of collaborating with Delvig's *Literary Gazette*,[27] Bulgarin's unpardonable allusions to Pushkin's ancestry, and his denunciations to Benckendorff, which had led to the suppression of *Literary Gazette* and aroused suspicions about Delvig's loyalty to the Tsar. Somov begins with remarks on the *Northern Bee*.

> *Northern Bee* also thought to mystify its readers with its literary essays. It reviled the good and overpraised the impossibly mediocre. Certain essays, noteworthy for their bad taste, weak knowledge of Russian, childish errors in style and boundless conceit were filled with indecorous jokes and ambiguous hints directed at true talents. It is amusing that the author of these essays, a certain F. B., asserted to his readers, "I know History! I know Chemistry! I know music!"[28]

The statement here about "indecorous jokes and ambiguous hints directed at true talents" alludes to Bulgarin's attack on Pushkin.

In this same survey Somov returned to Bulgarin in connection with the latter's ill-starred historical novel, *Dmitry the Pretender*. He led into his discussion by way of remarks on Mikhail Zagoskin's *Yuri Miloslavsky, or the Russians in 1612*, a historical romance which he felt was marred by anachronisms and lack of accuracy in the depiction of historical personages. However, he found the "general impression" good and was pleased by the author's obvious patriotism, his devotion to God and the Russian Tsar, and his native knowledge of Russian customs. This closing tribute was calculated by Somov to suggest a comparison between Zagoskin and the next author discussed, namely Bulgarin, whose service to the Tsar had been interrupted by an interlude as an officer in Napoleon's army.[29] Regarding the novel itself, Somov finds all the characters poorly delineated. The False Dmitry is depicted simply as an immoral opportunist and Boris Godunov emerges as a "vapid whiner." Bulgarin's fictional character, the Greek woman Kaleriya, is a poor imitation of Mrs. Radcliffe's vengeful Italian women. Although in his previous surveys Somov had commented positively upon Bulgarin's style, he now finds only negative qualities.

> Mr. Bulgarin writes like a foreigner who has mastered the mechanics of Russian; that is, one who knows the rules for arranging words, their mutual relations, the construction of sentences, but one who is unacquainted with all the means, all the abundance of this language, all its daring locutions. . . .[30]

Somov insists further that the novel is inartistic, dull and lifeless, a judgment which he feels is substantiated by the fact that the majority of readers are unable to finish the work—or even the first volume.

Somov's loss of critical objectivity and the increasingly polemical nature of his surveys, particularly reflected in his growing antagonism toward Bulgarin, diminished his usefulness as a critic. Pushkin certainly recognized this, and when discussing with Pletnyev the publication of the final issue of the almanac, which was to be a memorial to the deceased Baron Delvig, he recommended that no survey by Somov be included: "No survey of literature is necessary; is our literature possessed by devils that we have to abuse Polevoy and Bulgarin? Is such a hallelujah proper on Delvig's tomb?"[31]

The vigorous attack against Bulgarin which Somov launched in his last survey represented only part of a more general conflict, one which concerned the prestige of Nikolay Karamzin. The gentry coterie which more or less formed the central body of *Northern Flowers'* contributors were united much more closely than by mere collaboration on the same almanac—they frequented the same literary circles, encouraged the same young writers, published in the same periodicals, in general shared art for art's sake attitudes. Karamzin was their spiritual godfather, and they were quite aware of their indebtedness to him for his reform of the literary language, his contribution to Russian prose, and his *History of the Russian State*. With respect to this latter work, they approved both its style and tendency, and Pushkin, for one, put it at the head of his list of works which Russian literature might exhibit with pride before Europe.[32]

The strong pro-Karamzin editorial attitude of *Northern Flowers* is implicit from the first in its anti-Classical stance, its support of the Zhukovsky-Batyushkov current in poetry (which Karamzin's reform made possible), and in directly expressed admiration by several contributors. In his unsigned "Excerpts from Letters, Thoughts, and Remarks" ["Otryvki iz pisem, mysli i zameča'nija"], appearing in the 1828 issue of the almanac, Pushkin hailed the appearance of the *History*, but noted that no one in Russia was capable of evaluating the work. He dismissed some fatuous objections and expressed chagrin that no one thought to thank Karamzin for his twelve years of indefatigable labor.[33] In the same issue Nikolay Grech's "On the Life and Works of Karamzin" ["O žizni i sočinenijax Karamzina"] served as a formal eulogy for the recently deceased (May 22, 1826) man of letters. Grech praised Karamzin as a historian and then went on to underscore his contribution to the literary prose language:

> But if as a historian he is worthy of the praise and gratitude of the learned world, then no less, in our opinion, does he deserve fame as a man of literature and prose writer. In writing his *History* he had precursors and models of the famous writers of the past and present. But the new Russian prose, pure, light and noble, he created himself with the power of his talent and taste. His works, which seemed easy because they found many imitators—few of whom were successful—at first aroused opposition from men of letters accustomed to the prose of Lomonosov and his contemporaries. But with the passage of time the truly educated public generally ad-

mitted that Karamzin's style was not a capricious imitation of foreign examples but was based on a deep understanding of the qualities of the Russian language, purified by noble taste and based on the rules of universal grammar. . . . One may say decisively that for the lightness, clarity and correctness of contemporary Russian prose we are indebted to Karamzin.[34]

Northern Flowers' commitment to Karamzin automatically defined the role it would have to play in the controversy over Nikolay Polevoy's *History of the Russian People,* published in 1829. This very controversial work was, as the title might indicate, an attempt to refute Karamzin's *History of the Russian State,* but it was inferior to the latter work both with respect to accuracy and style. A journal as pro-Karamzin as was *Northern Flowers* could not remain indifferent to the challenge represented by Polevoy's work. Nor could it ignore the potential of various short-term *mariages de convenance* with other anti-Polevoy periodicals. Thus in his 1831 critical essay Somov commends the *Slav,* edited by the notorious literary pirate Alexander Voyeykov, for Russov's review of Polevoy's *History,* which "quite clearly put on exhibit all the incongruities and blunders of the new Historian."[35] In this same article Somov even makes temporary peace with Kachenovsky's *Messenger of Europe.*

> The editor, in his essays, continued to drink tea, smoke tobacco, and chat with Mr. Nikodim Nadoumka [Nikolay Nadezhdin] about Russian literature. However, one must give him his due: several remarks regarding the second volume of *History of the Russian People* were sound and even witty.[36]

The survey of that same year concluded with a lengthy and heated critique of Polevoy's *History,* which Somov asserted failed completely in its professed attempt to present a history of the Russian people.

> Here, besides several unimportant hypotheses, extraneous parenthetical opinions which often are completely irrelevant, and continuous contradictions of Karamzin—

contradictions expressed at times with unsuitable super-
ciliousness—nothing new is to be found. All is just the
same as in the work of previous historians: not one fresh
thought, not one essential hypothesis. And in contradict-
ing Karamzin, this new historian often contradicts even
himself, particularly with regard to chronology. And he
also contradicts himself in that having undertaken to
write *the history of the people,* nowhere does he bring
the people to the fore as an independent entity.[37]

If Somov was a vigorous opponent of Polevoy-the-his-
torian, he was more moderate regarding Polevoy-the-author-
and-editor. In general he is positive in his comments about
the *Moscow Telegraph,* as he is about Polevoy's prose, though
usually his remarks are tempered by a plea for greater attention to style. Polevoy's well-established limitations as a
translator receive attention also when Somov, with a measure
of malicious glee, makes note of the *Short Telegraphic
Dictionary* compiled by the editors of the *Northern Bee*
[Bulgarin, *et al.*] to acquaint the public with Polevoy's mis-
translations of French words.

If occasional hostilities with the pro-Romantic *Moscow
Telegraph* were impossible to avoid, then it was absolutely
inevitable that sooner or later *Northern Flowers* and the
Messenger of Europe would openly clash, the more so that
the latter was pro-Classicist and vigorously anti-Pushkin. The
Messenger of Europe, founded in 1802 by Karamzin, had
passed through the hands of a number of editors and in 1815
became the ward of M. T. Kachenovsky, a professor of history. Although Kachenovsky continued to print works of
Romantic writers—especially European ones—the journal
was officially conservative. It opposed Pushkin's *Ruslan and
Liudmila,* Vyazemsky's pro-Romantic preface to "The Fountain of Bakchisaray," Griboedov's *Woe from Wit,* and
resisted tendencies initiated by *Polar Star,* the *Moscow Telegraph,* and other periodicals with Romantic orientations. In
1828 Kachenovsky announced from the pages of his journal
that he was assuming the duties of publisher in addition to
those of editor, and in this connection he intimated that he
would become a savior who would lead Russian literature

from its state of helplessness. This pompous declaration was greeted with astonishment and derision by other journals, in particular by the *Moscow Telegraph,* in which Polevoy, over the pseudonym "Beninga," printed a deeply sarcastic assessment of Kachenovsky's intentions and literary accomplishments. A subsequent number of the *Messenger of Europe* contained a brief and ominous statement by Kachenovsky.

> I consider it fitting here to announce that I have no desire to quarrel with Beninga, having renounced forever fruitless polemics, and now I don't even have the right to do this [dispute], having taken other measures to preserve my reputation from the whimsical arbitrariness of this Beninga and others like him.[38]

What Kachenovsky alluded to as "other measures" was in fact his formal complaint against S. N. Glinka, the member of the Moscow Censorship Board who had approved Polevoy's text. Kachenovsky charged that such an obviously overt attack against his honorable service and rank should never have been passed. The Moscow Censorship Board, with the exception of V. V. Izmailov, a sometime contributor to Delvig's almanac, decided in favor of Kachenovsky, but this finding was subsequently overruled by higher authority.

The Kachenovsky-Polevoy conflict, despite its possibly serious consequences, had its burlesque aspects, and in the 1830 issue of *Northern Flowers* Pushkin, with delicious irony, reviewed the developments in this controversy in his "An Excerpt from Literary Annals" [Otryvok iz literaturnyx letospisej"].[39] Pushkin takes the position of an ingenuous bystander who observes the declarations and evaluations of both Polevoy and Kachenovsky with perplexity, now siding with the outraged professor, now defending his insistent antagonist. The ultimate result is that the pettiness and essential absurdity of both parties are delightfully illuminated.

Somov's treatment of Kachenovsky was more direct, and in his critical survey for the 1830 almanac he mocks the professor's pretentious expectations of delivering Russian literature from its pitiable state. These intentions, Somov asserts, have so far only been realized by the *Messenger of*

Europe's use of pre-Petrine orthography and the presence of literary criticism by the ex-student Nikodim Nadoumka (Nikolay Nadezhdin), who fractures Greek and Latin quotations and permits himself to comment on poems of Pushkin and Baratynsky. In a footnote Somov remarks that several journals have pointed out that the pseudonym Nikodim Nadoumka (which suggests Nickodemus the Advisor) should really be Nikodim Nedoumok (Nickodemus the Fuddled).

Northern Flowers' stance with respect to the *Moscow Herald* was ambivalent, certainly in part because it shared contributors with that journal, including Pushkin and Delvig. Founded in 1827 by a number of Russian author-critics interested in German idealistic philosophy, including S. P. Shevyrev, V. F. Odoevsky, A. S. Khomyakov, the Kireevsky brothers and others, with the historian M. P. Pogodin as editor, the *Moscow Herald* opposed the philistinism of Polevoy's *Moscow Telegraph* and the commercialism of Bulgarin's *Northern Bee*. Somov, in his first review of the newly founded journal, gave high praise to its literary content and its articles on literary theory, but he chided it for some careless errors and expressed hope that the editor would be less pedantic in his own essays. He concludes: "Despite these small exceptions, the journal is one of the best and represents varied, pleasant, and often useful reading."[40] This review was too positive for some and too critical for others, as Somov ruefully remarks in his survey the following year. And he adds, "My untimely solicitude gave rise to the uncontrolled ambition and the wholly unjustified arrogance which were the governing spirit of the *Moscow Herald*'s polemics during 1828."[41] Somov then proceeds to provide a *quid pro quo* for the less than positive assessment of *Northern Flowers for 1827* written by Stepan Shevyrev, chief critic for the *Moscow Herald*. Shevyrev is criticized for his translation of *Wallenstein's Camp* in which German soldiers use Russian proverbs and address each other with Russian diminutive names, and the same translator's rendition of Mickiewicz's *Konrad Wallenrod* into prose is termed "jejune and flaccid." It should be noted that Shevyrev, in reviewing *Northern Flowers*, had characterized Somov's story "The Holy Fool" as vulgar [prostonarodnyj] and had taken him to task for his strained witticisms. Somov responds to these charges with a measure of humor, but his smile disappears when he discusses the insufficiently positive attitude toward Baratynsky of the *Moscow Herald*, whose critics saw in the young poet only the talent of an immature novice.

The next year's surveys treated Pogodin and his journal with limited approval and tactful criticism. In general the poetic contributions, particularly those of Pushkin and other collaborators of *Northern Flowers*, were praised, though Somov noted some mediocre works. The attitude toward Pogodin himself was more negative, and his views on history were characterized as weak and not justifying their claim to originality. In passing it might be noted that in the 1830 issue of the almanac, Somov reviewed Pogodin's *The Fatal Malaise* [*Černaja Nemoč'*], a novel about a young man who committed suicide when his thirst for knowledge was frustrated by his father's contempt for learning. The critic found the plot fatuous and the hero's motivation improbable, but he admitted the value of the author's depiction of Moscow merchant life. Strangely, Pushkin had a much higher opinion of this work than Somov, but, of course, Pushkin held a much higher opinion of Pogodin and the *Moscow Herald* than did many others.[42]

In the war of periodicals skirmishes might be won, but total victory was an impossibility—editors and critics simply refused to die gracefully. Then, too, many of the new journals or almanacs—and several new ones appeared each year—entered the field with guns ablaze, seeking to wrest a bit of high ground from which to barrage targets of opportunity. In defending its positions of "free" art, the Karamzinian tradition and Karamzin, Romanticism, and Pushkin and his Pleiad, *Northern Flowers* was continually in the thick of battle. Not the least difficult of Somov's problems was to defend what was valuable against the onslaughts of tireless antagonists and at the same time remain true to his standards of objectivity. Each of his surveys is a demonstration of the complexity of his task and, it should be said, a testament to his generally correct literary judgement. It might be thought that it did not take any special acumen to support such poets as Pushkin and Baratynsky—perhaps not, from a perspective of almost a century and a half later. But in the twenties there were many critics who were far less enthusiastic about these poets than they should have been, and some were downright antagonistic. Somov may have chosen his side correctly, but still his task was not an easy one.

In 1827 Pushkin published his *Gypsies, The Robber Brothers* and Canto III of *Eugene Onegin,* and in the survey covering that year Somov gives them the place of honor in his critique of individual authors and works. In the 1829 issue of the almanac he lauds the recently published fourth, fifth, and sixth cantos of *Onegin,* noting the new element of action which makes the characters, previously viewed as portraits, come to life. In 1830 he again gives primary emphasis to Pushkin with a long assessment of two volumes of *The Poems of A. Pushkin,* focusing his remarks particularly on *Poltava.* A summary of the poem's content is followed by enthusiastic comments on the "beauty of detail," "the daring and power of expression," "the charm of the verses." In expressing his reservations about the work, the critic becomes more specific, objecting in particular to the torture and execution scenes on the grounds of plausibility and historical verisimilitude. Somov notes that Kochubey, under torture, when asked the location of his treasure, replies that he has three treasures: his honor, taken from him by torture; his daughter, stolen by Mazeppa; and sacred vengeance, which he is preparing for God. "Could Kochubey," queries Somov, "suffering from torture and preparing to be executed, voice enigmas or play with words?"[43] The critic also objected to the execution scene, pointing out that the playful posturing of the executioner and happy mood of the crowd were historically inaccurate; since the condemned, Kochubey and Iskra, were heroes to the Ukrainians and deemed guiltless by them, argues Somov, there could hardly have been a festive atmosphere at their martyrdom. These reservations are reasonable and they reveal the critic's objectivity, even when dealing with the poet whom he placed above all others.

It might be well to note here that in a number of places

Somov criticizes works on the basis of criteria which are certainly closer to the modern concept of realism than Romanticism. In his very first survey he had found fault with Kulzhinsky's *A Little Russian Village* on the grounds that it presented an idealized picture of Ukrainian rural life. His comments seem almost a plea for realism: ". . . but having the honor to be a countryman of Mr. Kulzhinsky, I shall remark to him that our precise age demands substantiality in descriptions, not dreaminess, fidelity of color and not delicacy, and accuracy of epithet, not excessiveness."[44]

In his final survey Somov returns to *Eugene Onegin*, prefacing his remarks on Canto VII with lengthy observations on those who cannot tell mediocre from good poetry. In this connection he applies Tatyana's question about Onegin, "Is he not indeed a parody?" to the *Northern Bee*, *Son of the Fatherland*, and the *Moscow Telegraph*, and then he goes on to outline the action of Canto VII and comment in general terms on its high poetic value.

It may well have been on behalf of Pushkin that Somov so vigorously castigated the newly formed *Galatea* [*Galateja*], established in 1829 by Semyon Raich. Despite the fact that the journal published two poems by Pushkin—and works by other contributors to *Northern Flowers* as well—it also contained several essays in which Pushkin was sharply criticized. In assessing the journal, Somov expressed distaste for its selection of fiction—"stories about bandits, murders, spirits, and spies, stories filled with terrible and revolting details"—and disgust with its prose style.[45] He grudgingly admitted that in some numbers one might find good poetry, but not often, and then asserted that "the distinguishing character of this journal is vacuity, vapidity, tastelessness, and breach of decorum."[46] This last remark was prompted by *Galatea's* unseemly polemics with the *Moscow Telegraph*, which shocked a number of people.[47] Somov then turns on Raich himself:

> The arrogant demands of the publisher were often quite amusing. For example, he said that only *artists* could judge his poetry. What have artists to do with his poetry, which only causes good folk to laugh? Alas! Better that he had kept completely quiet about his poetry.[48]

And to crush Raich utterly, the critic adds the following footnote.

> Sluggishness of imagination, punctilious affectation of feeling, absence of imagination and taste, frequent laughable choice of poetic meters—these are the characteristics of the verses of the gentleman editor of *Galatea*. He rides forth on his translation of *Jerusalem Delivered* and considers it something sacred and inviolable. But in vain![49]

Somov's efforts on behalf of Pushkin may have been unnecessarily zealous, since the poet was really quite able to defend himself and enjoyed sufficient popularity so that those who deprecated his work did so at considerable risk. However, the situation was otherwise with Yevgeny Baratynsky, whose talent was seriously underestimated by a number of contemporary critics. Therefore, the defense of this poet and the establishment of his reputation was one of the significant tasks undertaken by the critics of *Northern Flowers*. In the 1828 issue Peter Pletnyev devoted a short essay, "On the Poems of Baratynsky" ["O stixotvorenijax Baratynskogo"], to the campaign in support of the poet. In general he comments upon the ideational content of Baratynsky's poetry and, in particular, stresses his command of the Russian literary language. Regarding Baratynsky's style, he remarks that

> The works of Baratynsky represents a model of accuracy and style. He expresses his thoughts so faithfully that the reader can note and feel their lightest shades. There are no words which are out of place, unconsidered, or accidental. His verbal succinctness not only does not harm the clarity of his verses but lends them particular force. In the composition of his periods he is as varied as in the invention of new ideas.[50]

Pletnyev is impressed with Baratynsky's ability to resist the blandishments of contemporary European poetry, with its "seductive dreaminess," and he commends the poet for having rejected affectation and hyperbolic ornamentation. Though he is primarily an elegist, says Pletnyev, in his elegies "there is no dejection, no dreaminess, but rather (if one may say so) reflectiveness [razdum'e]." Sometimes close to tears, he stops them and smiles; on the other hand, his happiness sometimes shines through tears. Childlike sensitivity and the mind of the philosopher under the strict control of refined taste constitute his chief characteristics."[51]

At a time when much of Russian poetry was the work of Epigoni, Baratynsky's originality and freshness were as welcome as they were rare—at least to the critics of *Northern Flowers.*[52] The problem of originality had, incidentally, occupied Somov also, and his survey in the same issue as Pletnyev's essay made an eloquent plea for the abandonment of imitation.

> In the works of our young versifiers it is almost always possible to notice that the means of expression, the ornamentation of the verses, even the predilection for certain words and rhymes derive from one or another poet whom they have studied the most. Imitativeness becomes second nature to them. Therefore, the greater part of their elegies, epistles about the *languor of life, yearning for the better,* and so forth waft with an epidemic of boredom. An imitator never achieves the perfection of his model; he will always follow far behind, slip and fall, or crawl.[53]

The following year Somov vigorously returned to Baratynsky's defense, taking to task the *Moscow Herald* for judging Baratynsky as if he were "some immature youth with an undeveloped talent."

> The bard of *Eda,* of *Feasts,* of *Finland,* the creator of numerous elegies breathing with deep and true feelings, and epistles sparkling with free and unfeigned wit, deserves that when critics speak about his works they weigh their words with greater care and responsibility.[54]

He then went on to mock the *Moscow Herald's* critics for having mistaken Baratynsky's "The Last Death," which had appeared in *Northern Flowers,* as an excerpt from a longer work.

As one might expect, the critical posture of *Northern*

Flowers was to some extent determined by its contributors: authors favored by its editor would likely be praised by its critics. Such is the case, though Somov obviously reserved the right to speak forthrightly even about the almanac's closest collaborators. Next to Pushkin and Baratynsky, consistently favorable assessments were made about the poetry of Ivan Kozlov, Dmitry Venevitinov, Baron Rozen, Alexey Illichevsky, Fyodor Glinka, Nikolay Yazykov, and Ivan Krylov. Against Delvig's wishes, Somov also positively assessed his editor's poetry, particularly in the survey which followed the publication of *The Poems of Baron Delvig* in 1829. But collaboration was no guarantee that the almanac's chief critic would invariably react favorably to work published elsewhere. Thus Andrey Podolinsky, who appeared in *Northern Flowers* from 1828 to 1830, was unfavorably reviewed in the surveys of both 1830 and 1831. On the basis of the promise demonstrated by his *Div and Peri,* which had appeared in 1827 when he was just twenty-one, Podolinsky had been patronized by Delvig's circle and much was expected from him. But his next major work, *Borsky,* was a disappointment. In his critique of the work, Somov admitted that the verses themselves were "beautiful, free, and sonorous," but he took exception to the improbable plot, and one feels that he was even overly gentle in his appraisal of that ragout of parental curses, suspicion, murder, and madness. The following year his remarks about Podolinsky's *The Beggar* were more severe.

> In this new tale the author of *Div and Peri* and *Borsky* does not satisfy those expectations with which the first efforts of his young Muse lured his readers. . . . Confusion of narration, falseness of emotion and, in places, inaccuracy of expression—such are what these verses contain.[55]

Somov did remark that the verses were pleasing to the ear, but he withdrew his favor by adding that the work was deficient in intellectual and emotional content.

Among the interesting marginalia of literary history is the fact that Somov was the only critic to give encouragement to the young Nikolay Gogol following the fiasco of his *Hanz Küchelgarten*, the ill-fated narrative poem which marked Gogol's initial venture into literature.

> The eighteen-year-old versifier painted these eighteen pictures in which are revealed his still young imagination, immaturity of talent with respect to style, language and versification, and an extreme absence of creative precision. But there is in the author a visible talent which promises a future poet.[56]

Somov advised Gogol to avoid premature publication and predicted future success if the poet would give more diligent consideration to this work. Knowing Gogol's acute sensitivity and *amour propre*, one may imagine how this gently admonitory assessment must have affected him. Yet he doubtless was encouraged the following year when his "A Chapter from a Historical Novel" was accepted by *Northern Flowers*, marking his first piece of published prose.[57] In thus assisting Gogol, whose early works hardly gave a clue to his real talent, Somov was either gifted with second sight or, perhaps, simply sorry for his homesick young countryman. Apropos of historical novels, it should be mentioned that *Northern Flowers* certainly contributed to the popularity of this emerging genre by printing individual chapters of various novels as samplers. In 1829 Chapter IV of Pushkin's "The Moor of Peter the Great" appeared, in 1831 the aforementioned contribution by Gogol, and the following year there was a selection from I. Lazhechnikov's *The Last Novik*. Indicative of the growing popularity of imaginative prose in general, that last issue also presented "excerpts" from two other non-historical novels and three complete short novels [povesti].

The perspective provided by the passage of years makes it possible to view *Northern Flowers'* role in the general context of its time and see with a certain objectivity in what areas that role was particularly productive and also where it was apparently pointless. Obviously, much of the energy of the almanac's critics was needlessly expended in the polemics of the period, since the Bulgarins were incapable of reform and the Polevoys and Kachenovskys too stubborn to change.

Of course, in the late twenties Neo-Classicism still appeared to be a vigorous antagonist of Romanticism, though we now know that by that time it was already mortally wounded. Again, the defense of Karamzin, although praiseworthy, was hardly necessary: his reform of the literary language had been firmly established by the twenties and his *History*, like all classics, was its own best defender.

The real victories of the almanac's critics were not achieved in the lists by breaking lances with the black knights of other periodicals but rather by the consistent encouragement of good talents, by seeing that promising authors were printed and their virtues extolled in critical essays. Unquestionably, this had its cumulative effect upon public taste. As a critical force *Northern Flowers* also functioned, largely through the efforts of Orest Somov, to focus the attention of authors on the task of developing a supple and refined prose language. Connected with this was the conviction of the almanac's editors and critics that, if the public were to be attracted to the domestic literary product, authors would have to provide something which would compete with foreign imports. With some exceptions the prose and poetry sections of *Northern Flowers* demonstrated that Russian literature could provide such competition.

Chapter V

Poetry and Poets

The Major Contributors

The section of *Northern Flowers* devoted to verse consistently presented works of those who have come to be recognized as the leading poets of the period 1825–32. Of course, in the later twenties and early thirties many of these authors did not enjoy the indisputable reputations that they do today, but even at that time a number of them were established poets and, if not completely accepted by all the critics and the public, they at least were well known. A great deal of critical literature exists concerning their poetry, and therefore there is no need here to attempt an analysis of individual works; such an effort would not only be redundant, but, owing to the number of poems involved, necessarily superficial. However, some mention should be made of the major pieces which these important poets published for the first time in *Northern Flowers*, since these works are an indicator of the quality of the almanac's poetry section.

The dominant figure among the contributors to the almanac, both quantitatively and qualitatively, was ALEXANDER PUSHKIN (1799–1837), who published more than fifty poetic selections in the almanac's eight issues. Excerpts from *Eugene Onegin* [*Evgenij Onegin*] appeared on four occasions, beginning in 1825. As we know, Pushkin's "novel in verse" was published by individual cantos between 1825 and 1832, and therefore the selections in the almanac served to advertise forthcoming cantos and to whet the appetite of the public. This procedure was typical for the period, when journals and almanacs often presented fragments of longer prose and poetry to generate interest in complete versions available in separate editions. In the 1826 issue a portion of *The Gypsies* [*Cygany*] also was included, thus anticipating the publication of the complete work the following year. Among Pushkin's longer works which appeared in their entirety were the comic *Count Nulin* [*Graf Nulin*] (1828)[1] and one of his famous little tragedies. *Mozart and Salieri* [*Mocart i Sal'eri*] (1832). The important ballad, "The Lay of Wise Oleg" ["Pesn' o veščem Olege"] was the lead contribution of the poetry section in the almanac's first issue.

Among adaptations or imitations were "Proserpine" ["Prozerpina"] (1825), from Parny, the fourth verse from "Imitations of the Koran" [Podražanija Koranu"] (1826), "Two Ravens" ["Dva vorona"] (1829), from Scott, "Imitation of Anacreon" ["Podražanie Anakreonu"] (1829), and the famous "Poison Tree" ["Ančar"] (1832), suggested by Wordsworth's "It is a poison tree." Several of the contributions were addressed to his friends, including "The Skull" ["Čerep"] (1828), an epistle to Delvig which playfully established that the skull which Pushkin sent to his friend was that of Delvig's ancestor. "To Baratynsky" ["Baratynskomu"] (1826) was written in Bessarabia in 1822 as an expression of admiration for the young poet. "An Answer to Katenin" ["Otvet Kateninu"] (1829) was Pushkin's reply to Pavel Katenin's ballad "An Old Tale" ["Staraja byl' "], which was published in the same issue of *Northern Flowers* and contained an allusion to Pushkin. "October" 19 ["19 Oktjabrja"] (1827) was the first of several anniversary poems marking the opening of the lyceum at Tsarskoe Selo in 1811. Composed in 1825 while Pushkin was in exile at Mikhailovskoe, it is a poignant expression of the loneliness experienced by the poet as he pondered the fate of his schoolmates. Some other poems are also from the Mikhailovskoe period and allude to the poet's isolation, such as "Winter Evening" ["Zimnij večer"] (1830). Among the most famous of the very personal lyrics are "I loved you once" [Ja vas ljubil"] (1830), "To

" ("I remember the wondrous moment") ["K" ("Ja
pomnju čudnoe mgnoven'e")] (1827), a tribute to the inspiration provided the poet by Anna Kern, and "Elegy"
("Under the Blue Sky") ["Èlegija" ("Pod nebom golubym")]
(1828), believed to allude to the deceased Amalia Riznich.
"The Demon" ["Demon"] (1825), in which the poet
expresses regret for the cynicism and mistrust which his demon
(probably Alexander Raevsky) had inspired, had previously
appeared in the almanac *Mnemosyne*. Two poems published
in the 1831 edition of *Northern Flowers* concern the theme
of the poet and the crowd. "To the Poet: A Sonnet" ["Poètu:
Sonet"] exalts the poet as the best judge of his art, and "An
Answer to an Anonymous Person" ["Otvet anonimu"]
expresses the idea that the public views the poet as an
itinerant clown.[2] Among the better known poems on themes
of nature were two connected with Pushkin's journey to
Erzerum: "The Avalanche" ["Obval"] (1831) and "The
Monastery on Mount Kazbek" ["Monastyr' na Kazbeke"]
(1831). This listing by no means exhausts the titles of the
significant works Pushkin published in *Northern Flowers;*
however, it sufficiently emphasizes the extent and value of
Pushkin's poetic contribution to the almanac.[3]

PRINCE PETER VYAZEMSKY (1792–1878) was, next to Pushkin,
the most active contributor of poetry to the almanac. Thirty-
six selections, including just about all of his best poems written
between 1824 and 1831, with the exception of "The Russian
God" ["Russkij Bog"], were published in the various issues.
Of the famous collaborators on *Northern Flowers*, Vyazemsky
presents one of the most difficult problems of classification:
as a critic he was firmly behind the so-called Romantics, but
in his own poetry he reveals a basically Classical orientation.
A staunch defender of the Karamzin tradition (Karamzin,
incidentally, was married to an older sister of Vyazemsky),
he was one of the mainstays of the anti-conservative literary
society Arzamas (1815–18). In 1824 his controversial introduction to Pushkin's *The Fountain of Bakchisaray*. "A Conversation Between a Publisher and a Classicist," a manifesto of
Romanticism, called forth sharp reactions from the literary

traditionalists. Vyazemsky was also associated with Nikolay Polevoy's pro-Romantic journal, *Moscow Telegraph*, which he helped to establish. But despite his allegiance to the flag of Romanticism, Vyazemsky was essentially an eighteenth-century intellect in the Voltairian tradition, and his poetry clearly demonstrates this. In an age when his friends were innovators and experimenters, when genres were being hybridized, meters varied, the language of poetry expanded, his Muse remained slightly old-fashioned, formal, and rationalistic. He has been called "a poet of thought," an appellation which he would probably have approved.

> I dearly love and highly value the harmonious quality of others' verses, but in my own verses in no way do I pursue this harmoniousness. I shall never sacrifice thought to sound.[4]

This emphasis on ideas was obvious to his contemporaries, among them Pushkin, who wrote to him regarding "To the Supposed Happy Woman" ["K mnimoj sčastlivice"] (1826), a poem on the theme of *mariage de convenance:* "Your verses to the Supposed Beauty (Ach, excuse me, Happy Woman) are too intellectual. And poetry, God forgive me, must be feebleminded."[5]

A number of Vyazemsky's contributions to the almanac relate to the conflict between Classicism and Romanticism. Among these are three satirical epigrams, "To the Journalistic Twins" [K žurnal'nym bliznecam"] (1825), addressed to his critical antagonists Alexander Pisarev and Mikhail Dmitriev, "A Characterization" ["Xarakteristika"] (1826), a six-line lampoon directed at Mikhail Kachenovsky, conservative editor of the *Messenger of Europe.*[6] and "A Russian Romantic to a Russian Classicist" ["Russkij romantik russkomu klassiku"] (1828). Two longer works also relate to this conflict: "A Local Feature" ["Čerta mestnosti"] (1825) presents a brief dialogue in which a pompous critic (read *classicist*) advises that in the first line of a love lyric, "The house in which my sovereign sits," the word "house" be replaced by "temple" or "chamber" and the word "sits" be replaced by the more poetic "dwells"; the poet answers that a local feature prevents this: his "unhappy young beauty sits within the walls of a madhouse." In "To My Journalist Well-Wishers" ["K žurnal'nym blagoprijateljam"] (1831) Vyazemsky humorously accused his antagonists of ingratitude, since it was only the critical attention which he had given their works which had saved them from deserved oblivion.

Notwithstanding his pro-Romantic critical orientation, indicated by these epigrams and facetious poems,[7] Vyazemsky's verses often exhibited the qualities typical of Classical poetry: objective attitude, formal tone, complex syntax, Slavonicisms, conventional epithets, and archaic words. An example is "The Narva Waterfall" [Narvskij vodopad"] (1826), an ode which apostrophizes the waterfall and establishes parallels between it and a man excited by passion. But the work is intellectual rather than emotional, and Vyazemsky himself stated to Pushkin, to whom he sent the work in 1825,[8] that "the verses are somehow cold." In a longer ode, "The Sea" ["More"] (1828), the poet alludes to the fate of the Decembrists. This work, composed in the summer of 1826, when word reached Vyazemsky of the execution and exile of the conspirators, was also first sent to Pushkin, who did not miss its heavily veiled allusions to the tragic denouement of the December Uprising. A gloomy mood also pervades "Autumn 1830" ["Osen' 1830 goda"] (1831), a work in the classical iambic hexameter. It is preceded by an epigraph from Victor Hugo's *Le Dernier Jour d'un condamné* stressing the idea that nature has no beauty for a condemned person; this serves as a stimulus for the poet's own musing on the omnipresence of death behind nature's facade of beauty. Although this poem was written at a time when Vyazemsky and his family were threatened by a cholera epidemic, its pessimism is a reflection of the poet's personal *Weltanschauung* rather than a reaction to the menace of the disease. A similarly intellectualized melancholy appears in the lengthy "Parental Home" ["Roditel'skij dom"] (1831), in which the poet voices the thought that memories are dearer than actuality, since

> *In memories we are at home;*
> *But in the present we are slaves*
> *Of sudden storms, of hopes'*
> *Destruction, of accident and fate.*

V vospominanijax my doma;
A v nastojaščem my raby
Nezapnoj buri, pereloma
Zelanij, slučaev, sud'by.⁹

Vyazemsky also cultivated various forms of "light poetry" based on the late eighteenth-century French tradition, and here the poet's visage is considerably brighter than in his philosophic meditations. His friendly epistles are spirited, informal, witty, and even prosaic, and their language is that of ordinary speech, at times even racy. His "Epistle to A. A. B. on Sending My Portrait" ["Poslanie k A. A. B. pri posylke portreta"] (1829) is typical of this variety of light poetry. His contribution to *Northern Flowers* also includes a number of simple lyrical poems on a variety of subjects, all of them pleasing but none especially noteworthy.

BARON ANTON DELVIG (1798–1831), editor and publisher of *Northern Flowers,* was also an active contributor of poetry, and thirty-four of his works appeared in the first six issues of the almanac. Owing to his troubles with *The Literary Gazette,*¹⁰ he lost interest in literary affairs and contributed nothing to *Northern Flowers for 1831.* The five poems which appeared in the 1832 almanac were discovered among his papers after his death.

Delvig's poetry is quite distinct from that of Pushkin and other members of the Pleiad who collaborated on *Northern Flowers.* His best known pieces, many of which appeared in the almanac, belong to two distinct categories, the idyl and popular song. In his idyls Delvig presents an idealized vision of Arcadian shepherds, shepherdesses, satyrs, and venerable old men who sing of love, friendship, and wine. An antique impression is created by local color, conventional names, and reference to the gods of Olympus. Of these idyls "The Bathing Women" ["Kupal'nicy"], which appeared in the almanac's first issue, is probably the most famous. D. S. Mirsky characterized it as "unquestionably the highest achievement in Russian poetry in the more purely sensuous vision of classical antiquity."¹¹ In dactylic hexameters Satyr describes to the shepherd Mikon how he eavesdropped on Daphnis and Licoris as they bathed (with two swans!) and from their conversation learned that Daphnis was indeed in love with the shepherd. In the same genre, "The Friends" ["Druz'ja"] (1827), dedicated to Baratynsky, celebrates two old Greeks, famous for their lifelong friendship and knowledge of wines. In "The Invention of Sculpture: An Idyl" ["Izobretenie vajanija: Idillija"] (1830) the potter Likadas recounts how he unexpectedly created the image of his faithless Harita while aimlessly working his clay. This work displays the bright coloration and plasticity associated with so many of Delvig's idyls.

An interesting, if not entirely successful, attempt to Russify the idyl is "The Retired Soldier" ["Otstavnoj soldat"] (1830), which Delvig subtitled "A Russian Idyl." The work is structured as a dialogue, principally involving a soldier and two shepherds, and instead of the traditional dactylic hexameter the poet employs blank iambic hexameter. This is a short composition, less than one hundred and thirty lines, most of which are spoken by the soldier. The idyl opens with the soldier, who is returning home from Wilno after a year's convalescence, encountering two shepherds, who offer to share their food with him. As he eats he feasts his senses upon Russian nature, which he declares is unsurpassed by anything he has seen in all his campaigns. When the shepherds ask for a story, he describes to them the horrors of the French retreat from Moscow. As they talk an officer stops on the highroad nearby and asks for a light for his pipe. Seeing the soldier, he tells him that the war is over and Moscow revenged.

We know from Pushkin that Delvig outlined this work when they were still students at the lyceum, a time when the memories of the Napoleonic invasion and retreat were quite fresh. Though the language is largely that of simple folk, it was noted by Barataynsky, in his extensive comments to Delvig upon one of the manuscripts, that in places the poem revealed an inappropriate "Greek tone" or high style. Regarding the concluding lines,

> *Look how*
> *The Lord has comforted Mother Russia!*
> *Pray, brothers, have not God's wonders*
> *Been accomplished before our very eyes!*

Vot kak
Gospod' utešil matušku-Rossiju!
Molites', bratcy! Bož'i čudesa
Ne soveršajutsja l' pred nami javno![12]

Baratynsky said: "These lines conclude the piece somewhat lifelessly. At least put a cesura in the last line—to console my classical ear."[13]

Delvig's Russian songs, though they have a "national flavor" owing to lexical and grammatical elements from folk poetry, are as stylized in their own way as his imitations of the classical idyl. Six of these, bearing the generalized title "A Russian Song" ["Russkaja pesn' "], appeared in *Northern Flowers* in various issues. All of them are laments of young women with various causes for grief: they are loveless, have lost their loves, or their lovers have gone to war. Avian imagery is important in several of these poems, where rather sophisticated parallels between birds' habits and human affairs are developed. Folksong metrics are generally observed: in "The birdlet sang and sang" ["Pela, pela ptašečka"] (1825), for example, there is an alternation of lines of trochaic trimeter with dactylic clausula and trochaic dimeter.

Delvig's innovations with respect to meter represent an important aspect of his contribution to the development of Russian poetry. His experimentation with unusual metrical combinations is represented by a work appearing in the 1827 almanac, "Dithyramb (On the Arrival of Three Friends)" ["Difiramb (Na priezd trex druzej)"], in which his four, seven-line stanzas follow the same pattern of iambs, amphibrachs, and trochees, with a regularly imposed cesura. In one of his sonnets, which appeared in the last issue of the almanac, he employed trochaic pentameter, an unusual form for Russian poets—as was the sonnet itself, for that matter. The metrical variations which are characteristic for so many of Delvig's poems are also found in "Romance" ("A Solitary Moon was Sailing") ["Romans" ("Odinok mesjac plyl")] (1829). This ballad-like poem presents intricate lines of two-foot and three-foot meters combined with a fixed cesura. In six couplets the poet establishes his setting (foggy night, remote tumulus), introduces his central figures (a knight and his horse), creates

an ominous mood (the knight's premonition that something
has happened to his beloved) and resolves the situation with
the knight's discovery of a new grave. Romantic elements are
here in quantity: the medieval setting, the nocturnal scene
with the moon and fog, the knight and his "melancholy steed"
(unylyj kon'), the tumulus. Strangely, however, when the
light of day dispels the romantic mists the knight sees "a temple in an oak grove." Despite this, a romantic mood dominates, and there is true romantic mystery in the poem's last
line, where the new grave is not definitely identified as that
of the knight's beloved.

Delvig's other contributions to *Northern Flowers* are less
interesting; some are only epigrammatic couplets. One might
mention, however, "On the Death of V[enevitino]v" ["Na
smert' V——va"] (1828), mourning the passing of that talented young member of Delvig's circle, and, on a different
level of significance, "On the Death of a Dog: Amika" ["Na
smert' sobački: Amiki"] (1828), an imitation of Catullus's
ode on the death of a robin. The unrhymed aphorism "Death"
["Smert' "] (1828)

*We're not afraid of death, but we're sad to part with our
    body:
Just as we're not willing to replace an old dressing gown.*

  *My ne smerti boimsja, no s telom rasstat'sja nam žalko:
  Tak ne s oxotoju my staryj smenjaem xalat.*[14]

precipitated a reaction disproportionate to its worth: both
Semyon Raich and Nikolay Polevoy set upon this bit of prosy
philosophy, the latter twice parodying it.[15]

YEVGENY BARATYNSKY (1800–44) was another of the almanac's
generous contributors, and the eight issues of *Northern Flowers* contained twenty-five lyrics, two fairy tales in verse, and
selections from his narrative poem *The Ball* [*Bal*] and *The
Concubine* [*Naložnica*]. His talent was unique, a fact recognized by his contemporaries and explicitly stated by himself
in "Muse" ["Muza"], which appeared in the 1830 issue of the
almanac:

I am not blinded by my Muse,
She can't be called a beauty

. . . .

But the world will be momentarily struck
By the unusual expression of her face
And the value of her thoughtful discourse.

Ne osleplen ja Musoju moeju:
Krasavicej ee ne nazovut,

. . . .

No poražen byvaet mel'kom svet
Ee lica neobščim vyrazen'em,
Dostoinstvom obdumannyx rečej.[16]

Much of Baratynsky's poetry is, in effect, ideas in verse, or, put another way, poeticized philosophy. The works in *Northern Flowers* are quite typical and include several of his more famous poems of intellectual content. A number of these directly treat the theme of death: "The Skull" ["Čerep"] (1825), a reflection on life and death inspired by a visit to a crypt; "The Inscription" ["Nadpis'"] (1826), in which the face of a corpse is likened to a suddenly frozen cascade; "The Last Death" ["Poslednjaja smert'"] (1828), a vision of the world from which man, grown indifferent to life owing to the comforts provided by technological developments, has disappeared; "Death" ["Smert'"] (1829), an abbreviated version of André Chénier's *Elégie XXV* mourning man's fate; "The Old Man" ["Starik"] (1829); and "Faith and Unbelief" ["Vera i neverie"] (1830), a philosophical dialogue in which "He" expresses the anguished view that even the joys of life are poisoned by the inevitability of death, while "She" argues that the life-death pattern is part of a divine plan which one must accept. The only optimistic note in all of these selections connected with death is in Baratynsky's single contribution of 1832,[17] "My Eli ion" ["Moj Ėlizij"], an affirmation that the recently deceasc l Delvig would not be forgotten.

In others of Baratynsky's poems the intellectual content is as marked as in those concerned with death: "Little Star" ["Zvezdočka"] (1825) expresses the idea that friends who are separated may be joined by gazing at a celestial body visible to them both. A lighter tone is evidenced by the lengthy (one hundred and two lines) "To Bogdanovich" ["Bogdanoviču"] (1827), an apostrophe to the creator of *Dushenka*, a masterful adaptation of La Fontaine's *Psyche et Cupidon*. The attraction of Baratynsky to this work was not accidental, for he was to an important degree both a product and partisan of the late Neo-Classical tradition. His amusement at the stereotyped melancholy of would-be Romantic poets is wittily expressed in "To Bogdanovich."

> *The spleen of German Muses has joined their Muses.*
> *Zhukovsky is to blame: he was the first among us*
> *To become friendly with German bards*
> *And, having lost his fear of God, he began to convey*
> *Their disparagement of life in captivating verse.*
>
> . . . .
>
> *Everyone's brow became covered with melancholy,*
> The soul faded and the heart withered.

> *Pristala k muzam ix Nemeckix muz xandra.*
> *Žukovskij vinovat: on pervyj meždu nami*
> *Vošel v sodružestvo s Germanskimi pevcami,*
> *I stal peredavat', zabyvši Božij strax,*
> *Žiznexulen'ja ix v plenitel'nyx stixax.*
>
> . . . .
>
> *U vsex unyniem odelosja čelo,*
> Duša uvjanula i serdce otcvelo.[18]

The late Neo-Classical influence upon Baratynsky is also reflected in two fairy tales published in *Northern Flowers*. "Theleme and Makar" ["Telema i Makar"] (1827), an adaptation of Voltaire's *Thélème et Macare*, makes the point that one should be satisfied with a lover as he is, not as he might be. A more ambitious piece in the style of Voltaire's moral fairy tales is "The Transmigration of Souls" ["Pereselenie duš"] (1829); in lighthearted tones it recounts how an Egyptian princess exchanged bodies with a shepherdess in order to win the latter's lover, an arrangement which proved mutually satisfactory to both transmigrated souls.

His narrative poems, *The Ball* and *The Concubine*, excerpts of which appeared in *Northern Flowers* in 1828 and 1831, were completely different.[19] Set in contemporary society, they concern tragic love affairs, one of which ends in suicide and the other in poisoning, albeit inadvertent. *The Ball* in completed form was published in one volume with Pushkin's *Count Nulin*, the full version of which had previously appeared in *Northern Flowers for 1828*. The critic of the *Messenger of Europe*, Nikolay Nadezhdin, provided this blanket judgment of the two works: "These are pimples on the face of our Dowager Literature! They are rosy, and plump, and mature: but . . . *Che chi a duo' occhi il veda!*"[20] The same critic, commenting upon the excerpts of *The Concubine* in *Northern Flowers*, would not even mention the title out of deference to his female readers. In general, neither of these works of Baratynsky were well received by his contemporaries, although discerning critics, such as Pushkin, Pletnyev and Kireevsky, were very positive in their appraisals.[21]

The collaboration of IVAN KOZLOV (1779–1840) with *Northern Flowers* began with the issue for 1825, the same year that his literary reputation was firmly established by publication of the narrative poem *The Monk* [*Černec*]. Born into a wealthy Moscow gentry family, he received a private education and then served briefly in a Guards' regiment, from which he retired at the age of nineteen to enter the civil service. In his later twenties his health began to deteriorate, and by the time he was thirty-two he was both paralyzed and blind.

Of Kozlov's eighteen pieces in the almanac, over half are translations or adaptations of foreign poets. This emphasis is proper, since it was as a translator that Kozlov made his most significant contribution. His range of interest in foreign literatures was broad, but English seems to have been his favorite. Thus, for the almanac's first issue he translated from Thomas Moore's cycle of Irish melodies "As a Beam O'er the Face of the Waters May Glow," giving it simply the title "An Irish Song (from Moore)" ["Irlandskaja pesnja (Iz Mura)"] (1825). An unusual accomplishment was his later rendering of Moore's "Evening Bells" ["Večernij zvon"] (1828), which is unexpectedly faithful to the swinging rhythm of the original.

Kozlov's translation of Charles Wolfe's "The Burial of Sir John Moore" was mistakenly given the Russian title "On the Burial of the English General Sir John. From Moore" ["Na pogrebenie anglijskogo generala Sira Džona. Iz Mura"] (1826). Happily this error was noted in the errata, but the correct original author was never mentioned.[22]

Although none of Kozlov's justly celebrated translations of Adam Mickiewicz's incomparable *Crimean Sonnets* were published in *Northern Flowers*, one adaptation of an erotic sonnet by the Polish poet did appear in the 1829 almanac, entitled "Stanzas (A Free Imitation of Adam Mickiewicz)" ["Stancy (Vol'noe podražanie Adamu Mickeviču)"]. The 1826 issue contained Kozlov's adaptation of the dream scene from Tasso's *Gerusalemme Liberata:* Clorinda appears to Tancred and tells him not to grieve, since her love transcends death.[23] Desdamona's song from *Othello* was Kozlov's last contribution to Delvig's almanac. The translation was entitled simply "Desdamona's Song (From Engl.)" ["Pesnja Desdemony (S Anglij.)"] (1831) and Shakespeare was not mentioned. Kozlov successfully used amphibrach tetrameter to convey the rhythm of such lines as "The poor soul sat sighing by a sycamore tree," but he made no effort to vary the meter in order to reproduce the special rhythm of the refrain, "Sing willow, willow, willow."

As a translator, Kozlov's particular reputation was connected with Byron, and it was probably his desire to know the poet better that led him to learn English in 1818. It is interesting as well that Kozlov's first literary efforts were also connected with Byron—he translated *The Bride of Abydos* into French! Three of his selections from Byron appeared in *Northern Flowers.* His translation of the song from stanza 13, Canto I, of *Childe Harold's Pilgrimage* excellently captures the surging rhythm and defiant spirit of the hero's last "good night" to the elements. Similarly, his translation of stanzas 122 and 123, Canto I, of *Don Juan* are more than simply what the poet chooses to call a "free imitation" ["Iz bajronova *Don-Žuana (Vol'noe podražanie)*"] (1830). Less successful, however, is his "Hebrew Melody: From Byron" ["Evrejskaja melodija: Iz Bajrona"] (1826), which is close to the original in meaning but whose amphibrach meter is too sportive for the subject: the distinct and clear light of a star is like "joy remember'd well," for it also is distant and cold.

Although Kozlov's original lyric poems often allude to his personal affliction, the eight examples of his own poetry in *Northern Flowers* lack such personal references. In fact, the graphic imagery and extensive use of color would presuppose a poet with unusual sensitivity to visual stimuli. Of course, it may be that just such bright and form-filled poetry served the poet as a compensation for his loss of sight. The rich, image-evoking quality mentioned above is exemplified by "*The Sunset Has Faded*" ["Zarja pogasla"] (1829).

> *The sunset has faded; in the glades breezelets*
> *Waft among the shrubs,*
> *They pluck lily of the valley, cornflowers,*
> *And circling, with scarlet blossoms*
> *Like variegated butterflies,*
> *They spread them over the meadows.*
> *Thus half-naked young maids,*
> *Carelessly, with lilylike fingers*
> *Of playful hands,*
> *Strew emeralds, amethysts,*
> *Pearls and fiery rubies*
> *When they retire in the wee hours.*

> *Zarja pogasla, —veterki*
> *V poljane dujut mež' kustami,*
> *Sryvajut landyš', vasil'ki*
> *I vmeste s alymi cvetami,*
> *Podobno pestrym motyl'kam,*
> *Kruža raznosjat po lugam:*
> *Tak izumrudy, ametisty,*
> *Žemčug i jaxonty ognisty,*
> *Nebrežno rezvoju rukoj*
> *S lilejnyx pal'cev, v čas nočnoj*
> *Ložasja spat', polunagie*
> *Ronjajut devy molodye.*[24]

Another good example is provided by "Stanzas to Nikolay Ivanovich Gnedich (To the Caucasus and Crimea)" ["Stansy k Nikolaju Ivanoviču Gnediču (Na Kavkaz i Krym)"]

(1826), which creates very plastic and colorful scenes of the Caucasus, the gardens of Bakchisaray, the Hellespont, and other places that Gnedich, then traveling in those regions, was expected to visit. The combination of three lines of iambic hexameter followed by one of iambic trimeter gives a stately tone which excellently complements the grandeur and emotional appeal of the scenes of nature. Another contribution combining plasticity and emotional elevation is Kozlov's "Kiev" ["Kiev"] (1825), an apostrophe to the ancient capital of Rus which is both descriptive and historical. Kozlov's two poetic tributes to women of his acquaintance, "To Princess M. A. Golitsyna, née Princess Suvorova" ["K Kn. M. A. Golicinoj, uroždennoj Knjažne Suvorovoj"] (1825) and "To Princess S. R[adziwil]l" ["Knjažne S. R——l' "] (1826) are simply conventional, and one stanza of the latter even seems to have been composed according to the formula used in the former. Pletnyev appended a brief poetic footnote to the poem addressed to Princess Radziwill praising Kozlov for having achieved a true vision of his addressee.

In the 1827 issue of the almanac appeared a selection from Kozlov's *Natalia Dolgorukaya,* with an accompanying note announcing that the complete work would soon be finished. This portion, entitled "A Moonlit Night in the Kremlin (From the Narrative Poem: Natalia Dolgorukaya, dedicated to V. A. Zhukovsky)" ["Lunnaja noč' v Kremle (Iz poèmy: Natal'ja Dolgorukaja, posvjaščennoj V. A. Žukovskomu"] included stanza 7 of Part II of the complete work. In it Kozlov presents an atmospheric and graphic impression of the ominous and silent Kremlin. Similar effects are achieved in "The Betrothed's Dream: A Ballad" ["Son nevesty: Ballada"] (1825), which describes the nocturnal appearance to a young girl of her drowned lover. Unlike the ballad in the German tradition, there is no tragic or frightful outcome of the visitation; here the ghostly lover consoles his fiancée with a promise of their future happiness in heaven.

NIKOLAY YAZYKOV (1803–46) was represented in *Northern Flowers* by thirteen poems, but, unlike the contributions of the other first-rate collaborators, these poems are hardly his

finest product. When Yazykov began publishing in the almanac
in 1826, only a limited number of his works had previously
appeared, primarily in *Well-Intended* [*Blagonamerennij*] and
Voyeykov's *Literary News*. However, during the latter part
of the twenties, which was his most productive period, he was
widely published and attracted considerable critical attention.

From a well-to-do Simbirsk gentry family, Yazykov received his education first at home, then in the Gorny Cadet
Corps, and from 1822 to 1829 he was a student at Dorpat
University. It is with the Anacreontic aspects of his bachelor's
life there that much, but certainly not all, of his poetry is
concerned. The year 1833, when his first volume of collected
works was published, is usually considered to mark the end
of his so-called first period, the more so that Yazykov himself
at that time wrote that he was "crossing straight from the
tavern to the church."[25]

Unfortunately, the works of Yazykov which appeared
in *Northern Flowers* fail to demonstrate fully those real qualities upon which his reputation has been based. The 1826
almanac contained three selections, one a rather insignificant
expression of joy at no longer being in love, ironically entitled "Praise the Lord" ["Slava Bogu"]. The other two
were intended as parts of narrative poems on themes from
Livonian life and history. Perhaps Yazykov's lengthy sojourn
in Dorpat suggested these topics; in any case, Livonia was of
considerable interest to Russian Romantics owing to its historical involvement with Russia and the exotic quality of its
feudal past under the rule of Teutonic Knights.[26] "An Excerpt
from the Tale Ala" ["Otryvok iz povesti Ala"] was to serve
as an introduction to a work dealing with the war against the
Swedes under the leadership of the Livonian patriot Johann
Reinhold von Patkul. Despite Yazykov's intention of completing this narrative poem, and his special studies to that end,
the work remained unfinished. The other narrative poem,
which was to deal with Estonian superstitions, also never got
beyond a partial introduction, represented by "Two Pictures"
["Dve kartiny"] (1826). This is a diptych of morning and
night scenes on Lake Peipus, both full of color, motion, and
sound; there is no indication in the work itself that it was to

be a part of a more ambitious poem, a fact revealed in Yazykov's correspondence.[27]

Yazykov was extremely prolific as a writer of poetic epistles, and a significant part of his entire corpus is in that form. The tone of these poetic missives may range from light humor to rather formal apostrophe, depending upon his addressee and the subject at hand. Alexey Wolfe, Yazykov's school friend and relative, was the recipient of a number of these, including one published in the 1829 almanac entitled simply "To A. N. W[ol]fe" ["A. N. V——fu"]. This epistle, marking Wolfe's entrance into active army service, contains the poet's promise to sing of Wolfe's military triumphs as he used to sing of their convivial student life. More formal is "To Baron A. A. Delvig" ["Baronu A. A. Del'vigu"] (1829), which was a comment upon the unfavorable criticism of Yazykov's poetry appearing in the *Moscow Telegraph*. Here the poet expands on the idea that present-day critics have turned the temple of poetry into some sort of noisy street market, full of strident sounds and abusive language. Two epistles in the last issue of the almanac deserve mention owing to the importance of their addressees: "To K. K. Jaenisch" ["K——e K——e Ja——' "] is a series of compliments to the the poetess-translator (better known under her married name, Karolina Pavlova); the other epistle, "To I. V. K. (About I. V.)" ["I. V. K. (ob I. V.)"] is an admonition to Ivan Kireevsky to beware the charms of a certain I. V.

Yazykov spent the summer of 1826 at Trigorskoe, the estate of Alexey Wolfe's mother, Madam Osipova. At that time he became acquainted with Pushkin, who was still languishing in exile at nearby Mikhailovskoe. Both Pushkin and Yazykov allude repeatedly in their poetry to the memories of that summer. Two such poems by Yazykov appeared in *Northern Flowers*, both connected with Pushkin's nurse, Irina Rodionovna. "To Nurse" ["K njane"] (1828) was included in a letter to Wolfe in the spring of 1827, and in this original version Yazykov began "Vasilievna, my light, can I forget you?" Wolfe corrected him, and Yazykov accordingly changed the first line to "My light, Rodionovna, can I forget you?" The poem, although it does emphasize the hospitality and graciousness of the nurse, who used to arrange dinners, serve wine, and tell tales, is really a reminiscence of visits with Wolfe to Mikhailovskoe where they and Pushkin would pleasantly pass the summer evenings. In this poem iambic hexameter is used, but the lack of cesura, the constant pyrrhics, the matter-of-fact tone and the concreteness to detail give the piece the quality of pleasantly flowing prose. Irina Rodionovna, who died in 1828, was the subject of Yazykov's "Elegy (I shall seek the humble cross)" ["Ėlegija (Ja otyšču tot krest smirennyj)"] (1831), which again conjures up images of evenings with Wolfe and Pushkin at Mikhailovskoe. The poem consists of nine octaves, the first containing a promise to find her grave, the next describing the delapidated manor house and garden and the third introducing the young company. As the poet proceeds to describe their bibulous evenings, the mood becomes less sombre and the elegy is transformed into a lively drinking song. Towards the conclusion, as the poet returns to the motif of the nurse's grave, the tone becomes more subdued.

In 1823, when Yazykov was virtually unknown, Baron Delvig addressed to him a sonnet entitled "Young Singer" ["Mladoj pevec"], which contained a prophecy of future fame.

> *Young singer, up a pretty path*
> *You'll at Parnassian heights arrive.*
> *A wreath for you (believe my words)*
> *Will Cupid and a dulcet Muse contrive.*

> *Mladoj pevec, dorogoju prekrasnoj*
> *Tebe idti k parnasskim vysotam,*
> *Tebe venok (pover' moim slovam)*
> *Pletet Amur s Kamenoj sladkoglasnoj.*[28]

In the 1832 almanac Yazykov presented two memorials to Delvig, "A Song (He was a poet)" ["Pesnja (On byl poėt)"] and "To A. A. Delvig" ["A. A. Del'vigu"]. Both laud the deceased poet for his disinterest in mundane affairs, his love of friendship, wine, and leisure; the latter poem summarizes, as it were, the poetic-personal essence of Delvig.

> *Such he was, Apollo's ward,*
> *By soul and lyre an ancient Greek.*

> *Takov on byl, xranimij Febom,*
> *Dušoj i lìroj drevnij Grek.*[29]

With increasing rhetorical power the poem goes on to note
Delvig's passage to a better world, and the final stanza concludes with Yazykov's plea that this poem, which is his best,
be not forgotten.

> *Oh, let my poems*
> *Leave people's sweet memories*
> *For oblivion's terrible darkness.*
> *All, all may perish, all the rest,*
> *But let not perish this, the best.*

> *O! pust' moi stixotvoren'ja*
> *Iz miloj pamjati ljudej*
> *Ujdut v nesnosnyj mrak zabven'ja,*
> *Vse, vse! .... No lučšee odno*
> *Da ne pogibnet: vot ono!*[30]

The poet's evaluation, of course, was prompted by his desire
to keep alive Delvig's memory, and the poem does, indeed,
represent an impressive tribute to the almanac's late editor.

IVAN KRYLOV (1769–1844) was already a "grandfather figure"
in Russian literature when *Northern Flowers* made its debut.
His early career, which had begun in the eighties of the
previous century, had been devoted to the writing of dramas
and editorial work on various journals. Following the suppression of his own satirical journal, The *Spectator* [*Zritel'*]
in 1792, Krylov left the literary scene for a number of years,
returning in 1805 as an author of comedies. In 1809 his first
book of fables was published, and from that time his reputation was assured.

   The eight fables which Krylov wrote for *Northern
Flowers* reveal a poet with a fine eye for human foibles and
a rationalistic, commonsense approach to life. In "The Fly
and the Bee" ["Muxa i pčela"] (1825), on the theme of the

shameless persistence of certain parasitical types, a fly impudently recounts how, when chased from banquets by disgusted diners, it simply comes in another window.[31] "The Aged Lion" ["Lev sostarevšijsja"] (1825) and "The Fox and the Ass" ["Lisica i osel"] (1825) are so close in theme that one wonders why both appeared in the same issue of the almanac. In the first a lion which has grown old and feeble endures the revenge of a horse, a wolf, and a bull, but as an ass prepares to kick him, he appeals for a quick death.

> *"From this earth however painfully I pass,*
> *'Tis better than to suffer insults from an ass!"*

> *"Kak smert' moja ni zla,*
> *Vse legče, čem terpet' obidy ot osla!"*[32]

If the moral of this is "better death than dishonor," the point made by "The Fox and the Ass" is that the mean in spirit are the first to seek revenge. The fox, meeting the ass, learns that all the animals have been paying back the old lion for its previous domination of them, and even the stupid ass has had its turn.

A particularly pleasing feature of Krylov's animal fables, also noted in those just discussed, is the colloquial character of dialogue, the animals expressing themselves in the language of the urban lower classes, peasants, petty officials, or some other dialect suitable for the themes and the types chosen to dramatize them. Though his genre was classical and his diction often archaic, Krylov's masterful use of many levels of the living Russian language gave his fables qualities of *narodnost* that many a would-be Romantic might have envied. The natural and native quality of Krylov's language is proved by the fact that many of his pointed morals have become proverbial, and in some cases their literary origin is not even known by those who repeat them.

"The Poor Rich Man" ["Bednyj bogač"] (1829) recounts amusingly how a pauper declares that if he were rich he would enjoy his wealth and also use it to help others. Miraculously given a purse which provides an inexhaustible supply of coins, he is told he may remove as many as he wants, but he cannot spend any until he has first thrown the purse in the river. Every time he goes to dispose of the purse, he has second thoughts, and thus he passes his life in the joyless accumulation of useless wealth. On a somewhat similar theme is "The Rich Man and the Poet" ["Bogač i poèt"] (1825), which makes the point that immortality is in art, not wealth. "The Razors" ["Britvy"] (1829) has a subtext alluding to the government's self-defeating failure to make use of persons once suspected of Decembrist sympathies. The story recounts how two acquaintances, having passed the night, arise the next morning and one begins to shave. His dull razor causes him torments, but, when questioned by his friend, he admits that he is afraid of a sharp one. As is often the case, Krylov concludes here with a quatrain which pithily reinforces the point.

> *My story's point I'll now reveal at once:*
> *Though they'd demur, how many have you seen*
> *Who fear a mind that's keen,*
> *And thus by choice endure a dunce?*

> *Vam pojasnit' rasskaz moj ja gotov:*
> *Ne tak li mnogie, xot' stydno im priznat'sja,*
> *S umom ljudej—bojatsja,*
> *I terpjat pri sebe oxotnej durakov?*[33]

An admonition to officialdom is also implicit in "The Cannons and the Sails" ["Puški i parusa"] (1829), a naval fable in which self-important cannons on a warship hope for the destruction of the sails, which swell arrogantly every time the wind blows. The wish is fulfilled, but the helpless ship is then sunk by the enemy. Here the silly cannons represent the military, while the sails are the civil service, and the point is that the ship of state is safe only if there is cooperation between the two branches.

"The Parishioner" ["Prixožanin"] (1825) is a witty treatment of insensitivity to art, but it also contains a polemical dart for Prince Vyazemsky. On more than one occasion Vyazemsky had expressed a preference for the fables of Ivan Dmitriev to those of Krylov. Apparently feeling that there was little justification in this sort of comparison, Krylov answered with "The Parishioner." The work opens with a statement that some people remain unimpressed no matter how hard one tries to sing well. To elucidate, he presents an anecdote about a preacher famous for his eloquence whose sermon touched all his listeners except one. The other parishioners, who had been reduced to tears, suggested that their dry-eyed brother didn't understand the sermon, to which he replied,

> *"Of course I understood!*
> *But there's no reason I should cry:*
> *I'm from a different parish."*

> *"Nu, kak ne ponimat'!*
> *Da plakat' mne kakaja stat'!*
> *Ved' ja ne ètogo prixoda."*[34]

Quite different is Krylov's lyric poem "Three Kisses" ["Tri poceluja"] (1825), a refreshingly simple narrative account of his being rejuvenated by the kisses of three girls while he dozed on a couch. The poem is unusual in that it lacks the figurative ornamentation and emotional posturing which the subject matter would have permitted and which mundane minds might have expected. Touchingly simple, but more "poetic," is "An Epitaph" ["Èpitafija"] (1829), a quatrain which likens the brief life of a child to the transitoriness of morning dew, which, having smiled on the earth, rises quickly to heaven.

Krylov's "To Alexey Nikolaevich Olenin: On the Presentation of the Latest Edition of Fables" ["Alekseju Nikolaeviču Oleninu, pri dostavlenii poslednego izdanija Basen' "] (1828), is a poetic gesture of gratitude to one's patron. The poem is classical, but without the apparatus of muses, groves, temples, and lyres. Here Krylov used iambic lines of varying length, which gives the effect of cadenced periods of rhetorical address. However, since the language itself is simple, the total impression is one of genteel informality, which gives special meaning to the otherwise conventional declaration that the author is motivated not by a desire to flatter but rather to express sincere gratitude.

VASILY ZHUKOVSKY (1783–1852) had already passed the high
point of his fame by the time *Northern Flowers* first appeared. Nonetheless, he was still a valuable and productive
poet and, to some extent, a central figure in the tradition for
which the almanac stood. Zhukovsky's effect upon Russian
poetry was similar to that of Karamzin on prose: utilizing
Karamzin's language reform, Zhukovsky had transformed
Russian poetry by breaking from French Neo-Classicism
and bringing about a new orientation toward German and
English Romantic, or pre-Romantic, poets. His adaptation
of Buerger's *Lenore* in 1808 introduced an entirely new current into Russian poetry. In his original lyrical poems he
revealed the Russian language's unexpected potentials for the
expression of intensely personal emotional moods. Despite his
acknowledged talent and contributions, serious doubts began
to be voiced about the non-Russianness of Zhukovsky's poetry,
its Germanic mistiness, its repetitious melancholic moods, its
stock vocabulary. From the midteens to the thirties, and later,
the questions raised by Zhukovsky's poetry were vigorously
discussed. A number of the contributors to Delvig's almanac
were among those who publicly criticized Zhukovsky's poetry,
but this is not to say that they were unaware of his enormous
contribution or that they could not find important values in
his works. For the circle of *Northern Flowers'* collaborators,
therefore, Zhukovsky was a man whom everyone admired,
who was given courteous but often limited attention, who
was respected as a one-time revolutionary but who was believed to have had his day.

The ten poems which Zhukovsky published in *Northern
Flowers* are quite representative of his art, and among them
we find philosophical-emotional elegies, elegies on themes
from nature, an epistle, a ballad, and scenes from *The Iliad*.
"The Secret Visitor" ["Tainstvennyj posetitel'"] (1825) is
typical of Zhukovsky with respect to style and lexical elements, but—and this is true of many of his selections in
Northern Flowers—the mystical quality is more pervasive
than usual. In six eight-line stanzas the poet rhetorically
queries the "vision, the beautiful guest" which has come
whence no one knows, why no one knows, and has disap-

peared whither no one knows. In successive stanzas alternative possibilities for the identity of the guest are proposed: Hope, Love, Thought, Poetry, Presentiment, but no conclusion is reached.

> *Often it is so in life;*
> *Someone luminous flies to us,*
> *Raises the screen*
> *And entices us into the* distance.

> *Často v žizni to byvalo:*
> *Kto-to svetlyj podletit*
> *I podymet pokryvalo,*
> *I v* dalekoe *manit.*[35]

The last line here is characteristic: "I v *dalekoe* manit," with the adjective "distant" serving as the noun "distance." However, the adjectival form increases the indefiniteness: entices us into the distant *what?*

Fogginess, mystery, indistinctness are found in "The Phantom" ["Prividenie"], appearing in the same issue of the almanac. The lexical elements and the imagery are typical of this poet: "In the shade of trees to the sound of strings," "In the luminescence of the waning evening rays," "In white raiment, like mist," "An airy, azure shroud." Here again the poet seeks to focus upon a briefly revealed phantom which had enticed one thither. But it had quickly disappeared, and "The soul overflowed / With yearning for the dear phantom." The elegy "The Sea" ["More"] (1829) is an apostrophe to "the silent sea, the azure sea," whose animation is treated as a manifestation of its mystical love for the sky. This anthropomorphization of nature is often encountered in Zhukovsky, and other examples of it are found in "Night" ["Noc'"] and "The Butterfly and Flowers" ["Motylek i cvety"], both from the 1825 *Northern Flowers*. The latter was preceded by the note: "Verses written in the album of N. I. I. for a sketch of a butterfly sitting on a bouquet." Zhukovsky's balladic contribution included "The Battle with a Serpent" ["Sraženie s zmeem"] (1832) and "The Triumph of the Victors" ["Toržestvo pobeditelej"] (1829), a rather close translation of Schiller's *Das Siegesfest.*[36]

In the same 1829 issue of the almanac appeared six hundred lines of Zhukovsky's rendition of *The Iliad*, prefaced by the following statement, probably written by Delvig.

> This translation was made under certain special circumstances. The translator, not knowing Greek, tried only to divine Homer, having before his eyes the German translations of *The Iliad* by Voss and Stolberg. This attempt cannot be compared with and cannot stand comparison with the translation of N. I. Gnedich, who conveys the real Homer, having listened to his native tongue. Here, so to say, is the echo of an echo. The verses in italics belong to the translator himself: they serve to unite the fragments, which are translations of complete portions of Cantos VI, XVII, XVIII, XIX and XX of *The Iliad*.[37]

This note, obviously, was an attempt to avoid any implication that Zhukovsky was in competition with Gnedich, who had earlier translated a part of Canto XIV of *The Iliad* for the 1826 almanac. Nevertheless, Gnedich was displeased, apparently having conceived of himself as enjoying some sort of proprietary right to *The Iliad*, particularly so since his complete translation of that work was on the point of being published. Subsequently, Zhukovsky abandoned *The Iliad* to Gnedich and focused his talents upon *The Odyssey*; his translation of that work is considered one of his most significant literary achievements.

After 1829 Zhukovsky was not represented in *Northern Flowers* until the final issue, in which appeared one poem, "An Answer to Ivan Ivanovich Dmitriev" ["Otvet Ivanu Ivanoviču Dmitrievu"]. Ivan Dmitriev (1760–1837), a sentimental poet in the Karamzin tradition, was well out of date by the thirties, but, notwithstanding some important divergencies in their critical views, he was still regarded with affection by most of the circle connected with *Northern Flowers*. Zhukovsky's poem to Dmitriev is a companion piece to the latter's work in the same issue, his only contribution to the almanac, entitled "To Vasily Andreevich Zhukovsky, on the Occasion of the Receipt from Him of Two Poems on the Capture of Warsaw" ["Vasiliju Andreeviču Žukovskomu, po slučaju polučenija ot nego dvux stixotvorenij na vzjatie Veršavy"]. In his poem Dmitriev asserted that his time had passed, that he had lost his poetic voice. To this Zhukovsky graciously responded with assurances that "the bard of two generations" would sing to yet a third; then he declared his gratitude to Dmitriev for having introduced him to poetry. He concluded by linking Dmitriev to "the sacred name, Karamzin" and reiterating his indebtedness to Dmitriev as the teacher of his youth.

Mental illness removed KONSTANTIN BATYUSHKOV (1787–1855) from the active literary scene around 1820, and thus his contributions in *Northern Flowers* were all composed a number of years before the almanac first appeared. But his importance in the development of Russian poetry, which rivaled that of his contemporary, Zhukovsky, made it almost a *sine qua non* that he be represented. Naturally, Delvig preferred to print works of Batyushkov which were not already known to the public, but these, understandably, were not easy to find. The three works which he did locate had not previously been published, but they are far from outstanding and give no real clue that their author was virtually the father of the Anacreontic tradition in Russian poetry, the famous exponent of "light poetry," and the poet who exerted the most influence upon the young Pushkin.

"To N. N." ["K. N. N."] (1826) is a poetic epistle to S. S. Uvarov complimenting his poetic taste. Apparently, it was written in 1817 when both Batyushkov and Uvarov were members of Arzamas, that convivial fraternity of the disciples of Karamzin. "An Imitation of Ariosto" ["Podražanie Ariostu"] (1826) is a translation of a stanza from *Orlando Furioso*, from which it takes its motto *La verginella è simile alla rosa*. The final poetic contribution, actually composed in 1819 or 1820, is entitled "Elegy" ["Èlegija"] (1828), but it is in fact an adaptation of stanza 178 from the last canto of *Childe Harold's Pilgrimage:* "There is a pleasure in the pathless woods." Interestingly, Batyushkov takes Byron's nine lines and expands them to twelve, partly in order to convey the full meaning of the original and partly to communicate an additional idea. Thus, Byron declares,

> *I love not Man the less, but Nature more,*
> *From these our interviews, in which I steal*
> *From all I may be, or have been before,*
> *To mingle with the Universe, and feel*
> *What I can ne're express, yet cannot all conceal.*

but Batyushkov, in his paraphrase, expands "From all I may be, or have been before," to "that which I was, when I was young and that which now I have become *in the chill of years* ["I to, čem byl, kak byl molože,/ I to, čem nyne stal pod xolodom godov"]."[38] One senses here a poignant allusion to that progressive melancholy which culminated in total insanity a year or so after these lines were written.

DMITRY VENEVITINOV (1805–27) early displayed unusual promise in the fields of art, music, and literature. Following an excellent private education, he audited courses at the University of Moscow from 1822 to 1824, during which period he became one of the central figures in the Lovers of Wisdom society (Obščestvo Ljubomudrija), a group interested in German idealistic philosophy.[39] In 1824 he assumed a post in the archives section of the Ministry of Foreign Affairs, serving in Moscow until the fall of 1826 and then in Petersburg. There, much to the dismay of Pushkin, Delvig, and other leading literary figures, he died suddenly in the spring of 1827. His known poetic works consist of less than fifty poems, three of which were published in *Northern Flowers*.

"The Greek's Song" ["Pesn' Greka"] (1827) is the *profession de foi* of a young Greek who swears to avenge the Turks' destruction of his native village, the death of his parents, and the slaying of his sister as they sought to escape. The poem is presented as a retrospective narrative in simple, declarative statements. The exotic setting and dramatic events (Greek village, Turkish attack, flight by boat, attempt to pass the Turkish fortress in the moonlight, the fatal shot from the fortress walls) make this poetic tale particularly effective. In some ways it reminds one of the confession of the novice in Lermontov's *Mtsyri*.

"Three Roses" ["Tri rozy"] (1827) pleasingly establishes a contrast between the three flowers, the first which blooms day and night, the second every day but only for a moment, and the third, the most fragrant, which blooms but once and quickly fades: the roses on the cheeks of a maiden in love. "Testament" ["Zaveščanie"] (1829) is an emotion-laden work which "was written in 1827 with a clear presentiment of imminent death."[40] The "lyric I," in the "hour of final suffering," sends brief greetings to his friends and then continues with a compelling admonition to his lover that she dare not forget his memory. This poem, along with two other last works which also treat the theme of impending death, "To My Ring" ["K moemu perstnju"] and "Consolation" [Utešenie"], suggests that the poet may have intended suicide, an hypothesis which is strengthened by our knowledge of his hopeless infatuation with Princess Zinaida Volkonskaya and the despondency expressed in his last letter (March 7, 1827, to Mikhail Pogodin) over his loss of poetic inspiration. However, it would appear that his death was due to a rather unromantic case of pneumonia.

PAVEL KATENIN (1792–1853) is the last of the poets who may, on the basis of reputation or representation, be considered major among the contributors to Delvig's almanac. Following an excellent domestic education, he served in the Ministry of Education until 1810 and then accepted a commission in a cavalry regiment. He took part in various campaigns during the Napoleonic invasion and accompanied the Russian army to Paris. After the conclusion of peace, he continued in the military service until 1820, when he was suddenly retired at the order of the Tsar. Two years later he was exiled from both capitals owing to his involvement in a petty scandal.

As a poet he is remembered for his innovations in verse forms and for his efforts to introduce elements of *narodnost* into Russian poetry. In this connection he was severely criticized for his *Olga*, an adaptation of Buerger's *Lenore* remarkable for its realistically crude language and striking imagery. Katenin, whom Pushkin called "one of the first apostles of Romanticism and the first to introduce folk elements and popular speech into the sphere of elevated poetry,"[41] abandoned the Romantic ballad just at the time when the genre was becoming popular and gradually assumed a conservative literary stance which allied him with the camp of Admiral Shishkov. Nonetheless, Pushkin valued him highly as a critic and solicited his collaboration with Delvig's *Literary Gazette*, for which he wrote a series of essays on poetry and the theatre. Katenin was also important as a translator of Corneille and Racine.[42] In 1832 appeared his collection entitled *Poetic Works and Translations of Pavel Katenin;* he published little subsequently, and by 1836 seems to have completely abandoned literature.

Only two of his works appeared in *Northern Flowers,* but together they represent almost six hundred lines, which makes him a major contributor if only on the basis of quantity. *An Old Tale* ["Staraja byl'"] has already been mentioned in connection with Pushkin's "Answer to Katenin." As an editor's note indicates, Katenin sent this work (and also his "Elegy," which appeared in *Northern Flowers for 1830*) to Pushkin to publish when and where he thought best. This rather long and lightly humorous poem concerns a singing match arranged by Prince Vladimir in honor of his military victories and his marriage to the Byzantine princess. The first prize is won by a Greek bard, who sings the glories of the Prince and his bride; the Russian competitor concedes defeat, claiming that he can sing only of heroic knights and of love, but not of great tsars and princesses. As his prize the Greek receives a fabulous steed, and the Russian is given a goblet. When this work was sent to Pushkin by Katenin, he included a poetic epistle in which he pretended that the goblet had been preserved and was in Pushkin's possession. Noting that a real poet need not first fill it with wine, Katenin invited Pushkin to drink from it. But the epistle and the poetic tale itself led Pushkin to suspect that the figure of the smooth-tongued Greek bard was supposed to represent himself. Thus, in his "Answer to Katenin" he declined the invitation and suggested that Katenin

> *fill the goblet*
> *And reap the laurels of Corneille and Tasso,*
> *Alone with your hangover.*

> *kubok nalivaj*
> *I lavr Kornelja ili Tassa*
> *Odin s poxmel'ja požinaj.*[43]

In view of the miraculous power of the goblet to fill itself for true poets, the indication that Katenin would have to fill it for himself had additional meaning.

Katenin's lengthy "Elegy" ["Ělegija"] (1830) is interesting both from its formal characteristics and its personal content. The imperfect dactylic meter (of which, obviously, Katenin was aware) and unrhymed lines provide a Hellenic flavor which nicely suits the ancient Greek setting. Eudorus, a soldier turned poet, complains that Phoebus and the Muses are the most cruel of the gods, and owing to their harsh treatment of him he has determined to hang up forever his traitorous lyre on an oak tree. Then follows his biography, which is simply a stylized version of Katenin's own—military service under Alexander (in the poem, it is Alexander of Macedonia), loss of favor, retirement to his patrimony, his devotion to poetry and the ultimate indifference of the crowd. Here Katenin covertly criticizes the younger generation of poets belonging to the so-called Pushkin Pleiad.

> *These youths did not respect their great predecessors;*
> *In their eyes Homer was naked, Aeschylus lacked art;*
> *Sophocles was weak in talent and Pindar in intelligence;*
> *Praising one another, and exaggerating to the stars,*
> *The youths (seven in number) called themselves the Pleiad.*
> *Among them Eudorus respected only Theocritus.*

> *Junoši te predtečej velikix ne čtili;*
> *Nag byl v glazax ix Omir, Èsxil ne iskusen,*
> *Slav darovan'em Sofokl i razumom Pindar;*
> *Drug že druga xvalja, i do zvezd veličaja,*
> *Junoši (sem' ix čislom) nazyvalis' Plejadoj.*
> *V nix uvažal Evdor odnogo Feokrita.*[44]

(Theocritus, of course, is Pushkin.) The gods hear Eudorus' complaint, and Calliope, in the image of Eudorus' deceased fiancée, descends to earth and exhorts him to reconsider his decision. He takes down his lyre and returns home.

The conception of the poem was ingenious, and Katenin masterfully introduced numerous references to ancient Greek personalities and gods. At the same time, in the biographical content there is an unpleasant evidence of arrogance, vanity, and even envy. The poet did not sufficiently sublimate his personal feelings to achieve an example of truly first-class art.

The Minor Contributors

The eleven poets previously discussed together provided about two hundred individual poems to the almanac. The poets treated below, who are perhaps arbitrarily classed as minor, were collectively responsible for about the same number; thus, they played an important role in determining the overall value of the poetry sections. Some of these poets were excellent, and some excellent at times, but in general they have remained in the shadows cast by the really imposing figures heretofore discussed. Since many of this group are not well known, and some indeed almost forgotten, more literary-biographical information will be included with the discussion of their works than for the previous group.

FYODOR GLINKA (1786–1880) was one of the most prolific of the regular contributors to *Northern Flowers*, and, with the exception of 1829, when he didn't appear at all, every issue contained at least one prose work and several poems. His total contribution of twenty-five poems and twelve pieces in prose indicates the extent of his effect upon the general character of the almanac.

Born in 1786 to a Smolensk gentry family, Glinka was educated in the First Cadet Corps and commissioned in 1803. He took part in the campaign of 1805–6 against Napoleon, but in 1806 retired from the army to devote himself to literature. The first of his *Letters of a Russian Officer* [*Pis'ma russkogo oficera*] was published in 1808. When Napoleon invaded Russia in 1812, Glinka again entered the army, resuming his previous position of adjutant to General Miloradovich, with whom he served until the end of the war. In 1815–16 six more volumes of his *Letters* appeared, and from that time on his works constantly were published in the leading journals.

Glinka cannot be identified with any particular literary group or school, though the term conservative might be applied without injustice both to his choice of themes and their execution. Lomonosov was his master, at least for his more solemn pieces, but he also evinced a full acquaintance with Sentimentalism and some aspects of Romanticism. Pushkin made special note of Glinka's originality in his review of *Karelia*, published in 1830: "Of all our poets, F. N. Glinka, perhaps, is the most original. He professes neither ancient nor French Classicism, he follows neither Gothic nor contemporary Romanticism."[45] Glinka himself had earlier averred an impartiality to either Romanticism or Classicism in his allegory "Two Sisters, or: Whom Should One Prefer?" But though Glinka at times seemed to set foot in the Romantic camp, for example in *The Maid of the Karelian Forests*, a narrative poem with at least a superficial resemblance to Pushkin's *Prisoner of the Caucasus* or Baratynsky's *Eda*, even there he was more a Sentimentalist than a Romantic.

Glinka played an important role in organizing the Free Society of Lovers of Russian Literature (Vol'noe Obščestvo Ljubitelej Rossijskoj Slovesnosti), established in 1816, and served as its president from 1819 to 1825. Through this organization, if not elsewhere, he came into contact with many of the future Decembrists, whose confidence he enjoyed. Although he was not a conspirator himself, he was arrested when the uprising was suppressed and exiled for a time to the Olonets region in northwest Russia. There he wrote the narrative poem *Karelia, or the Encarceration of Marfa Ioannovna Romanova* (whose title is deceptive since Marfa appears simply as an auditor for the tales of various other narrators). Meanwhile, Glinka's *Attempts at Sacred Poetry* [*Opyty svjaščennoj poèzii*] and *Attempts at Allegories or Parabolical Descriptions in Verse and Prose* [*Opyty allegorij ili inoskazatel'nye opisanija v stixax i v proze*] had appeared in 1826; these are his best known works. Throughout the thirties he

continued to be very active, but thereafter his productivity
and popularity waned.

The twenty-five poems of Glinka in the almanac show
him to be a competent poet-craftsman. Unafraid of experimentation, he is often very free in the length of his lines, and
it is not unusual for tetrameter, pentameter, and hexameter to
be combined in one poem. His alliterative effects are often
good. Yet, as a poet-thinker he is very uneven, and his contributions are too often marked by trite ideas and cosmic
commonplaces. About a third of the works in *Northern
Flowers* are on religious themes, and these include imitations
or adaptations of the Psalms, poems of nature with mystical
overtones, such as "Not Our Side" ["Ne naša storona"]
(1830), "A Comforting Feeling" ["Otradnoe čuvstvo"]
(1831), "Yearning for Him" ["Toska o nem"] (1831), "To
the Blue Sky" ["K sinemu nebu"] (1831), and "Contempla-
tion" ["Sozercanie"] (1832). His "Poverty and Consolation"
["Bednost' i utešenie"] (1831) which begins "Don't cry,
wife!" suggests that God himself be godfather to their children. This rather bizarre idea, coupled with the fact that
Glinka was not even married, caused Pushkin to suspect that
the poet had taken leave of his senses.[46]

The poems on themes connected with nature, or those
parts of other poems connected with nature, are often pleasing,
despite their sentimentality and quite conventional diction. In
this category are included "The Vision in the Moon" ["Videnie v lune"] (1825), "The Features of Autumn" ["Čerty
oseni"] (1826), and "Steppe Life" ["Stepnaja žizn'"] (1826),
the latter permeated with a nostalgic longing for Poland.
"Autumn and Village Life" ["Osen' i sel'skoe žit'e"] (1831) is
a typical Sentimentalist's idealization of the cozy and carefree
life of the peasants, who enjoy freedom from the backbiting
and anxieties which trouble more sophisticated people. Two
of the selections for 1832 are fragments from the narrative
poem *The Maid of the Karelian Forests* [*Deva karel'skix
lesov*]: "Forest Wars" ["Lesnye vojny"] is on the unusual
subject of a battle between black and red ants; the other
fragment concerns a recluse who justifies to his daughter his
withdrawal from a vicious society. "The Death of Figner"

["Smert' Fignera"] (1826), subtitled "An Attempt at Popular Poetry" ["Opyt narodnoj poèzii"], is a rather long poem of eight parts in which are recounted the almost legendary deeds of the partisan hero. Notwithstanding the subtitle, it reflects none of the characteristic features of the Russian folk tradition.

Glinka's typical themes of religion, historical greatness, and man's imperfection comment upon the essential seriousness of his Muse. His poems themselves, which are so often didactic and rhetorical, reveal no trace of wit or humor. There is little melody for its own sake, no lightness of touch, and certainly none of his works in *Northern Flowers*, including his prose, reflects the slightest departure from an intensely sober, almost sombre mood. He eschewed the "petty" genres of epigram, the playful epistle, or the love lyric, since poetry was for him an almost divine occupation which was to be at the service of superior truths—this may explain the success of his "Psalms." Generally, however, he lacked the divine insights and divine inspiration of the truly great poet.

Alexey Illichevsky (1798–1837), son of a governor of Tambov, attended the lyceum at Tsarskoe Selo and while there acquired the reputation of a poet. Later he was associated with the literary circle which met twice weekly at Baron Delvig's home, and he became an active contributor to *Northern Flowers*, which published eighteen of his poems and two prose works from 1826 to 1829. A small collection of original and translated poems, *Attempts of the Anthological Sort* [*Opyty v antologičeskom rode*], which appeared in 1827, attracted courteous but cursory attention.

As a poet Illichevsky had a limited range, his particular forte being witty, epigrammatic quatrains. Over half of his poems in the almanac are of this type, exemplified by amusing but essentially frivolous trifles such as "To N. N., On Bringing Her an Apple" ["N. N., podnosja ej jabloko"] (1826), "Madrigal" ["Madrigal"] (1826), and "Epitaph" ["Epitafija"] (1826).

> *Damon had creditors galore,*
> *But in the earth at last he lay.*

He settled up but one account:
His debt to nature he did pay.

Ostavja kreditorov polk,
Damon skončalsja v prošlom gode:
Odin on tol'ko otdal dolg.
To est', poslednij dolg prirode.[47]

Illichevsky's unidealized view of man finds expression in two poems of 1827: "On an Ancient Vase" ["Na drevnjuju vazu"] makes the point that a vessel of mere clay may last through the ages, while proud mortals live but a moment; "Eagle and Man" ["Orel i čelovek"] contrasts the daring bird, which looks straight at the sun and laughs at thunder and lightning, to humans, who seek to rival gods while crawling in the mud. "The Power of Hope" ["Sila nadeždy"] (1828) is another brief comment upon the human condition:

We always sing the selfsame song,
Each curses fate more than the other;
But every day we wait and hope
That there will be another.

My vsjakij den' poem vse pesnju tu že,
Branim sud'bu odin drugogo xuže;
No vsjakij den' nadeemsja i ždem
I vsjakij den' dlja zavtrago živem.[48]

In quite a different style are Illichevsky's translations. "The Village Orphan," subtitled "An Elegy of Soumet"[49] ["Sel'skaja sirota: Èlegija Sume"] (1827), which he translated in Paris in 1824, is an orphan's soliloquy lamenting her friendless childhood and expressing a longing for the mother who abandoned her on the church doorstep. The work is in the sentimental tradition, but it is poignant rather than lachrymous. Illichevsky's choice of it for translation betrays a soft heart complementing the more obvious rationalistic mind. Translations of three of Mickiewicz's *Crimean Sonnets* appeared in the 1828 almanac, another indication of the enthusiastic reception of this cycle by Russian poets,[50] as well as a sign of Illichevsky's poetic sensitivity.

PETER PLETNYEV (1792–1865) is remembered today largely because of his long and close association with Pushkin. Born into a clerical family, he received his education at the Central Pedagogical Institute, and in 1814 he became a teacher of literature in Petersburg. His acquaintance with Pushkin began prior to the latter's graduation from the Tsarskoe Selo lyceum, and their friendship was maintained until Pushkin's death. Pletnyev served as Pushkin's agent in Petersburg, as well as advisor and confidant. In Pletnyev's own words, "I was for him everything: relative, friend, editor, and cashier."[51] Pushkin's affection for Pletnyev and gratitude for his many services is evidenced by the dedication to him of *Eugene Onegin.*

Pletnyev's association with the Free Society of Lovers of Russian Literature brought him into constant contact with Bestuzhev and Ryleev, and in fact he was acquainted with most of the leading authors of the twenties and thirties. Zhukovsky, Baratynsky, Delvig, and later Gogol sought his criticism before publishing their works. His innate modesty and tact were widely admired, and he was one of the few journalists, if not the only one, who took no part in the vicious polemics which became so typical of periodicals in the late twenties. His critical essays were published in the Free Society's journal, the *Emulator of Enlightenment* [*Sorevnovatel' Prosveščenija*], and his poems appeared in every issue of Ryleev and Bestuzhev's *Polar Star.*[52] He was an active contributor to *Northern Flowers,* in which appeared two pieces of criticism and eighteen poems. After Delvig's death in 1831, Pletnyev assisted Orest Somov and Pushkin in publishing the 1832 issue of the almanac on behalf of Delvig's widow and two young brothers. Pletnyev was also associated with Pushkin's *Contemporary* [*Sovremennik*] and became its editor after Pushkin was killed. In the following nine years he wrote more than fifty articles for the journal, and his commitment to that publication, coupled with the demands of his academic career, was one of the reasons that he ceased writing poetry in the late thirties. It should be noted that his professorial career was very successful: in 1832 he was made Professor of Literature at the University of Petersburg, and in 1840 he became Rector of that institution, holding the post until his retirement in 1861.

None of the poems which Pletnyev gave to *Northern Flowers* are particularly memorable, but they are pleasant and reveal a modest talent. Several, such as "Betrayal" ["Izmena"] (1825), "To I. I. Kozlov" ["K I. I. Kozlovu"] (1825), and "Explanation" ["Ob'jasenie"] (1826) concern themes of un-achieved expectations, the "confusion of hopes" that is life.[53] Memory of a better past provides the only release from the weight of disappointed hopes. This melancholic attitude was probably not a romantic pose—Pletnyev longed to be a great poet, but he lacked the special gifts of genius. This was evident to Pushkin, who wrote to his brother Lev the following appraisal of Pletnyev's powers: "In general my opinion is that for Pletnyev prose is more fitting than verse—he has no feeling, no liveliness. His style is as pale as a corpse."[54] This critique became known to Pletnyev, who, with admirable restraint and unusual diffidence, responded to Pushkin with a dignified epistle in verse acknowledging acceptance of Push-kin's judgment: "Away with pretence. In my profession I have not achieved what is worthy of a poet."[55] This same feeling was expressed later in his epistle "To N. I. Gnedich" ["K N. I. Gnediču"] (1831).

> Why hide it? In my poetry
> There remains only a tale of delusions,
> A play of passions repugnant to the mind,
> There is no fire of heavenly inspiration.
>
> *Začem skryvat'? V poèzii moej*
> *Ostanetsja liš' povest' zabluždenij,*
> *Postydnaja umu igra strastej,*
> *A ne ogon' nebesnyx vdoxnovenij.*[56]

A more cheerful note was sounded in such brief pieces as "Stanzas to D***" ["Stansy k D***"] (1826), "The Ideal" ["Ideal"] (1826), "The Gardener" ["Sadovnik"] (1827), where he speaks of the joy of rural leisure, or in "Night" ["Noč'"] (1827), a nocturnal description in an elegiac mood.

As were many of the poets discussed in this section, Plet-

nyev was a reasonably good poetic craftsman, but his verse
lacked *élan* and was not characterized by melodiousness. Pushkin, as usual, was probably correct—Pletnyev's strength was
in prose.

MIKHAIL DELARYU (1811–68) first appeared in *Northern
Flowers for 1830,* and the last three issues of the almanac
contained sixteen of his poems. The son of an important government official, he was born in Kazan (hence his pseudonym,
"D. Kazansky"), and there he received his early education.
From 1820 to 1829 he attended the Tsarskoe Selo lyceum,
where he manifested an interest in classical studies and poetry.
The year of his graduation he published his *Transformation
of Daphnis* [*Prevraščenie Dafny*], translated from Ovid, and
thereafter appeared not only in Delvig's almanac but in *Literary Gazette* and other important journals and almanacs of
the thirties and early forties.

As a poet, Delaryu was a disciple of Delvig, and much of
his mature work is thematically and technically similar to
that of his master, at least insofar as the classical element in
Delvig's poetry is concerned. His most ambitious piece in
Northern Flowers was a translation of some two hundred lines
of Ovid's *Metamorphoses* concerning Myrrh's incestuous love
for her father and her subsequent transformation into a tree.
The dactylic hexameters used here are employed in other
poems, such as "To the Neva River" ["K Neve"] (1830), and
"To My Guardian Angel" ["Angelu-Xranitelju"] (1830),
where the classical meter is reinforced by diction that wafts
of the eighteenth century. Like Delvig, Delaryu experimented
with verse forms and meters, as, for example, in his tribute to
Venevitinov, "The Poet's Tomb" ["Mogila poèta"] (1831),
where a combination of dactylic pentameters and hexameters
is employed. "The Fading Rose" ["Uvjadajuščaja roza"]
(1832), in quatrains of amphibrach bimeter, has a tumbling
rhythm which is reminiscent of Poe, while the consolatory
"To Lizanka Delvig" ["Lizan'ke Del'vig"] (1832) represents
an unusual combination of trochaic tetrameter, with an aBaaB
rhyme scheme. Even a poor translation (of the fifth and final
stanza) conveys the special quality of his form: having as-

serted that her father has returned to the child as an angel, the poem concludes

> *Let not this angel leave you ever!*
> *As a pleasant way you wind*
> *Down life's path that darkens never,*
> *With your soul which loves forever,*
> *Heaven here on earth you'll find.*

> *O, da budet že s toboju*
> *On vovek! i ty projdeš'*
> *Žizni put' dobra stezeju,*
> *I vseljubjaščej dušoju*
> *Nebo na zemle najdeš'.*[57]

This motif of angels who manifest their presence on earth plays a role in several other of Delaryu's poems considered here: "Recovery" ["Vyzdorovlenie"] (1831) ascribes the cure from a serious illness to the ministration of an angel; "The Tear of Love" ["Sleza ljubvi"] (1830) reports that an angel was seen carrying to heaven the tear of a praying maiden; "Dream and Death" ["Son i smert'"] (1831) is a dialogue between two angels, in which Death insists that by taking an innocent child he has protected it from eventual betrayed love. Betrayed love is itself alluded to in many of these selections.

"The Poet" ["Poèt"] (1830), a sonnet, is Romantic in its linking of poetic and divine powers, but its Classical essence is revealed by its formal, old-fashioned diction: "Not in the strait life-path of his mundane brethren" ["Ne v tesnoj judoli zemnyx svoix bratij"]; "And the words of heaven" ["I neba glagoly"]; "And with an angelic visage he pours forth his song" ["I s angel'skim likom sol'et svoe pen'e"].

Pushkin appreciated Delaryu, but he saw the weakness of his poetic art. Writing to Pletnyev in 1831, he declared

> Delaryu writes too smoothly, too correctly, and is too stiff for a young lyceum student. I don't see a drop of creative power in him, although there is a good deal of art.[58]

Had there been no Delvig, Delaryu might have become better known. Certainly he must have appeared to his contemporaries, irrespective of the pleasure his poetry may have given them, simply a skillful imitator of a greater master. Living in an age of great poets, his own considerable talent was insufficient to gain him enduring fame.

Delaryu's post-*Northern Flowers* literary career was marked by an incident which is indicative of the special problems faced by editors and authors with respect to the official censorship. In 1834 Delaryu published in *Library for Reading* [*Biblioteka dlja Čtenija*] a translation of Victor Hugo's "À Une Femme," in which the author declares that if he were tsar he would give up his earthly dominion for one glance of his beloved, and if he were God he would give up paradise for one kiss. This ludicrous bit of hyperbole was in an equally ludicrous manner interpreted as an act of *lèse Majesté* and *lèse Dieu*. Delaryu was arrested and relieved of his government post, but there were apparently no further serious consequences, other than the translation having attracted more attention than it deserved, since everyone was bound to read it after Delaryu's arrest. Delaryu published a volume of his poems in 1835, but his literary career was virtually ended by the advent of the forties. In 1841 he retired from his position as inspector of the Richelieu Lyceum in Odessa, and he spent the remainder of his life in Kharkov or its environs.

PLATON OBODOVSKY (1805–64) is remembered—when remembered—as a writer and translator of dramas. While still quite young he was associated with the Free Society of Lovers of Russian Literature, in whose journal he published, and a few of his early poems on religious themes appeared in *Polar Star*. Excerpts from his Persian verse tale, *Orsan and Leila*, were accepted for *Little Star*, but were not published there owing to the almanac's suppression. A narrative poem, *The Orphan of Chios* [*Xioskij Sirota*], composed in 1828 to help raise the ransom for a youth held captive by the Turks, received a good review in Orest Somov's critical survey in *Northern Flowers for 1829*.

Obodovsky is represented by eleven pieces in *Northern Flowers* from 1825 to 1830. Five of his contributions are translations, among which are scenes from Adolf Müllner's tragedy *Die Schuld* ["Otryvok iz Mjul'nerovoj tragedii: *Die Schuld*"] (1827), Schiller's *Don Carlos* ["Otryvok iz Šillerovoj tragedii: *Don Karlos*"] (1829). In the 1830 issue of the almanac there also appeared Act III, scene 1 of *Romeo and Juliet*, but it is not possible to state categorically that the translator was Obodovsky since the piece is unsigned.[59] This interest in Romantic drama, represented by translations of Shakespeare,[60] Müllner, and Schiller, would suggest that Obodovsky belonged to the Romantic camp. There does, indeed, seem to be a Romantic attraction to exotic natural settings in his original works, such as the two selections from the Persian tale *Orsan and Leila*, both of which appeared in 1826 under the titles "A Persian Romance (From the tale: *Orsan and Leila*)" ["Persidskij romans (Iz povesti: *Orsan i Leila*)"] and "Excerpts from the Persian Tale: *Orsan and Leila*" ["Otryvki iz Persidskoj povesti: *Orsan i Leila*"]. The emphasis here is upon luxuriant local color and the unusual cultural background. "Hermione (A Rustic Elegy)" ["Èrminija (Sel'skaja èlegija)"] (1830) is an anguished lover's soliloquy heavily burdened with nature imagery and shows Obodovsky's close acquaintance with the elegiac tradition of Zhukovsky.

Obodovsky's contributions to *Northern Flowers* (as those to *Polar Star*) reveal a deep interest in religious themes, and in his works of this sort we find a poetic language heavily seasoned with Slavonicisms to impart a biblical flavor. The titles here are characteristic: "Spring Hymn to the Almighty (During the First Thunder)" ["Vesennij gimn Vsederžitelju (Vo vremja pervogo groma)"] (1825); "The Grandeur of the World (An Imitation of Schiller)" ["Veličie mira (Podražanie Silleru)"] (1827), a translation of Schiller's "Die Grösse der Welt"; "The Demise of the Benefactor" ["Končina Blagotvoritelja"] (1828), a poem on the crucifixion; and "Prophecy of the Messiah" ["Proročestvo o Mesii"] (1828).

VASILY TUMANSKY (1800–60) was one of the many talented, if not brilliant, poets who contributed to that durable poetic canvas against which the more original designs of poets such

as Pushkin, Baratynsky, Delvig, and others stood out so
strongly. From a Ukrainian gentry family, he was educated at
the Kharkov Lyceum and then at the Peter and Paul School
in Petersburg. On completion of his course there, he went to
Paris, where he audited classes at the Collège de France. On
his return to Petersburg, he joined the Free Society of Lovers
of Russian Literature, and at this time his works began to
be published in the leading literary journals. In 1823 he took
a government post in Odessa, and it was there that he became
acquainted with Pushkin. Tumansky, who was a close friend
of Ryleev and Bestuzhev, contributed to all issues of their
Polar Star, and he was also personally responsible for solicit-
ing Pushkin's collaboration for the 1824 edition of that
almanac.[61]

Pushkin's relations with Tumansky were at first characterized by some reservations on the part of the former, particularly with regard to Tumansky's quality as a poet. Writing
to Bestuzhev in January, 1824, Pushkin said of Tumansky,
"He is a really fine fellow, but, as a poet, I don't like him.
God grant him some sense!"[62] However, in August of the
following year, Pushkin wrote to Tumansky from Mikhailovskoe: "What about you, what about your verses? Do
us the favor of not forgetting your talent. I am afraid the
prose of your life has overcome life's poetry."[63]

The ten poems of Tumansky in *Northern Flowers* appeared in four issues, beginning in 1825, when his two contributions were signed simply "T." Most of his poems are
personal and elegiac, concerned with love or his attraction to
the natural beauties of his native south. Typical of his art
are such works as "My Love" ["Moja ljubov'"] (1825): the
beauties of Tavrida, which are described, have little effect
upon the poet, who is absorbed with thoughts of his beloved.
"Thoughts of the South" ["Mysl' o juge"] (1831) is an
enthusiastic comment upon the charms of the southern landscape and southern girls. The trochaic tetrameter gives a
lively movement to the stanzas.

> *There is luxury, refulgence,*
> *Fragrant perfumes, captivation.*
> *Haughty northland, haughty northland,*
> *Can you give me consolation?*

> *Tam garmonija, sijan'e,*
> *Blagovon'e, naslažden'e:*
> *Sever gordyj! sever gordyj!*
> *Čto ž' ty daš' mne v utešen'e!*[64]

It might be noted that Tumansky's partisanship for the natural surroundings of his native region led him to the creation of idealized landscapes. In "Onegin's Journey," Pushkin humorously remarks that

> *Our friend Tumansky described*
> *Odessa in harmonious verse,*
>
> . . . .
>
> *With his charming pen*
> *He sang the praises of Odessa's gardens.*
> *It's all very nice, but the fact is*
> *That the steppe is bare all around* . . . .
>
> *Odessu zvučnymi stixami*
> *Naš drug Tumanskij opisal,*
>
> . . . .
>
> *Očarovatel'nym perom*
> *Sady odesskie proslavil.*
> *Vse xorošo, no delo v tom,*
> *Čto step' nagaja tam krugom* . . . .[65]

At his best Tumansky was a competent poet, but there is neither depth nor particular significance to his verse. Of his other contributions to *Northern Flowers*, one might mention as particularly melodious, probably owing largely to the amphibrach meter, "To Beautiful Eyes" ["Prekrasnym glazam"] (1828) and "Romance" ["Romans"] (1831), the latter "To the Tune of a Beethoven Waltz."

By profession Tumansky was a diplomat, and in this career he saw service in Moldavia and Wallachia, took part in the drafting of the Treaty of Adrianople with the Turks, and served after 1836 as Secretary to the Russian Legation in Constantinople. Later he transferred to the Government Council, from which he retired in 1846. The last years of his life were spent in attempts to improve the conditions of peasants in the Poltava region. Poetry, therefore, was for him an avocation, and he might have achieved more had he shown greater devotion to his Muse. Or perhaps it was the inconstancy of his Muse that gave his poetry its tone of restrained sadness and led him to sing of unrequited love.

FYODOR TUMANSKY (1800–53) represents the rare example of a poet who wrote too little. Less than a dozen of his poems have been preserved, and eight of these appeared in *Northern Flowers* during the years 1825–30.[66] From the Ukrainian gentry, Fyodor Tumansky was a cousin of the more productive but less talented Vasily Tumansky. When he finished the course of the preparatory school attached to the University of Moscow, he entered the Ministry of Foreign Affairs, in which service he remained until his death. As Russian consul in Jassy, he was often in Kishinev, and there he met Pushkin in the early twenties. Pushkin's "Answer to Tumansky" ["Otvet Tumanskomu"] was written in response to a composition of this author which has not been preserved.

Tumansky's poetry is sensitive, unforced, and technically pleasing, but it remains undistinguished by superior ideas or special vision. All of his pieces in some way directly concern personal reactions or attitudes, with the exception of "To A. S. Pushkin," a less self-focused work intended as a tribute to his friend. In general an elegiac tone dominates, and two of the poems appearing in the 1826 almanac are simply titled "Elegy" ["Èlegija"]; both concern old age's attraction to the memories of youth. Perhaps his best work, and best known, is "The Birdlet" ["Ptička"] (1827), which relates in two uncomplicated quatrains how a bird, which he released from captivity, seemed to be praying for him as it disappeared singing into the radiance of the blue sky.

It is said that as a person Fyodor Tumansky was as reticent as his Muse. Had he been able to maintain the quality of his verse while increasing its production, he would be well known today.

STEPAN SHEVYREV (1806–64) was recognized as a poet and critic even before he contributed to *Northern Flowers* (1826 and 1831), but his later achievements as a professor of literature, biographer, and art scholar were still to come. Born into a Saratov gentry family, at the age of twelve he was enrolled in the Moscow University preparatory school (Gentry Pension), from which he graduated with honors. He then assumed a position in the archives of the Ministry of Foreign Affairs in Moscow. In the early twenties he was associated with the literary-philosophical circle of Semyon Raich, a teacher of literature at the Gentry Pension whose group included Vladimir Odoevsky, Mikhail Pogodin, Vladimir Titov and the brothers Kireevsky. At the same time Shevyrev was involved in the Lovers of Wisdom society, a group interested in German idealistic philosophy.[67] Shevyrev met Pushkin at the poet Venevitinov's house in 1826 at a reading of *Boris Godunov,* and the following year, when Shevyrev became chief critic for Pogodin's newly formed *Moscow Herald,* he reviewed Pushkin's drama very favorably —in contrast to the negative appraisal of most critics. In 1828 Shevyrev again gained Pushkin's gratitude by sharply criticizing Bulgarin's prose sketches of Russian mores.[68]

Shevyrev's health required a better climate, and so in 1829 he went to Rome as tutor to the son of Princess Zinaida Volkonskaya, noted patroness of the arts and a sometime contributor to *Northern Flowers.* He stayed abroad, primarily in Italy and Switzerland, for the next two and one-half years, and during that period he assiduously studied foreign languages and literatures, art and music. Following his return to Russia in 1832, he finished a book on Dante and his age, and the next fall he joined the University of Moscow as a teacher of literature. In later years he became a professor of that institution and a member of the Russian Academy. During the thirties he was a critic for the *Moscow Observor* [*Moskovskij Nabljudatel'*], and in 1841 he joined the staff of the *Muscovite* [*Moskvitjanin*], where he was chief critic for a time. Ill health forced him abroad in 1863, and he died in Paris in 1864.

There is little striking or original about Shevyrev's eight poems (two are translations) which appeared in *Northern Flowers.* The contributions of 1826 include a translation of Schiller's "Der Abend" ["Večer (Iz Šillera)"], the choice of

which may reflect the influence of Raich's circle, and "The
Lily and the Rose" ["Lilija i roza"], a floral allegory on in-
nocence and love. The six poems of 1831 were doubtless all
written while Shevyrev was abroad, and several of them reflect his experiences there, such as "The Reading of Dante"
["Čtenie Danta"] and "Sirocco" ["Širokko"]. The translation,
"Horace's Last Ode (IV, bk. 16)" ["Oda Goracija poslednj-
jaja (IV, k. 16)"], and "The Trinity" ["Trojstvo"] a brief
piece honoring Homer, Dante, and Shakespeare, are connected
with Shevyrev's study of ancient and modern literatures.
"Two Songs: Love Before and After Happiness" ["Dve pesni:
Ljubov' do sčastija i posle"] contrasts the moods of a lover
who first begs the sun to slow its movement but when later
disaffected is bored by the tedious passage of the day.

Formality and restraint, allusions to mythology, intellectual content make Shevyrev's poetry quite distinct from
that of other lyric poets where mood and melody dominate.
He has been characterized as a "poet of thought," and a comparison has been made between him and Fyodor Tyutchev,
a poet of much greater accomplishment whose personal history also was connected with the Lovers of Wisdom. Notwithstanding the possibility of such a comparison, it must be
stated that Shevyrev's real contribution to Russian literature
was in the field of criticism and scholarship.

ALEXANDER VOSTOKOV (1781–1864), the illegitimate son of
Baron Osten-Saken, studied first at the Cadet Corps and then
at the Academy of Arts. A deep interest in literature led to
his membership, from 1801, in the Free Society of Lovers
of Literature, Science and Arts (Vol'noe Obščestvo Ljubitelej
Slovesnosti, Nauk i Xudožestv), and at about the same time
he began to publish his verses in various periodicals. In the
second decade of the century Vostokov made important contributions with his scholarly works of a philological nature,
such as his study of tonic verse and his efforts in the field
of Slavic linguistics. A reflection of these activities is found
in the eight "Serbian Songs" ["Serbskie pesni"] which he
translated for *Northern Flowers'* first three issues. These were
accompanied with his explanatory notes. His only original

work for the almanac was "To My Friends" ["K druz'jam"] (1826), a brief poem written as a dedicatory introduction to a collection of his verses.

VASILY SHCHASTNY (dates unknown), a disciple of Delvig's and editorial secretary of the Baron's *Literary Gazette*, belonged to a slightly younger generation than most of those who were attached to the circle of *Northern Flowers'* contributors. He frequented Delvig's literary evenings, and there he met Pushkin and other of Delvig's lyceum comrades. It is probable that his encounter there with the Polish poet Adam Mickiewicz in the winter of 1827–28 inspired him to translate Mickiewicz's "Faris"; Shchastny read this effort before that company, and it met with general approval.[69]

Apparently it was through his connection with Delvig that seven of Shchastny's works appeared in *Northern Flowers* in the 1829, 1831, and 1832 issues.[70] Five of these are lyrical poems, adequate, perhaps, but not unusual. Their titles indicate the subject matter: "Colloquy of a Sweet Maid" ["Beseda miloj devy"] (1829), "Two Wishes" ["Dva želanija"] (1832), "The Hearth" ["Kamin"] (1832). The last poem, eight lines of trite sentiment, speaks for itself. In the almanac's last two issues were included scenes two and three from the second act of the dramatic poem of Jósef Korzenowski, *The Hermit* [*Otšel'nik*]; the turgid, blank verse of this translation casts serious doubts upon the quality of the original Polish. Shchastny's "Turkish Song" ["Tureckaja pesnja"] (1832), in the form of a maiden's complaint that her lover has deprived her of the peace of soul which she had known before meeting him, is lilting but trivial and, as other Shchastny poems, contains barely acceptable rhymes.

BARON YEGOR ROZEN (1800–60) was well known during the thirties for his various activities as poet, playwright, and editor of literary almanacs.[71] He was the first to translate *Boris Godunov* into German, which, according to his own testimony in a letter to Shevyrev, earned Pushkin's "enthusiastic gratitude and the praise of Zhukovsky."[72]

In *Northern Flowers* for 1829, 1830, and 1832 Baron

Rozen published seven poems, two of which concern the flower from which his family took its name: "The Secret of a Rose (An Imitation of the Arabian)" ["Tajna rozy (Podražanie arabskomu)"] (1829) and "The Rose of the Grave" ["Mogil'naja roza"] (1830). Both poems develop the idea of a mystical union between a rose and a maiden. The latter, in amphibrach tetrameter, is sweetly and sadly melodious. "The Path of Love" ["Put' ljubvi"] (1830) and "The Wedding Ceremony" ["Venčal'nyj obrjad"] (1830) both conclude on the pessimistic note that marriage ultimately leads to a chilling of passion and the loss of childhood joys. Moralistic admonitions are sounded in "The Shepherd's Horn in Petersburg" ["Pastušij rog v Peterburge"] (1832) and "Damnation" ["Prokljatie"] (1832), and the final selection, "To a Greek Maid" ["Grečanke"] (1832) concerns a speculative passion. It is remarkable only in that it is presented entirely in the conditional mood.

NIKOLAY GNEDICH (1784–1833) was one of the major "minor contributors" to Delvig's almanac. Author, poet, academician, he had been a successful literary figure for almost a quarter of a century prior to his participation in *Northern Flowers*. Today he is remembered principally for his translation of *The Iliad*, published in 1829, which was the first complete translation from Greek to appear in any language.

Born in Poltava, he received his early education at seminaries and then studied for two years at the University of Moscow, after which he assumed a minor post in the Ministry of Education in Petersburg. His earliest literary efforts, which began to appear at the first of the century, included an original novel, *Don Carrado de Herrera*, and a translation of Schiller's drama *Die Verschwörüng des Fiesko zu Genua*. These, as well as his original poetic works of the period, were quite in harmony with the liberal and civic attitudes of the Free Society of Lovers of Literature, Science and Arts with which Gnedich was closely associated. His literary activities merited his being elected to the Russian Academy in 1811, and the same year he was given a sinecure in the public library to enable him to work on his translation of *The Iliad*.[73]

Gnedich began his translation of *The Iliad* from the seventh book, originally intending to complete the task begun by Yermil Kostrov (d. 1796). However, he soon became dissatisfied with the Alexandrine verse form utilized by Kostrov, and in 1813 he abandoned his work and began anew from the first book, this time duplicating the Greek epic meter. Ill health forced him to go to the Caucasus in the mid-twenties, and then he settled for a time in Odessa. Greatly improved, he returned to Petersburg in 1828, and the following year his complete *Iliad* was published. In 1832, a year before his death, the first collection of his poems appeared.

Although essentially Gnedich was a Classicist and literary conservative, he remained independent of any strong allegiance to such stolid fraternities as Admiral Shishkov's Colloquy of Lovers of the Russian Word (Beseda ljubitelej russkogo slova). In fact, his membership in that group did not prevent him from composing the parodistic catechism for Colloquy members which so delighted Arzamas, that informal gathering of Karamzin's followers which had as its major purpose the lampooning of Shishkov's disciples. Gnedich did not approve of Sentimentalism or of the foggy Romanticism exemplified by Zhukovsky which replaced it, yet he was progressive enough to take part in the meetings of the Green Lamp (*Zelennaja Lampa*) and to accept membership in the Free Society of Lovers of Russian Literature, of which he was vice-president from 1821 to 1823.

Gnedich first appeared in *Northern Flowers* in 1825 with three of his "Greek Popular Songs" ["Grečeskie prostonarodnye pesni"], translated from contemporary Greek.[74] The following year he treated the almanac's readers to an excerpt from his translation of the fourteenth book of *The Iliad*. "Cyprian's Belt" [*"Pojas Kipridy"*]. "The Fishermen: An Idyl" ["Rybaki: Idillija"] (1827) is a rather prosaic work about a young Neva fisherman whose ability on the pipe gains him the patronage of a boyar. The tone is lofty, the dialogue stylized, the descriptions conventional, and the unrhymed amphibrach pentameter becomes tedious after twenty pages. Incidentally, there is some indication that the work contains allusions to Count Stroganov's patronage of Gnedich.[75] In the 1828 issue of the almanac appeared an excerpt from Gnedich's epistle to Pletnyev, and the complete poem, along with Pletnyev's poetic answer, was included in the 1831 issue. In rather bombastic tones, the "master" seeks to encourage his young correspondent; the prose translation conveys the tone.

> *The most impartial judge of Poets,*
> *Their real mother, is Nature.*
> *Stand before her face*
> *At the hour of the sun's solemn ascent,*
>
> . . . .
>
> *Let thy genius question nature*
> *And if thou art her worthy neophyte*
> *She will speak to thee*
> *In a tongue which is simple, though incomprehensible*
> *To the masses, and most eloquent to the heart.*
>
> . . . .
>
> *With a daring hand touch the dumb strings;*
> *They shall become enflamed with the fire of the soul,*
> *They shall speak, and from thy fingers*
> *Living songs will pour forth.*

> *Est' bezpristrastnejšij Poètov sudija,*
> *Ix sobstvennaja mat', Priroda.*
> *Predstan' pered lice ee*
> *V čas solnceva toržestvennogo vsxoda,*
>
> . . . .
>
> *Pust' genij tvoj prirodu voprošaet;*
> *I esli ty ee dostojnyj neofit,*
> *Ona k tebe zagovorit*
> *Svoim prostym, no černi neponjatnym,*
> *Krasnorečivejšim dlja serdca jazykom;*
>
> . . . .
>
> *Rukoju smeloju kosnisja strun nemyx:*
> *Oni ognem duši zažgutsja,*
> *Zagovorjat, i ot perstov tvoix*
> *Živye pesni razol'jutsja.*[76]

Gnedich's presence in *Northern Flowers* certainly contributed to the popularity of the almanac, since his verses, despite their formal and old-fashioned qualities, were still admired by the public. Further, as one of the grand old men of Russian letters, his name lent an aura of respectability to the publication and certainly enhanced its prestige.

VICTOR TEPLYAKOV (1804–42) was of gentry origin, but little is known of his early years other than that he received a good education prior to entering the Ministry of Foreign Affairs, in which he served until his death. Something of an eccentric, he seems to have delighted in the constant changes of residence which his career as a diplomat necessitated. Pushkin, with whom he became acquainted in Kishinev and Odessa, dubbed him "Melmoth the Wanderer,"[77] not only for his peregrinations but because of the unusual sack coat, rumpled hat (which Teplyakov called Fortunatus' cap), and heavy iron cane (inscribed *memento mori*) which he constantly affected. Teplyakov accompanied the Russian army to Varna, Bulgaria, in 1829, and later served in Petersburg, Constantinople, Athens, and finally Paris, where he died. From all these cities he made constant excursions and trips, to such an extent that even his close friends were often in doubt as to his whereabouts.

Although Teplyakov published during the twenties, it was in the thirties that his reputation as a poet was established.[78] *Northern Flowers* played a significant role in the establishment of his prestige, because it was in this almanac, beginning in 1830, that several of his best works, or excerpts from them, appeared. "The Wanderers" ["Stranniki"], his contribution for 1830, is a dialogue in which one speaker extols life spent at home among familiar scenes and seasons, while the other lauds a rover's life. The verse is light, alliterative, and quite rhythmical. In 1831 appeared "Setting Sail" ["Otplytie"], his "First Thracian Elegy" ["Pervaja Frakijskaja èlegija"]. The poem presents a voyager's impressions as a boat carries him away from his homeland. Although the traveler's thoughts at parting are elegiac, the selection is far from sombre. The poem combines iambic hexameters with tetrameters in stanzas of various forms with a free rhyme scheme, which enhances the impression of lightness, movement, and action. The quality of this poem was duplicated by others of the series, and when the collection of *Thracian Elegies* was published in 1836, it rated a special article by Pushkin in the *Contemporary*.

"A Rumelian Song" ["Rumilijskaja pesnja"] (1831) consists of seven quatrains which in passionate terms express the longing of a woman for her absent lover. G. Niklevich's music for this song is included on the almanac's final pages. The 1832 almanac contained two pieces sharply contrasting in mood. "The Terrible Apparition" ["Žestokij prizrak"], of some seventy-one lines, is an empassioned apostrophe to an ominous vision, forever "transfixed" to the poet's soul "like Prometheus' vulture and chains," which capriciously plays with his emotions and destroys his peace of mind. "The Blue Stockings," whose title is given in English only, is a less sombre declaration of the pleasure to be derived from teasing women, most especially those "full of mysticism, politics, and romanticism." Strangely, though both of his contributions appear over his name in the 1832 almanac, he is absent from the index of contributors.

ANDREY PODOLINSKY (1806–86) contributed to *Northern Flowers* during 1828–30, the very years that his reputation as a poet was at its zenith. He then fell from grace, and in the late thirties disappeared completely from the literary scene. Educated at the preparatory school attached to the University of Petersburg, he had completed his schooling and at the age of seventeen was on his way to Kiev when he chanced to encounter Pushkin at a posting station in Chernigov. Owing to Pushkin's casual dress, Podolinsky mistook him for a waiter, and, to his subsequent complete mortification, he was disdainful of Pushkin's friendly questions. Several years later, when they met again in Petersburg, Pushkin had forgotten the incident.[79]

In 1827 Podolinsky published his first work, the narrative poem *Div and Peri* [*Div i Pèri*]. It was an immediate success and led to the poet's acquaintance with the leading figures of the Petersburg literary scene. Delvig became his patron, and during the winter of 1827–28 Podolinsky was frequently present at Delvig's literary evenings. Podolinsky's next two verse tales, *Borsky* [*Borskij*] and *The Beggar* [*Niščij*], which appeared in 1829 and 1830, were sharply criticized by Pushkin, Ivan Kireevsky, Nadezhdin, Somov, and even Delvig, who stated that *Borsky* was imitative and caustically commented that "melodious verses which lack ideas do not indicate poetic talent but rather a well-developed organ of hearing."[80]

Despite the critical reaction to his narrative poems, Podolinsky continued to enjoy favor as a lyric poet, and his works appeared in many of the periodicals of the thirties. A collection of his poetry published in 1837 was well received, but after 1839 his Muse remained silent until 1855, when the events of the Crimean War inspired a final poem, "The Allies" ["Sojuzniki"].[81] A second edition of his poetry appeared in 1860.

It was the melodiousness, the apparent freedom and ease of Podolinsky's poems which appealed to his contemporaries, and these qualities were appreciated even in his unsuccessful narrative poems. The six pieces contributed to *Northern Flowers* cover a wide range of themes. "Firdausi" ["Firdousi"] (1828), uses the Persian poet's biography as the background for an aphoristic conclusion regarding the continued need for fame once it has been acquired. "The Orphan" ["Sirota"] (1829) is a dramatic poem about a young girl found weeping at night on the grave of her brother. Given shelter, she sleeps, and in a dream her brother tells her to cease her mourning. A year later she visits his grave, which now is covered with grass and flowers, and at its center is a bird's nest. The dialogue is pleasing and the narrative interpolations are good, but the point of the work is not evident. "The Two Wanderers" ["Dva strannika"] (1829) recounts the arrival in Rome of a pair of hungry and exhausted pilgrims. While one begs, the other feasts his eyes on Capitoline Hill, and the glories of the ancient city parade before his imagination. He prostrates himself before the sacred shadows—he is the "creator of Jerusalem."

The ballad "Houri" ["Gurija"], of thirteen stanzas, exactly reproduces the form of Pushkin's ballad of 1828, "The Drowned Man" ["Utoplennik"].[82] In simple and sensuous verses, the poet recounts how a young warrior abandons his beloved and seeks death in a holy war in order to obtain the favors of the maid of Paradise.

Notwithstanding Podolinsky's considerable talent for writing verses, he lacked the originality which characterizes the really good poet. In an age when poetry had to progress in order to survive, he continued to produce verse on old lasts. In so doing he was in direct competition with the many really fine poets of the period, and thus he was necessarily relegated to a secondary position.

LUKIAN YAKUBOVICH (1805–39) is almost totally forgotten, but if his contribution of seven poems to *Northern Flowers for 1832* provides any basis for a judgment of his talent, he was certainly not the least important of the almanac's poets. From a gentry family of means, he studied at the Moscow University preparatory school. Then, after a brief period in the government service, he resigned to devote himself exclusively to literature. He received little or no help from his family, and his earnings from literature were very modest. Thus, he was forced to endure physical privations which ultimately affected his health. Shortly before his death, he received a large inheritance, but it came too late to make possible the restoration of his health.[83]

Yakubovich's poetry appeared widely in the thirties, and it was, in fact, almost *de rigueur* to have him represented in one's journal or almanac. Pushkin enjoyed him as a person and appreciated his poetry, some of which was published in the *Contemporary*.[84] Yakubovich seems to have mastered the techniques and styles of his times, but he added little that was new or original. Yet, he did have an ability for the creation of melodious and pleasing verse, and he was able to evoke emotional response with considerable economy of words.

In *Northern Flowers* his poorest poem, "A Prayer" ["Mol'ba"], in heavy iambic pentameter, is a plea to the Muses that his poetry not be forgotten. Trite in conception

and weak in execution, it is the least likely of his seven contributions to the almanac to persuade anyone that he should
be remembered. "Iran (From Hafiz)" ["Iran (Iz Gafiza)"] is
a local-color piece celebrating the beauty of Persia; the work
may be a translation, but even if so it is a typical Romantic
stylization of Eastern poetry—foreign terms, artificial locutions, native flora: "And the heavens, like the glances of
houris, are eternally pure" ["I nebesa, kak vzory Gurij,
večno-čisty"]. "Music" ["Muzyka"] is a conventional piece
which likens the effect of music to that of an angel of peace
descending into one's soul; "Winter" ["Zima"] proceeds from
a description of a snow-shrouded landscape to the thought
that, just as the vital forces of nature will revive, so the dead
will also ultimately be resurrected. The two "Ukrainian
Melodies" ["Ukrainskie melodii"] are charming poems in the
tradition of the popular folk song. The first, a lilting apostrophe to one's personal lot or fate, resists a translation which
might render its essential content and rhythm: "Gde ty,
dolja, moja dolja./Na gore ili sred' polja?" ["Where art thou,
fate, my fate,/ On a mountain or in fields?"] The second is a
short dialogue between two lovers, whom neither rivers nor
time can keep separated. It also is very musical, notwithstanding its (intentionally) imperfect metrical pattern. Perhaps
the most interesting of his selections is "The Wood Demon"
["Lešij"], a brief dramatic narrative filled with atmosphere—
night, a demon howls in the forest, there is dancing in the
village; an old man boasts of the gay escapades of his youth,
but his wife cautions him that the laughter and howling in
the forest signify a demon's intention to carry him off.

ALEXANDER IZMAILOV (1779–1831) was a well-established
figure in literary circles long before he began contributing
to *Northern Flowers*, on whose pages he appeared six times
from 1825 to 1830. Of gentry origin, he attended the Gorny
Cadet Corps and later entered the Ministry of Finance. In
1799 he published his famous prose work, *Eugene, or the
Results of Bad Upbringing and Society* [*Evgenij, ili pagubnye
sledstvija durnogo vospitanija i soobščestva*], in which vice is
detailed with loving care. Two years later he played a major

role in organizing the Free Society of Lovers of Literature, Science and the Arts and became its permanent president. In the years 1818–26 he edited the society's journal, *Well-Intended* [*Blagonamerennyj*], and in 1826 and 1827 he edited its almanac, *Calendar of Muses* [*Kalandr' Muz*]. From 1818 he was associated with the Free Society of Lovers of Russian Literature.

While very active in literary matters, Izmailov pursued a career in the civil service; he was for two years Vice-Governor of Tver and later held a similar post in Archangel. He retired from government service in 1830 and died the following year.

Considerably older than the writers who dominated the literary scene in the twenties, Izmailov understandably was not a partisan of "new Romanticism" in either literature or politics.[85] He is remembered particularly for his fables, which, although lacking the high perfection of Krylov's, nonetheless were appreciated by his contemporaries and later generations for their national and naturalistic elements; the latter gained for Izmailov the title of "the Russian Teniers." A first edition of these fables appeared in 1814, and three more editions were published during his lifetime.

To the first issue of Delvig's almanac Izmailov contributed two brief album pieces honoring a name day and a birthday. Far more interesting were his fables, which reveal their author's common sense and somewhat sardonic humor. "The Shooters" ["Strelki"] (1826) is a dialogue in which a duelist who has been wounded in the eye tells of his hopes to be more successful now that he has a better pistol. He is advised to treat his injury and keep quiet. "The Miser and the Oculist" ["Skupoj i okulist"], subtitled "A Fairy Tale" ["Skazka"] (1829), humorously recounts how a miser, having agreed to a price for the restoration of his sight, stops the oculist when one eye has been operated upon and then pays only half the stipulated amount. "A Beastly Judgment" ["Skotskoe pravosudie"] (1830), is a satirical fable in which a dutiful dog is punished and a criminal wolf is rewarded by a judge who is an ass. "Deceptive Appearance" ["Obmančivaja naružnost'"] (1830) attacks the contemporary

misuse of poetry for personal vilification. The fable's narrator visits a rich wastrel who houses pigs and snakes in a
temple. When the poet remonstrates at this abuse of a work
of art, the spendthrift points out that poets do the same,
with the difference that his pigs besmirch no one and his
snakes don't bite, whereas poets hide dirty pigs and poisonous
snakes under the flowers of their poetry. Notwithstanding
the aptness of Izmailov's observation, the fable is excessively
contrived and the point is thereby vitiated. It must be said
that these particular fables are rather pedestrian and lack the
pithiness of statement, the conciseness of exposition, and the
special wit which are required for success in the genre.

VASILY GRIGORIEV (1803–76) received his education at the
Petersburg Government High School. Upon graduation in
1820, he assumed a modest position in the Treasury and
served there until his death. His literary activity began while
he was still in school, and he was first published in 1821. Two
years later, on the recommendation of Ryleev and Orest
Somov, he was accepted into the Free Society of Lovers of
Russian Literature and his works began to appear in its journal,
the *Emulator*. Through his connection with Ryleev, several
of his poems were published in *Polar Star*.

There is, unfortunately, little to recommend Grigoriev on
the basis of the five poems which appeared in *Northern
Flowers*.[86] "The Lament (An Israelite Song)" ["Setovanie
(Izrail'skaja pesn')"] (1828) is a dirge on the loss of the
Jewish homeland. "Epistle to N. F——v." ["Poslanie k
N.F——vu"] (1828) expresses an enthusiastic attitude toward
the beauties of the Volkhov region, the homeland of his
addressee. "Mount Beshtau" ["Beštau"] (1827) and "The
Georgian Maid" ["Gruzinka"] (1829) were probably inspired by Grigoriev's experiences in the Caucasus, where he
served for several years. The former in a rather hazy manner
links the eternal qualities of the mountain with the immortality gained by a poet who successfully makes a sacrifice to
inspiration. "The Georgian Maid" laments the fate of a
beautiful girl whose brief days of childish pleasure must be
followed by the slavery of marriage. In none of these works

does Grigoriev go beyond the conventional means and themes of his period. Certainly he failed, at least in *Northern Flowers*, to bring to inspiration's altar a sacrifice which would grant him the immortality of the truly creative artist.

ALEXANDER KRYUKOV (1803–33)[87] was a poet and writer of prose, and both aspects of his literary art are represented in *Northern Flowers*. Very little information is available concerning his life and work; it is known, however, that in 1827 he published "The Orenburg Exchange" ["Orenburgskij menovoj dvor"] in *Notes of the Fatherland* [*Otečestvennye Zapiski*] and "The Khirgiz ["Kirgizcy"] in Delvig's *Literary Gazette*.[88]

The 1829 issue of *Northern Flowers* contains three poems of Kryukov, "Night" ["Noč' "], "The Moon" ["Luna"], and "Death" ["Smert' "], which appear in sequence and are numbered consecutively. The first is a plaintive plea to night in which the "lyric I" begs for a vision of his loved ones so that he might forget his imprisonment. The second apostrophizes the moon, which brings consolation to the prisoner's cell—he sees it as a link between him and his distant friends. "Death" is the longest of the three (five stanzas of six lines) and contains speculations on the nature of death. The same issue also contains his "Unexpected Meeting" ["Nečajannaja vstreča"], in which he likens his sudden encounter at night with his addressee, a woman, to an encounter between the spirit of darkness (himself) and a peaceful angel. Since there is no particular reason to give a metaphysical interpretation to such a prosaic incident, this poem is less effective than the others. But in all cases, Kryukov reveals a competence to express himself movingly in verse.

DMITRY STRUISKY (1806–56), who used the pseudonym "Trilunny," contributed two poems and one prose work to each of the last two editions of *Northern Flowers*. Born of a serf mother, he was legitimized by his gentry father, the son of a minor eighteenth-century author. Struisky-Trilunny was rather prolific, and his literary activity involved prose, poetry, and criticism of literature and music. His works appeared in many of the better almanacs and journals of the thirties and forties, and as early as 1830 he had published an almanac collection of his verses.[89]

The four poems which appeared in *Northern Flowers* should be considered in connection with his prose contribution of 1831, "Excerpts from a Notebook" ["Vyderžki iz zapisnoj knižki"]. This work consists of semiphilosophical observations on man and nature in a sentimental style recalling Karamzin of *Letters of a Russian Traveler.* The following passage conveys the mood which seems to underlie his considerations.

> Each time when I delve into the moral being of man, I find an inexhaustible source of sadness in my heart. Give me all earthly blessings, embody in me all dreams of happiness, and that sadness, that element from which I have been created, remains always within me.[90]

His comments upon modern poetry detail his conviction that man has lost his primitive ability to express himself naturally.

> Now we live in an age in which all feelings are hidden under a mask of decorum. Raptures no longer exist; they have disappeared along with primal human life. With the invention of spoken language, feelings have become enfeebled, and only music alone serves them with its weak echo. Only in it alone do I hear the lofty language of prayer. Haydn's *Creation of the World,* Mozart's *Requiem,* Beethoven's *Mass* (C major), these are the representatives of the fine arts of the Christian world. They have convinced me of the divinity of the human soul, and modern romantic poetry cannot stifle in my heart the seeds sowed by these works. Look objectively at the chaos of our poetry: with what can one compare it? With a worm feeding on the grave's dampness. Unhappy Faust, unhappy Manfred—these are the representatives of our age! One stamp has been put upon them, and this is it:

> *Doubt in the heavens, scorn for the earth;*
> *A storm in the soul—the stamp of melancholy on the brow.*[91]

It must be said that the stamp of melancholy was not absent from Struisky's own poetry, though it was not from grief born of romantic revolt but from an awareness of the transitoriness of man and mankind's moral imperfection. "Alpine Pines" ["Al'pijskie sosny"] (1831) notes the anchoritic life of these isolated trees, but the poem leads to a conclusion that their remoteness gives safety from fire and axe and provides friendship with eagles and thunder. "Tears" ["Slezy"] (1831) insists that for someone who has lost his sight the "entire beautiful world is buried" and that for the blind man all that remains are tears. "Resurrection" ["Vozroždenie"] (1832) expresses the not so profound idea that humans replace one another on earth like ivy which grows on the columns of an abandoned temple. There is little in any of these selections to inspire enthusiasm for Struisky's art; however, his "Darkness (An Imitation of Byron)" ["T'ma (Podražanie Bajronu)"] (1832) reveals considerable talent. More an adaptation than imitation, it resembles the original only with respect to the basic idea and general scene— deprived of sunlight, the inhabitants of the world go mad and all living things perish. Struisky does not closely reproduce the particular imagery of Byron's apocalyptic scene but substitutes his own equally forbidding details. What is special, however, is that while Byron ends

> *The winds were wither'd in the stagnant air,*
> *And the clouds perish'd; Darkness had no need*
> *Of aid from them—She was the Universe.*

Struisky continues

> *But Someone lives as eternity!*
> *There is an inaccessible, peaceful world*
> *And grateful prayers!*
>
> *No Kto-to večnost'ju živet!*
> *Tam—nepristupnyj, mirnyj svet,*
> *I blagodarnye molitvy!*[92]

This conclusion significantly alters the whole effect of the poem, since it provides at least a vague note of hope in contrast to the crushing despair of the original.[93]

VASILY VERDEREVSKY (dates unknown) contributed to numerous journals and almanacs beginning in the mid-teens. In his lengthy career as a government official, he held a number of responsible positions, but in 1865 he was found guilty of embezzlement and was sent to Siberia.

His contribution to *Northern Flowers* consisted of five odes from Horace, which he adapted from French translations of the originals. These were published from 1828 to 1831 and included Odes 15 and 25 from Book I, Ode 5, Book II, Ode 23, Book III, and Ode 3, Book IV. Although Delvig manifestly appreciated Verderevsky's talent, Polevoy did not, and his *Moscow Telegraph* contained more than one negative comment regarding the renditions of Horace.[94]

ALEXANDER ROTCHEV (1813–73), a graduate of Moscow University, was an active translator and a sometime original poet. His four contributions to Delvig's almanac were the efforts of his adolescence. His first appearance there was in 1827 with "An Imitation of the Arabian" ["Podražanie arabskomu"], which was mistakenly signed "Tyutchev," thus attributing the work to a poet who was subsequently to become known as second only to Pushkin.[95] Delvig corrected his error in a public notice.[96]

Rotchev's "To a Would-Be Classicist" ["Mnimomu klassiku"] (1829) is a four line epigram chiding some "old dandy" for affecting caprine feet in his verselets. "In an Album to K. N. U——va" ["V Al'bom K. N. U——voj"] (1830) is a weak and imperfect example of album verse, distinguished only by its variety of meters. Rotchev's "Darkness (From Lord Byron)" ["T'ma (Iz Lorda Bajrona)"] (1829) is much closer to the original than Struisky's "adaptation," but somehow it lacks the apocalyptic quality which Byron conveyed. The terrible vision of the triumph of Darkness found in Byron is unsuccessfully conveyed by Rotchev's concluding lines.

> *The whirlwind became still—and all the earth*
> *Bore the stamp of destruction!*
>
>   *Vixr' onemel—i vsja zemlja*
>   *Pečat' nosila razrusen'ja!*[97]

As he approached this conclusion, Rotchev himself seems to have been running out of light: unlike the greater part of his translation, his conclusion is rather a condensation than a close rendition of the content of the original.

Later in life Rotchev was involved in several journalistic enterprises in those various localities where his government service took him.

NIKOLAY STANKEVICH (1813–40) began publishing when still a student in the Voronezh Preparatory School. His collaboration with *Northern Flowers* coincided with his first two years at the University of Moscow, where he remained from 1830 to 1834. There he became deeply interested in German philosophy and was the central figure in a student philosophical circle.[98] Following graduation, he served for a brief period as Honorary Inspector of the Ostrogozhsk District school system and then went to Berlin to continue his studies. Ill health, which had plagued him from childhood, drove him to Italy, where he died before his twenty-eighth birthday.

Two of Stankevich's three selections in *Northern Flowers* are translations. These include Goethe's "Gesang der Geister über den Wassern" ["Pesn' duxov nad vodami (Iz Gete)"] (1832) and the work of an unidentified poet entitled "The Eagle-Owl (A Translation)" ["Filin (Perevod)"] (1831). It is possible that the latter was actually Stankevich's original work and that its seventeen-year-old author called it a translation in order to lend authority to his effort. The poem is an apostrophe to an ominous nocturnal bird who sings of death. An Ossianic, elegiac mood prevails, as it does in several of Stankevich's early poems. His original work, "Striking of the Hours on the Spassky Tower" ["Boj časov na Spasskoj bašne"] (1832) is again a mood piece inspired by the nocturnal chiming from the Kremlin tower. It is unusual for its period owing to the combination of four-, five-, and six-feet iambic lines. Notwithstanding a certain talent as a poet, Stankevich is remembered today primarily for his philosophical interests.

KONSTANTIN MASALSKY (1802–61) was educated at the preparatory school of the University of Petersburg and then served in the Ministry of Internal Affairs. He became popular in the thirties, particularly owing to his historical novels, among them *The Streltsi* [*Strel'cy*] (1832), *The Black Box* [*Černyj jaščik*] (1833), and *The Regency of Biron* [*Regenstvo Birona*] (1834). He contributed three poems to Delvig's almanac. "Sea and Earth" ["More i zemlja"] (1825) is a translation from Greek in dactylic hexameters. "To the Brook" ["K ruč'ju"] (1829), from the Spanish of Villegas, loses much of its value due to the disturbing insistence of the iambic trimeter lines. "Ruins" [Razvaliny"] (1826) is original, but it is a quite conventional elegiac treatment of the hackneyed theme of life's transitoriness.

ALEXANDER KRYLOV (1798–1829) took an active part in the Free Society of Lovers of Russian Literature, and his poems were printed in the *Emulator*. His three brief lyrics in *Northern Flowers* are simple expressions of personal moods: "In the Album of N. N. V——a" ["V Al'bom N. N. V——oj"] (1825), "To the Maple (An Imitation of Parny)" ["K Klenu (Podražanie Parni)"], and "To A. A. K——a" [A. A. K——oj] (1829). These works are pleasant but quite typical of the casual verse of the period.

N. I. SHIBAEV (dates unknown) first appeared in *Northern Flowers* in 1831 with two poems, "Elegy" ["Èlegija"] and "Naples" ["Neapol' "]. The following year he contributed "Consolation (From A. Chénier)" ["Utešenie (Iz A. Šen'e)"]. There is little noteworthy about any of these works.

Poetesses of *Northern Flowers*

There is no particular justification for relegating, or elevating, the poetesses to a separate subsection. In general, there were very few of them, they contributed little, and the quality of their contributions, with one exception, were not impressive. If the publication of Delvig's almanac coincided with a period remarkable for its abundance of great poets and its plethora of Epigoni, it was a period in which poetesses were primarily imitative dilettanti.[99] It is evident that some of their works were published more as a gesture of friendship on Delvig's part than for their intrinsic worth. Yet, one must not be too harsh: certainly the ladies show a capacity for poetizing which is not worse than that of many of the male contributors.

NADEZHDA TEPLOVA (dates unknown) was the most prolific of the almanac's poetesses; her three poems appeared in the 1832 issue. The works reveal an ability to versify, and, although hardly significant with respect to content, are pleasantly melodious. "The Language of Eyes" ["Jazyk očej"] insists upon the eloquence of the organs of sight, and "Love" ["Ljubov' "] stresses the capacity of the tender passion to restore the authoress' spirit and waft her upwards from her earthly cell. "To Her" ["K nej"] is a poem in lilting amphibrachs commenting upon the insouciance of the addressee, whose life has been "a joyful feast." This poem may have been addressed to her sister, Serafima, also a sometime poetess, whose "To My Sister in an Album" ["Sestre v al'bom"] appeared in *Northern Flowers for 1832*.

ANNA GOTOVTSOVA (dates unknown) began publishing her poems in the mid-twenties, but her poetic activity ceased when she married at the end of the decade. Two of her epistles were published in Delvig's 1829 almanac. The first, addressed to Yury Bartenev, and titled simply "To Y. N. Bartenev" ["K Ju. N. Bartenevu"], expresses gratitude for his interest in her Muse and modestly discusses the "capricious visits" with which inspiration occasionally favors her. Her other contribution, "To A. S. P." ["A. S. P."], addressed to Pushkin, appeared between poems addressed to her by Prince Vyazemsky and Pushkin. The former's poem contains conventional praise for her talent as a poetess and her qualities as a person. Her poem to Pushkin lauds him to the skies, but ends on an enigmatic note.

> *Your judgment is unjust;*
> *But we do not dare to blame you:*
> *We know how to pardon genius—*
> *Silence will express reproach.*

Nespravedliv tvoj prigovor;
No poricat' tebja ne smeem:
My geniju prostit' umeem—
Molčan'e vyrazit ukor.[100]

Pushkin's "Answer" ["Otvet"], written in response to Prince
Vyazemsky's request to him for a poetic acknowledgement of
Gotovtsova's epistle, reveals his uncertainty regarding the
reasons for her censure. When he sent his poem to Delvig, in
his letter of November 26, 1828, he reiterated this uncertainty.

> Here is your answer for Gotovtsova (Devil take her).
> How do you like *ces petits vers froids & coulants?* What
> did my Vyazemsky write to her? She has little to profit
> from me. And, indeed, what is she censuring me for?
> For being impolite to the fair sex, or for obscenity, or
> disorderly behavior? Lord knows what she has in mind.[101]

PRINCESS ZINAIDA VOLKONSKAYA (1792–1862), well-known
patroness of the arts and intimate friend of the leading literary
figures of her time, placed two poems in the 1832 almanac.
Neither is significant. "The Funeral Song of the Slavic Gusli
Player" ["Nadgrobnaja pesn' slavjanskogo gusljara"], an
adaptation of a South Slavic popular song, is accompanied by
an editor's note giving details about the gusli, the folk instrument of the Illyrian Slavs, and about their most famous
composer-singer. The poem itself contains several words
which are deliberately misaccented to accommodate the folk
rhythm. "To My Star" ["Moej zvezde"] is a sentimental
apostrophe to the poetess's mystical, celestial soul mate.

It is worth noting that Vissarion Belinsky considered
Nadezhda Teplova, Anna Gotovtsova, and Princess Volkonskaya among the four most remarkable women of Pushkin's times.[102] The only other poetess appearing in the almanac
who was identified by name was Maria Dargomyshkaya (dates
unknown), whose "Two Worms (A Fable)" ["Dva červjaka
(Basnja)"] (1825) is no great credit to the genre.

EKATERINA TIMASHEVA (1798–1881), née Zagryazhskaya,
whose work was identified only by the letters "K——a

T——sheva" (K——a T——ševa) was the author of "An Answer" ["Otvet"], which appeared in *Northern Flowers for 1831* in response to the work immediately preceding it, "A Christmas Joke" ["Svjatočnaja šutka"] by Prince Vyazemsky. Both poems contain obvious allusions to some private knowledge of the two authors. In his poem Vyazemsky banteringly asks his addressee what sort of a devil she has associated with; and did she take a leaf from his book or did he learn from her? She replies by denying that she has seen any devil, and declares that she is not frightened even by Asmodeus (the king of demons who destroys matrimonial happiness; also Vyazemsky's Arzamas nickname). She continues

> *Hosts of hellish devils are not frightening*
> *We can exorcise them with a cross;*
> *But earthly devils—we secretly*
> *Tremble at their insight.*
> *There are many of them: one wears glasses,*
> *He lacks talons, he isn't frightening,*
> *In prose he is cutting, and in poetry*
> *He expresses the whole fire of passion.*

> *Ne strašen adskij sonm besov:*
> *Ot nix krestom my otčertimsja;*
> *Besov semnyx že, ix umov*
> *Nevol'no v tajne my strašimsja.*
> *Ix mnogo est': inoj v očkax,*
> *On bez kogtej, on ne pugaet,*
> *On kolok v proze, on v stixax*
> *Ves' plamen' strasti vyražaet.*[103]

This description nicely fits Vyazemsky himself. She concludes by disparaging society devils, who are merely talkative, but she expresses real fear of quiet, calculating devils.

Although Modzalevsky, in his notes to Pushkin's collected letters, states that only two of Timasheva's poems are known (including "An Answer"),[104] it is quite possible that the 1832 issue of *Northern Flowers* contains two other of her works. Both of these appear over the letters "E. Ti——va." "To a Bashful Person" ["K zastenčivomu"] asserts that a quiet and timid glance is more eloquent than

words. This poem has a quite unusual clarity and forthright-
ness, perhaps due to the absence of verbal ornamentation.

> *Oh, don't envy that cold art*
> *Of aimlessly expressing love in empty words.*
> *Leave that gift to others, be satisfied,*
> She *will understand you.*

> *O! ne zaviduj ty xolodnomu iskustvu*
> *Bez celi vyražat' ljubov' v pustyx slovax,*
> *Ostav' sej dar drugim, dovolen bud' soboju;*
> Ona *pojmet tebja.*[105]

The other work signed "E. Ti——va" is "To An Unforgettable Person" ["K nezabvennomu"], a declaration that
although her addressee still affects her emotionally, yet this
is not the emotion of love but rather friendship. Both of these
works represent a significantly different kind of emotional
expressiveness than that found in the usual stale bonbon of
love poetry. They have a tension, or elasticity, they are like
crystal glass rather than colorfully ornamented china. Had
Ti(mashe)va been more productive, she might have exerted an
important influence upon the development of poetic diction.

Finally, COUNTESS YEVDOKIA ROSTOPCHINA (1811–58), née
Sushkova, a poetess who was to enjoy a substantial reputation
during the later thirties and forties, was represented by one
work, "Talisman" ["Talisman"], which appeared in the 1831
edition of the almanac over the signature "D——a——."
The poem was, incidentally, her first published work.

Peripheral Contributors

Several other poets published only once or twice
in the almanac, and thus their effect upon the general quality
of the almanac was obviously quite limited. Nonetheless, some
of these contributors were well known at the time, or were
to become well known, and their connection with *Northern
Flowers* is therefore not without significance. In any case,
it would be well to provide a complete roster of identifiable
contributors.

SEMYON RAICH (1792–1855) exerted a considerable influence upon Russian literature through his activities as poet, journalist, and teacher of literature at the Gentry Pension (preparatory school) of the University of Moscow. He is credited as the focal figure in a literary-philosophical circle which included V. F. Odoevsky, Mikhail Pogodin, Dmitry Oznobishin, A. N. Muraviev, Stepan Shevyrev. Fyodor Tyutchev, the Kireevsky brothers, and V. P. Titov.[106] Raich edited several almanacs, including *New Muses* [*Novye Aonidy*], *Northern Lyre* [*Severnaja Lira*], and was publisher-editor of the journal *Galatea*. Orest Somov severely criticized Raich's translation of *Jerusalem Delivered* and mocked his literary pretensions.[107] Raich published only one poem in the 1826 *Northern Flowers:* "To Leda: An Imitation of K. Hall" ["K Lide: Podražanie K. Gallu"].

IVAN KOTLYAREVSKY (1769–1838) is recognized as an important figure in the establishment of Ukrainian literature. His "A Little Russian Song" ["Malorossijskaja pesnja"] (1830) is typical of his interest in the folklore of his native region.

PRINCE ALEXANDER SHAKHOVSKOY (1777–1846), dramatist and producer, was a staunch defender of the classical tradition. He satirized Karamzin in *A New Sterne* [*Novyj Stern*], a comedy of 1805, and his *A Lesson to Coquettes, or Lipetsk Spa* [*Urok koketam, ili lipeckie vody*], which appeared in 1815, ridiculed the sentimentalist tradition as exemplified by Zhukovsky. Shakhovskoy was a member of Admiral Shishkov's Colloquy and a vigorous opponent of Arzamas. As someone close to the Arzamas group, Pushkin initially was hostile to Shakhovskoy, but subsequently modified his opinion. It may well have been Pushkin's decision to include Shakhovskoy's two poems in *Northern Flowers'* final issue: "Step-children: A Fable" ["Svodnye deti: Basnja"] and "Inscriptions for Two Groups of Work by I. P. Martos" ["Nadpisi k dvum gruppam tvorenija I. P. Martosa"].

VLADIMIR IZMAILOV (1773–1830), author, translator and journalist, was an ardent disciple of Rousseau and follower of

Karamzin. He was an honorary member of the Free Society
of Lovers of Russian Literature. He contributed one fable
to Delvig's almanac: "The Horse and the Foal: A Fable
(From Florian)" ["Kon' i žerebenok: Basnja (Iz Florijana)"]
(1828).

ALEXEY KHOMYAKOV (1804–60), poet and playwright, is
remembered principally as a Slavophil philosopher and a
central figure in that movement. After three years in the
military service, he went abroad to study. On his return in
1826, he was closely associated with the Lovers of Wisdom
society. At the time of his collaboration with *Northern
Flowers*, he was involved in editorial work for Mikhail
Pogodin's *Moscow Herald*. His "Farewell to Adrianople"
["Proščanie s Adrianopolem"] appeared in *Northern Flowers
for 1830*.

ALEXANDER ARDALIONOVICH SHISHKOV (1799–1832), author,
playwright, and translator, was known as "Shishkov the
Second," to distinguish him from his uncle, Admiral Alexander
Shishkov, to whose literary and political views he was
diametrically opposed. He was a close friend and literary
disciple of Pushkin. Shishkov's military career was marked
by a number of disciplinary actions, and he was knifed to
death in the streets of Tver by an officer whom he had
challenged for insulting his wife. His "The Elf" ["El'fa"],
a dramatic dialogue involving the title figure and forest birds,
appeared in 1830.

IVAN VELIKOPOLSKY (1797–1868), poet and playwright, was
an active member of the Free Society of Lovers of Literature,
Science and Arts and the Free Society of Lovers of Russian
Literature. He retired from the military service with the rank
of major in 1827. His *To Erast: A Satire on Gamblers*
["Èrastu: Satira na igrokov"], published the following year,
occasioned some difficulties with Pushkin, but the two were
subsequently reconciled.[108] Velikopolsky contributed two
poems to *Northern Flowers:* "To a Bestowed Tress" ["K

podarennomu lokonu"] (1826) and "Remembrance (From Lamartine)" ["Vospominanie (Iz Lamartina)"] (1827).

DMITRY OZNOBISHIN (1804–77) was an original poet and also a translator from Western and Near Eastern literatures. In 1827 he was coeditor with Semyon Raich, of the almanac *Northern Lyre*. To Delvig's almanac he gave: "The World of Fantasy" ["Mir fantazii"] (1826) and "Violet (An Imitation of Ibn-Rumi)" ["Fialka (Podražanie Ibn-Rumi")] (1827).

NIKOLAY OSTOPOLOV (1782–1833) was a poet, translator, and theoretician of Russian Classicism. He belonged to both Free Societies and was also a contributor to *Polar Star*. His "The Cat and the Squirrel (A Fable)" ["Kot i belka (Basnja)"] appeared in the first issue of *Northern Flowers*.

MIKHAIL SUKHANOV (1801–43) was a peasant poet whose reputation was based on his songs and fables in the popular tradition. His *Fables, Songs and Various Poems of the Peasant Mikhail Sukhanov*, published in 1828, earned him a silver medal from the Russian Academy. He was also active as a collector of folk literature. In 1828 *Northern Flowers* included his "The Flower and the Thorn Bush: A Fable" ["Cvetok i ternovnik: Basnja"].

MIKHAIL ZAGORSKY (1804–24), poet and translator, died the year of his graduation from the University of Petersburg. Primarily an elegist, he published in the *Emulator*, *Well-Intended* [*Blagonamerennvj*], *Polar Star*, and elsewhere during his lifetime. His posthumous contribution to *Northern Flowers* was "The Glove (From Schiller)" [Perčatka (Iz Šillera)] (1825), a translation of "Der Handschuh."

YEFIM ZAITSEVSKY (1801–60) was an officer, and later diplomat, who wrote primarily elegies. His works appeared in many periodicals from the twenties to the fifties. Contributions to Delvig's almanac included "Uchan-Su" ["Učan-su"] (1828), the title of which is the Tatar name for a Tavrida waterfall, and "To B. F. R——a" ["B. F. R——oj"] (1829). Zaitsevsky took part in the Russo-Turkish war of 1828–29, and it was he who led the volunteers who successfully stormed the fortress at Varna.

MIKHAIL YAKOVLYEV presents some difficulties, since the works signed with that name may be from the pen of Mikhail Lukianovich Yakovlyev (1789–1868), the poet and musician who was a schoolmate of Delvig and Pushkin at Tsarskoe Selo lyceum (and who wrote music to their poetry), or Mikhail Alekseevich Yakovlev (1798–1853), an editor of the *Neva Spectator* [*Nevskij Zritel'*] and author of prose, verse, and drama. The recent discovery of the latter's personal archives revealed that Pushkin's schoolmate had incorrectly been credited with a number of Mikhail Alekseevich's works.[109] In any case, one of them contributed "Elegy" ["Èlegija"] (1826) and "Epigram" ["Èpigramma"] (1827).

VASILY PUSHKIN (1767–1830), uncle of Alexander Pushkin, was a follower of Karamzin and author of light verse and humorous narrative poems. He played an active role in Arzamas. His works appeared in many journals and almanacs from the nineties of the previous century until his death; his collected poetry was published in 1822. His one contribution to *Northern Flowers* was "A Fragment from the Tale: Captain Khrabrov" ["Otryvok iz povesti: Kapitan Xrabrov"] (1829), the second chapter of an indifferent narrative poem.

ALEXANDER A. KOMAROV (n.d.–1874), a teacher of Russian literature at the Petersburg Military School, contributed "Night" ["Noč'"] and "An Excerpt from a Rural Narrative Poem: Masha" ["Otryvok iz sel'skoj poèmy: Maša"] to the 1832 almanac.

DMITRY GLEBOV (1789–1843), a translator and author of patriotic verses, published in Delvig's almanac the translation "A Dream (From Byron)" ["Son (Iz Bajrona)"] (1827).

MIKHAIL VRONCHENKO (1805–55), an administrative official primarily remembered for his translations of Shakespeare,

Byron, Mickiewicz and Goethe, presented one of his translations in the 1829 issue, "Irish Melodies (From Moore)" ["Irlandskie melodii (Iz Mura)"].

There were a few additional contributors who today are simply names in indexes. Certain of these may have been important outside the field of literature as such, but since they were only modestly talented and hardly prolific, they have been almost forgotten. Their names and their contributions follow. Alexander Glebov: "A Fairy Garden (A Poetic Fantasy)" ["Volšebnyj sad (Stixotvornaja fantazija)"] (1827); "August" ["Avgust mesjac"] (1827). Valentin Shemiot: "Elegy (From Parny)" ["Èlegija (Iz Parni)"] (1827); "To My Friends" ["Druz'jam"] (1830); Prince Alexander Vasilievich Meshchersky: "Stanzas" ["Stancy"] (1832); P. Sklyarevsky: "A Dance (From Schiller)" ["Pljaska (Iz Šillera)"] (1827); Ivan Ballyo: "To an Unfortunate" ["Nesčastnomu"] (1827); Platon Volkov: "A Dream ["Mečta"] (1831); T. Volkov: "Undines" ["Rusalki"] (1831); and N. Stavelov: "The Wanderer" ["Strannik"] (1832).

Finally, there are several authors whose identities are hidden behind initials or elliptical versions of their names: A. Og——v: "My Epitaph (An Imitation of Scarron)" ["Moja èpitafija (Podražanie Skarronu)"] (1826); M.: "The Bee and the Butterfly" ["Pčela i motylek"] (1828); ——ch [——č]: "Midnight" ["Polnoč"] (1832); Z——ya R——a [Z——ja R——a]: "I Loved" ["Ljubila ja"] (1831).

Chapter VI

The Prose in *Northern Flowers*

If the poetry sections of *Northern Flowers* consistently present the good and the great talents of an era known for its rich stock of poets, the prose sections represent a more modest contribution to Russian literature. Yet the almanac is of great interest for the scholar in that it provides material for a study of one of the most critical periods in the development of Russian prose. Some preliminary indication of the real significance of *Northern Flowers* in this area may be gained from the knowledge that both Pushkin and Gogol published their first fiction[1] in this almanac: namely, Pushkin's "Chapter IV from a Historical Novel," in the 1829 issue, and Gogol's contribution of 1831, "A Chapter from a Historical Novel," signed "o o o o," a pseudonym apparently derived from Nikolay Gogol Yanovsky.

A surprising number of genres are represented by the prose in *Northern Flowers*, and, in fact, one may find examples of virtually every form of prose extant at that time. First, let us deal briefly with a rather heterogeneous group of contributions which may be loosely categorized as essays, some of which belong to lettres and some to literature, depending upon subject matter, the emphasis on information or amusement, and the author's concern with style for its own sake. Largely of an informative nature are Vasily Grigorovich's two long essays, "On the State of Art in Russia" ["O sostojanii xudožestv v Rossii"], appearing in 1826 and 1827, Dmitry Dashkov's articles on the manuscripts in the Seral library (1825 and 1826), Mikhail Pogodin's "Something about Science" ["Nečto o nauke"] (1832), or M. Maksimovich's "On the Life of Plants" ["O žizni rastenij"] (1832). Literary criticism was an important element in the prose section and involved, in addition to Somov's annual surveys, a number of other critical essays, but these have been discussed elsewhere in this study. Of minor significance are two works on historical subjects, which must be classified as lettres despite their authors' obvious concern for style. These are Faddey Bulgarin's "Peter the Great in the Naval Expedition from Petersburg to Vyborg (1710)" ["Petr Velikij v morskom poxode iz Peterburga k Vyborgu (1710 goda)"] (1829) and Fyodor Glinka's "The Advance of the Main Active Army to the Position near Tarutino" ["Vstuplenie bol'šoj dejstvuščej armii na poziciju pri S. Tarutine"] (1830). The former is so patently a contrived and false treatment of fact that it could hardly be justified even in a collection of patriotic tales for children. Glinka's work is a more objective, but overly laudatory, account of Kutuzov's and Miloradovich's activities during the French invasion. This piece, along with other parts of Glinka's *Letters of a Russian Officer*, from which it is excerpted, merits attention as a source for Tolstoy's treatment of Kutuzov and the French invasion in *War and Peace*. One might also mention Fyodor Glinka's "Ancient Castles" ["Drevnie zamki"] (1825), a superficial and naïve essay on the general development of European social classes, commerce, towns, and so forth.

Within the genre of essay, but quite different from those previously discussed, is Alexey Illichevsky's "A Remarkable Blind Man" ["Primečatel'nyj slepoj"], which appeared in the 1827 issue of the almanac. A modern equivalent of this type of sketch is represented by the *Reader's Digest* contributions entitled "The Most Unforgettable Character . . . ," although the heavy sentimentalism of these is happily not a feature of Illichevsky's work. In a matter-of-fact manner the author describes the background and accomplishments of a certain Chesnokov, a blind artisan with whose unusual history the

author became acquainted while in Siberia. Chesnokov, who
went blind at the age of three, early developed a number of
manual skills, progressing from carpentry to the designing and
making of clocks; he even was successful in teaching reading
to those with normal sight. Illichevsky provides some other
interesting details of Chesnokov's unexpected accomplishments, and he concludes laconically that Chesnokov "it seems,
is satisfied with his lot."[2]

Another biographical essay, but one with a more obvious
emphasis on narrative structure and style than Illichevsky's
informational sketch, is "Firdausi," an anonymous contribution of 1826 concerning Abul Kasim Mansur, author of the
Persian national epic *Shah Namah*. Having noted that probably even the name of this "Persian Homer" is unknown in
Russia, the writer proceeds to outline the historical background and essential details of Firdausi's life. The Turkish
Sultan, Mahmud, having achieved domination of Persia, sought
to consolidate his position by becoming the patron of the
intellectual elite. When he had won their favor, he suggested
that his reign be immortalized by one of their poets. At an
informal competition there appeared an unknown youth,
Firdausi, who manifested a talent surpassing that of all the
other poets, and he was subsequently promised a rich reward
by Mahmud if he would devote his art to the monarch's
glorification. As court poet, Firdausi gained the respect and
admiration of all, but when Mahmud's most brilliant young
favorite fell under the sway of the poet and manifested indifference to the ruler, the latter became intensely jealous.
When Firdausi finished his monumental commission, Mahmud
deliberately paid him much less than promised, whereupon the
outraged poet composed verses insulting the ruler and fled.
Later Mahmud repented his action and sent rich gifts to en-
tice Firdausi to return, but his messengers arrived to find
the poet had just died.

Almost all that is known about Firdausi derives from
traditional accounts of his life, and the author of this particular treatment departs even from these. The fictitious nature
of most of this biography is evident from the obvious elements of legend which are employed by the author: the

appearance of an unknown youth who easily bests the established poets, the patronage of the ruler followed by his unjustified animosity, the fame and respect which the poet almost
universally enjoys, the ruler's change of heart which coin-
cides with the death of the mistreated artist. Even the conclusion wafts of legend: Mahmud was stricken with grief and
sought to indemnify the poet's sister, but she would accept
nothing and "finished her life near the grave of her dear
brother."[3] Incidentally, the Firdausi tradition mentions a
daughter, but the author of the present work, in keeping with
his emphasis on the image of youthful genius, reconstructs a
family tree more suitable to his purposes. This piece of secular
hagiography is presented in a style involving a certain sentimental strain common to the mid-twenties.

> All the nobles and those close to the ruler not only did
> not envy his [Firdausi's] excellent fortune, of which he
> was worthy, but they felt some sort of inexplicable re-
> spect for him, some sort of special love, resembling the
> impression which remains in our soul when examining the
> most perfect work of sculpture or art. This period of
> Firdausi's life was without doubt the most happy.[4]

But the author, in the early stages of his narrative, manifested
an unusual laconicism.

> Firdausi lived in the middle of the eleventh century. He
> was born in the town of Tus. His father was a gardener.
> For his first acquaintance with poetry he was indebted to
> his teacher Essedi, who, after Firdausi's death, finished
> his epic *Shah Namah*. A strange story is told of the dis-
> covery of this poet's talent.[5]

Among the nonfiction contributions to the almanac, one
of the most intrinsically interesting, both from the point of
view of content and style, is Alexander Kryukov's "The Kirghiz Raid" ["Kirgizskij nabeg"] (1830), the account of an
adventure which befell the author while in charge of a survey
party on the Russian-Kirghiz frontier near the confluence of
the Ural and Ilek rivers. As an introduction to his anecdote,
the writer characterizes briefly the turbulent life of this region,

where the warlike Kirghiz nomads constantly sought to break through the Russian defense line in quest of plunder and prisoners. He then gives a brief description of the survey convoy with its fearsome-appearing Cossack guards arrayed à la Stenka Razin, the dilapidated Sergeant Moshnin and the morose and attenuated Lieutenant K. riding in a steppe carriage resembling a hearse. While camped for lunch the group was suddenly attacked by a band of Kirghiz horsemen. After a brief skirmish the enemy was driven off, enabling the survey party to strengthen their defenses. Shortly, a horde of nomads appeared and made a series of unsuccessful attacks. The rather bizarre Sergeant Moshnin was conspicuous in the action, attacking the enemy with wit and weapon; the gloomy lieutenant ran about shouting orders, which everyone ignored, and waving a long pistol, which, it subsequently developed, was without flints. The Kirghiz were finally driven off after one of their more daring leaders was killed, and the survey party returned safely to Ural.

Kryukov is a modest narrator with an unusual story. He opens by noting that his adventure is of a special sort

> worthy of occupying several stanzas in some Byronic-romantic poem: for in it the novelty of the situation was united with unexpectedness and terror. What a pity that I don't know how to write narrative poems! In any case I shall relate to you my poetic adventure simply, as a prosaic anecdote. And if I merit the attention enjoyed by the narrators of town news and other harmless mundane rubbish, then I shall be as satisfied as can be. And so, please listen.[6]

It is questionable that Kryukov was serious in suggesting that a poetic form would better have suited his anecdote, but certainly literature was not poorer for his having told it as he did. In a period when many writers of prose thought to walk with lofty steps but stumbled on the cobbles of cliché, Kryukov's unpretentious style and comfortable manner were rather exceptional. The above quotation indicates the conversational tone of his narrative, which throughout was marked by many elements common to the spoken language: direct address to the auditor (reader, in this case), rhetorical questions, emphatic statements, as well as an abundance of those phrases and words which are widely used in oral narration, such as the linking formulae "and so," "finally," "meanwhile," and statements such as "I must admit that," "it is true that," "it is necessary to know that," "in my opinion," and so forth. The naturalness of Kryukov's expressions, his avoidance of "literary" metaphors, his refusal to sentimentalize his experience—all of this makes his writing rather unusual for the period. And regarding the question of sentimentality, this is how he describes the death of the Kirghiz brave.

> Soon after this, several of the most lively attackers, drawing apart from the crowd and as if reproaching their comrades for lack of spirit, began quietly to approach our camp. . . . In front of all rode a conspicuous youth. He was proudly erect in the saddle and in one hand held a long lance and in the other a heavy *ai-balta* (battle axe). Apparently he was already prepared to fling himself at our camp . . . when at that moment the Cossack Kolesnikov aimed his long weapon at him . . . the shot resounded, the bullet hummed—and the Ordynetz quietly tumbled from his steed. With joyous cries our side swept forward. . . . Shots sounded. The Kirghiz became confused and showed us their heels! Contrary to custom, they even did not succeed in taking with them their fallen leader, whom Moshnin dragged by a leg to our camp. The slain Kirghiz was young, handsome, and stout. The bullet had passed through both cheeks below the temples. The Cossacks, by old custom were not slow in stripping him to the skin, and having noticed certain signs of life in him, in consideration for his suffering or more probably because of an evil feeling of hostility, hastened to finish off the victim with his own battle axe.[7]

In Tolstoy's *The Cossacks* there is a similar situation, but the treatment is entirely different. Kryukov, clearly, was an unneurotic pragmatist; to him this was a question of life or death—his life or death. No mercy could have been expected at the hands of the Kirghiz.

Essays primarily of a literary nature were only modestly represented in *Northern Flowers*. The first issue contained the brief contribution of Eugene Baratynsky entitled "The History of Coquetry" ["Istorija Koketstva"] a lightly humorous biographical sketch of this goddess, whose mother was Venus and whose father was Mercury, Apollo, Mars, or Vulcan—in any case, the young child had features of all these possible sires. Having achieved majority, Coquetry secured Jupiter's permission to settle among mortals, subsequently living in Greece and Rome, then wandering through Asia and Africa. In the eighteenth century she appeared triumphantly in Italy and France, accompanied by a daughter, Fashion. But it was on the banks of the Seine that her temple was raised. Her circle of male admirers was enormous, including even Frederick II and Voltaire. Baratynsky adds, "I will not speak about the women. One may call Coquetry the politics of the fair sex."[8] However, following the French revolution she apparently renounced her divinity and now "lives alone, reads edifying books, and sighs over her previous delusions. Time will tell whether the rumors about the sincerity of her reformation are true."[9]

This work is sufficiently pleasant, but it has very little to recommend it for a second reading. Baratynsky's exposition is uninvolved, and, although many of his sentences are rather long, this is really a function of his liberal use of colons and semicolons. The piece, as befits its satirical purpose, is devoid of any sentimentality.

The other essay, "Three Epochs of Love" ["Tri èpoxi ljubvi"], (1829), is less than three hundred words and is worthy of attention not because of its literary merits but because it is a contribution of Dmitry Venevitinov, whose death in 1827 at the age of twenty-two robbed Russian literature of a very promising poet, critic, and potential philosopher. This piece, which bears the subtitle "An Excerpt from an Unfinished Novel" ["Otryvok iz nekončennogo romana"] and is dated 1826, speaks of the first stage of love as an "epoch of rapture" when all things are equally beautiful to a youth, the second stage as that of love's focusing upon one object—a maiden. But reality causes youth to abandon his image of the ideal, and, disillusioned, he "pays dearly for the rapture of his second love."

> He is reticent and thoughtful. Oh, if then on another brow, in other eyes he reads the traces of the same feelings, if he overhears a heart beating in accord with his own—with what joy he gives his hand to that fellow being! And how clearly they understand one another! That is the third epoch of love: that is the epoch of meditation.[10]

One suspects some deep emotional experience motivating the expression of this gloomy philosophy, and the notes to this fragment in the 1934 Academia edition of Venevitinov's complete works substantiate the autobiographical nature of the piece.[11] But that, of course, has no relevance to its artistic value. Apparently, this bit of philosophical rhetoric actually was taken from an unfinished novel on which the poet worked in the last year of his life as an experiment to determine whether to abandon poetry for prose. An outline of this novel, based on the author's verbal synopsis, was presented in the preface to the first collection of Venevitinov's prose works, which appeared in Moscow in 1831.[12] The plot is not unduly original, and one can discern the shadowy outlines of Faust, Melmoth, and some Byronic types underlying the sketch of the hero, a brilliant youth who poisons his rival, inadvertently kills his beloved, and destroys the innocent daughter of his benefactor. Eroded by passions and tormented by conscience, he ultimately becomes a sort of animated corpse, unable to find anything to solace his empty soul. It might have been a good novel, but, if one may judge by the synopsis and the emotional lyricism of the fragment which remains, the work would not have contributed greatly to Russian prose. However, one must not forget the poet's age or that he, as did Lermontov, probably would have matured artistically in the course of writing further prose works.

To judge by the number of examples appearing in the early issues of *Northern Flowers*, the sentimental allegory was a quite popular genre in the mid-twenties. However, thanks to the prodigious efforts of Fyodor Glinka, who was responsible for almost all of the contributions of this type in the almanac, the editor's and probably the reading public's appetite was quickly satisfied—as well it might have been. The single allegory of 1825, "The Unknown Woman" ["Neuznannaja"], a brief prose poem on conscience, was followed by three similar pieces in 1826. "The Inexplicable Union" ["Neponjatnyj sojuz"], presented as a tale told by old Abufar during a caravan stop, deals with the inseparability of a black, greedy, irreligious, and dull *he* (body) and a white, devout, patient *she* (soul). "The Inseparables" ["Nerazlučnye"], another "Eastern" allegory, unites poverty and pity. "The Guide" ["Vožaty"] concerns a miraculous cicerone who leads the narrator into the interior of the earth and shows him everywhere the spirit of life and the secrets of nature— this guide is Imagination. "The Miraculous Companion ["Čudesnaja soputnica"], on the subject of fancy, continued the tradition in 1827, and after 1828, when Glinka presented only one allegory on Classicism and Romanticism, "Two Sisters, or: Whom Should One Prefer?" ["Dve sestry, ili: kotoroj otdat' preimuščestvo?"], the genre was not again represented by him until 1832, when his "An Important Question" ["Važnyj spor"] appeared. Definitely unimportant, this tedious piece concerned some vague conflict between black and white, the former of whom—or which—is pleased when people waste time playing cards, an activity much to the sorrow of white.

These moralistic bonbons are pretentious and tedious, and Glinka's attempts at purple prose convey only an impression of artificiality. Alas, the same thing must be said about his two "pictures from nature," "Autumn Days" ["Osennie dni"] (1827) and "Sunrise on a Stormy Autumn Morning" ["Vosxoždenie solnca v burnoe osennee utro"] (1828), both of which are pathetic bouquets of gaudy wax flowers. The first of these remarks how wonderful summer days are, but adds, "I admit that autumn days are dearer." In both works we encounter fatuous metaphors, banal philosophizing, ponderous and vapid turns of speech. From "Sunrise"

The minutes before sunrise possesses something solemn, something marvelously calming. It seems that along with the darkness of the night everything that is dark passes away. I don't know whether it is because of one's attention to the rising star or some other reason that all the soul orients itself to the line of the east and, like a bride fixedly gazing at the door from which her bridegroom must appear, joyfully sinks in nameless sensations, in pleasures which it is impossible to touch or to buy for all the gold of Peruvian mines, for all the diamonds of India, in pleasures which the Merciful Lord offers free to all who are not detained by sloth and sleep in the hours of the bright appearance of the universal guest of nature, the magnificent Divine sun.[13]

After this anything would be anticlimactic, and that is, in fact, a good way to characterize Glinka's effort of 1831, "The New Assay Tent" ["Novaja probirnaja palatka"], a dream about a foreigner from the East who can tell truth from falsehood; hence, women will not enter his tent. Unfortunately, Orest Somov seems to have become infected by Glinka's allegorical-dream style, for in the last issue of the almanac there appeared his "A Living Person in the Cloister of Eternal Bliss" ["Živoj v obiteli blaženstva večnogo"], a dream of heaven and *Him*. Somov, who, after all was a competent writer, would have done much better to stick to criticism and conventional fiction. This effort, as well as all of Glinka's similar pieces, was mercifully brief.

Autobiographical travel accounts are heavily represented in the early issues of *Northern Flowers,* but, after 1827, their number is considerably diminished, an indication that this particular genre was reaching a point of saturation. Usually presented either as accounts of journeys or parts thereof, or in the form of letters presumably written while traveling, this genre embraced a wide variety of content. Descriptions of exotic locations, comments on local customs, sketches of interesting persons encountered en route, anecdotes of adventure, cultural and historical information, among other things, were commonly found in this type of literature. The "grab bag" nature of the genre leads to certain difficulties, for some of the adventures or anecdotes interpolated in these travel accounts might rightly be excerpted and treated simply as short stories. Some authors obviously took considerable pains to give a "literary" quality to the episodes within their accounts, and it is evident in a few cases that the demands of structure and plot became more compelling than a strict adherence to the facts themselves.

The sentimental travel account, an attempt to imitate the style of Karamzin's *Letters of a Russian Traveler*, is represented by the contributions of Voyeykov and Princess Volkonskaya. Alexander Voyeykov[14] (1778–1839), a literary Jack-of-all-trades whose modest success was largely a result of Zhukovsky's patronage, contributed only one piece to the first issue of *Northern Flowers*. His "An Excursion in Kuskovo Village" ["Progulka v sele Kuskove"] concerns a visit in 1811 to an estate of the fabulously rich Sheremetev family. Descriptions of the grounds, with its parks, groves, caves, ponds, fountains, canals, streams, grottoes, arbors, and zoo are combined with details of the interiors of the manor house, the Italian and Dutch cottages with their paintings by famous European masters, the Hermitage with its table for sixteen served automatically from below. Voyeykov lets emotion seize him in the portrait gallery.

> How many glorious and grievous memories there are in the portrait gallery of the Kings and Queens of Europe, contemporaries of CATHERINE the Great. They are depicted full size, and it appears as if they were alive, as if they gaze upon the entering visitors. Here is Frederick the Great! Here is Joseph II, well-intentioned but impatient: he began everything but finished nothing. . . . I turned away from the corrupt free-thinker, the Regent of France: he destroyed her![15]

Having parted sadly with the "famous European Monarchs and Russian Boyars, who ushered in the glittering age of CATHERINE and ALEXANDER," the author "feasted his eyes upon the enchanting views around Kuskovo: Gothic churches with lofty bell towers, outlying houses, villages, the highway, copses, meadows, the ponds, rivers, the fields," but these "charming pictures" were not enough: "All is beautiful,

striking, opulent; but, I admit, the soul is oppressed." All this
is too ordered, too formal, and so the author and his companions "cried forth from joy" when they entered the
"dreamy shadows of the English garden" with its "capricious
brook, flowing according to its own fancy." His sensitive
soul was soothed by his return to unfettered nature, and, as
he does from time to time throughout his essay, he reinforces
his prose with some lines of heavy poetry. He closes with an
emotional—but withal conventional—exposition of the "sweet
reverie" he enjoyed in the light of the full moon.[16]

The rhetorical emotionalism and the turgid style of this
piece suggest that it was written at least two decades before
its publication in *Northern Flowers*, at a time when this type
of sentimental exposition was in vogue. Appearing in 1825,
it seems dated and pompous.

Of less merit is Princess Volkonskaya's "Excerpts from
Travel Notes" ["Otryvki putevyx zapisok"] (1830) concerning her travels in Weimar, Bavaria, and the Tyrol. Her language is painfully and unnaturally florid, and the information
she conveys is so lacking in specifics that the whole thing
might easily have been fabricated had she never left Russia.
Goethe is described by an extended simile likening him to a
town incorporating Hellenic and Gothic features of architec-
ture. The Bavarian landscape is rendered by ponderous and
nonfunctional metaphors.

> Young Bavaria. Here mountain rises beyond mountain,
> forest beyond forest, higher and higher, like green pyra-
> mids; and beyond them bare cliffs, and on them lies un-
> thawing snow. Like the eyes of a kind father on his un-
> grateful children, the sun beats upon them in vain![17]

This conventional and essentially trite piece is not improved
upon by Princess Volkonskaya's contribution for the following year, under a similar title, which, however, had the ad-
vantage of being only four pages long.

Far more intrinsically interesting are the unpretentiously
factual travel accounts, whose authors simply describe as ob-
jectively as possible their own experiences and impressions. In
some cases these contributions were written by persons with-

out apparent literary aspirations, as, for example, the two
pieces by an anonymous author (probably Dmitry Dashkov),
"Mount Athos: An Excerpt from a Journey Through Greece
in 1820" ["Afonskaja gora. Otryvok iz putešestvija po Grecii
v 1820 godu"] (1825) and "Russian Pilgrims in Jerusalem
(An Excerpt from a Journey Through Greece and Palestine
in 1820)" ["Russkie poklonniki v Ierusalime (Otryvok iz
putešestvija po Grecii i Palestine v 1820 godu)"] (1826). In
the former the author discusses the social, political, economic,
and historical aspects of monastic life on Mt. Athos, adding
some details regarding internal feuds, secret libraries, and other
incidental information gleaned during his ten days' stay. He
also reports the rather paradoxical fact that one of the monks
knew Buerger's *Lenore* by heart. In his other selection the
author enumerates the holy places in Jerusalem and presents
an extensive account of the squabbles between the various
Christian religious groups for custody of the holy sites and
sacred relics. In general this author employs a direct manner
of exposition, but there are occasional lapses into a personal-
sentimental style:

> At the first glance at these ancient walls—the city of
> David, Herod, and Godefroy—a thousand memories, each
> more sacred than the other, flock into one's soul. Let cold
> intellects laugh at the raptures of the pilgrims! Here, at
> the foot of Zion, everyone is a Christian, everyone a be-
> liever who but preserves ardor in his heart and love for
> greatness.[18]

In 1825 and 1827 appeared selections entitled "Excerpts
from Letters from Italy" ["Otryvki pisem iz Italii"], both
written by the same correspondent but only the first identified as the work of a certain P——y [P——ij]. The first contribution was accompanied by an editorial note explaining that
the letters were not written for the public and that their
composer never expected to be an author in Russian, since
French was a more natural means of expression for him. "But,"
the explanation continues, "they are written so intelligently
and in such a pleasing style that we decided to print several
excerpts."[19] The two pieces are indeed pleasing and reveal, at

the very least, the talent of a gifted amateur. The author structures his letters around personal encounters, anecdotes, and episodes into which he injects facts and descriptive content. The style is pithy and often humorous, and the information at times unusual, especially the second contribution which deals with Sicily. The description of the capital, Palermo, though perhaps overly critical, is nonetheless vivid and informative. The discussions of convents, monasteries, and the Sicilian cult of Saint Rosalia, albeit tinged with a certain anti-Catholic prejudice, provide much intrinsically interesting information. He notes a visit to a monastery near Palermo where the monks, all from prominent families, live in real luxury, an excursion to a Capucin monastery, famous for its caves where the dead are suspended along the walls, and a Trappist monastery where he had an unexpected encounter.

> The richest man in the kingdom is . . . the Prince of Butera. In his garden he has built a Trappist monastery of twenty cells. Each is supplied with a bed, clean linen, a kitchen, and all cooking gear. The cleanliness of this house is remarkable: two men constantly sweep the corridors. There is exemplary quiet and order in the cells, where the monks pass days and years in a monotonous but peaceful life. I found some reading, others sleeping or walking about. But imagine my surprise: In one cell I found a young nun! She sat at a little table holding a pen in her hand and before her lay a sheet of paper. I approached her, took the paper and pen and wrote a frank opinion regarding the founder of this monastery. The nun looks like Eloise: she is waxy, like the other Trappists, not excluding those sweeping the corridors.[20]

Similarly factual travel notes are presented by Alexey Illichevsky and Victor Teplyakov, who are both also represented in the poetry sections of various issues of the almanac. Illichevsky's "A Journey from Saint Bernard" ["Putešestvie iz Sent-Bernard"], appearing in 1826, contains fascinating information about the life of the Bernardine monks at their life-saving station on the Alpine pass. Apparently the first Russian to visit these monks, he was very impressed with their humanitarian dedication, their hospitality, and their hardihood. In a direct manner, with touches of light humor, he describes the ascent to the monastery, the severity of the climate, the activities of the monks and their famous dogs. A careful observer and engrossing reporter, he pictures the monastery, its church and library, and the grim *caveau*, where the bodies of perished travelers are kept in a natural deep freeze.

Teplyakov's "Letter III from Turkey" ["Pis'mo III iz Turcii"] was written in connection with his expedition to Varna in 1829 with the Russian army and appeared in the 1831 almanac. In a lightly humorous tone he reports an excursion which he made, under the protection of a military convoy, to the monastery of Saint Constantine in the environs of Varna. Typical of the travel sketch, the piece includes details of the somewhat dangerous journey, comments on the unusual persons encountered on the way, and a description of the picturesque monastery ruins on a cliff overlooking the sea. The exotic quality of the subject matter provides the main interest, but the piece is hardly something one would wish to read more than once.

Probably the most matter-of-fact example of travel notes is provided by Nikita Bichurin's "Baikal" ["Bajkal"], subtitled "A Letter to O. M. S.——" ["Pis'mo k O. M. S——"] (doubtless Somov), which appeared in the almanac's final issue. Bichurin was an important Orientalist and translator from Chinese and Mongolian, and, as a note explains, this letter was written in connection with a journey he made to Baikal for reasons of health. At the time he made his trip the Lake Baikal region was virtually uninhabited, and he notes that there were just two small settlements of a few houses each along the whole western shore. This letter is really a piece of descriptive geography, and although there are occasional emotional passages about nature, the author is primarily concerned with heights, widths, distances, and other facts of interest to the natural scientist, such as the abundance and types of fish in the lake.

Konstantin Batyushkov's "A Letter to S. from Gothenburg" ["Pis'mo k S. iz Gotemburga"], appearing in the 1827 almanac, was actually written in 1814. This humorous and at times emotional epistle describes his journey from London to Gothenburg, paying particular attention to the delights of nature and the eccentricities of his traveling companions.

> On the fourth day a favorable wind swelled the sail and my illness passed. The sailors sang, the captain joked with the Jew, but the Swede became more intolerable and boring by the hour. Where could one hide from him? . . . His bad German and French accents brought me to despair. At every movement of the ship he paled. Now it seemed to him that the captain had drunk too much rum, now the compass could not be trusted, now the sail not in place, and this was not right and that was wrong. . . . Now he gave advice to the captain, who answered him with a goddamn, he saw a whale in the sea, a mouse on the deck, or a tomtit in the air. He bored everyone, and the humanitarian Jew proposed that we throw him into the sea, like the godless Diagoras, as food for the sea monsters.[21]

This selection is frankly sentimental, but in the best sense of the word, for the sentiment rings true and, although obviously influenced by literary tradition, appears as an organic component of the style rather than a pretentious attempt to achieve grandiloquence.

> On this day, never to be forgotten by my heart, one of the travelers, learning that I was a Russian, invited me for a stroll. We wandered along the seashore among sweet-smelling pastures and forests which bless the environs of Garich. Crowds of happy villagers in holiday dress walked along the road or rested on the grass. Through the thick greenery of hazel groves or elms the pleasant huts of the coastal dwellers looked out and the evening sun illuminated a magnificent picture. Everything attracted me, everything captivated me. I feasted my eyes on England and tried to stamp on my memory all the objects surrounding me.[22]

Batyushkov's contribution, since it was the product of an earlier period, functions in *Northern Flowers* rather as an anthology piece than as an example of contemporary prose. And certainly his modest sentimentality is far more attractive than that of Voyeykov or Princess Volkonskaya, whose anachronistic attempts in the sentimental vein appear so inadequate when compared with a good original example.

Pushkin also contributed to the travel accounts published by *Northern Flowers*, though it is to be suspected that his "An Excerpt from A. S. Pushkin's Letter to D." (Delvig) ["Otryvok iz pis'ma A. S. Puškina k D."] in the 1826 almanac, was published for reasons other than its purely literary value. This very short piece, embracing only six pages, describes the return part of a Crimean journey he made with the Raevsky family (although they are not mentioned). The tone is very matter-of-fact and the details minimal.

> From Asia we traveled to Europe [from Taman to Kerch] by ship. I immediately set off for the so-called Mithridates sepulchre (ruins of some tower); there I plucked a flower as a memento and lost it the next day without regret. The ruins of Panticapaeum did not act upon my imagination any more strongly. I saw traces of streets, an overgrown ditch, old bricks and that was all. From Theodosia to Yurzuf I traveled by sea. I didn't sleep all night; there was no moon; the stars shone; before me in the fog stretched the southern mountains. . . . "There is Chatyr Dag," the captain said to me. I couldn't distinguish it, and in fact wasn't curious.[23]

Following an interpolated poem addressed to Peter Chaadaev, Pushkin continues: "I arrived at Bakchisaray ill. I had previously heard about the strange monument of the infatuated khan. K** poetically described it to me; she called it *la fontaine des larmes*."[24] In using the letter "K" to identify the person who had related to him the legend of the Bakchisaray khan (which served as an inspiration for his *The Fountain of Bakchisaray*), Pushkin was attempting to throw off the track those who had suspected that Maria Raevskaya had been his informant. This deception was necessitated by the fact that Bestuzhev and Bulgarin had tactlessly printed some of Pushkin's poetry and private correspondence alluding to a secret attachment for the one who had provided him with the legend. Pushkin was desperately anxious that this attachment not become public knowledge and, more important, that Maria herself be given no cause to think that he had discussed his interest in her with his friends.[25] Perhaps Pushkin's composition of this letter and its subsequent publication were motivated by these considerations.

"The Inn Stairs" [Traktirnaja lestnica"] (1826) was the work of Nikolay Bestuzhev, brother of Alexander Bestuzhev (Marlinsky), and appeared over the pseudonym "Alexey Korostylev." The work, essentially, is a rather unsuccessful hybrid combination of travel account and biographical sketch. Presumably, when visiting Copenhagen in 1815, the author became acquainted with an enigmatic old derelict who shared his inn. After winning his confidence, the narrator was rewarded with the old man's confession, which is presented in the first person. The story he tells concerns his clandestine affair with a married lady which culminated in the birth of a son. Following the death of the woman, her husband learned that he was not the father of her child, and from that time he manifested an increasing hostility to the boy. The latter developed very badly and was finally disowned by his legal father. Subsequent efforts of the real father to establish ties with his son were unsuccessful, since the boy rejected him. The distraught father's health then failed, and thenceforth he had been an invalid whose whole life was confined to observing silently what passed by his chair at the foot of the inn stairs.

This is a moral tale in the sentimental manner, though the expected tumid exposition is absent. In fact, the narration is rather direct and uncomplicated, notwithstanding many tearful interludes. As an attempt to create a credible characterization of the old man, the work fails, for his psychology is arbitrary and his motivation unclear. The story closes, as one might have anticipated, with the traveler-narrator returning to the inn to find that the old man has died. The piece is further weakened by extraneous material, such as the lengthy excerpt from the narrator's diary describing his wanderings about Copenhagen, his impressions of nature, and a sentimental encounter with an old soldier happily ensconced in the bosom of his admiring family.

Although an absolute failure from the artistic point of view, this work is interesting as an example of the difficulty faced particularly by an amateur author at this stage in the development of prose literature. Wishing to provide verisimilitude for his fictional tale, he put it within the more credible form of travel account, but the travel element then asserted its rights and he was obliged to provide more of the ingredients expected from this genre; hence, the diary excerpts. The result was a literary Topsy, whose main characteristics are size and awkwardness.

Bestuzhev's biographical sketch framed by travel notes is paralleled by the form of Faddey Bulgarin's military memoir "The Almodavar Ruins" ["Razvaliny Al'modavarskie"], appearing in 1827. Here again the factual details forming the frame seem to have been employed to lend verisimiliture to the putatively true events of the central story.

In the story's frame the narrator (presumably Bulgarin) relates some of the details of the Spanish resistance to the invasion by Napoleon's army, in which he served as a cavalry officer. One night, having left his troop bivouacked near Almodavar, he had an almost fatal adventure while exploring the ruins of an ancient castle.

> A sudden noise broke my reverie: sand and rubble sifted down from the top of a half-ruined vault. I looked around and saw a woman in a black dress with unkempt hair. She stood above my head and held a huge rock in her hands, ready to strike me! Our eyes met, and her wild look produced in me the same feelings as the glitter of a dagger over the head of a man suddenly awakened from sleep. An involuntary tremor ran through my veins, my blood congealed and my heart contracted. "Did you kill him," she cried in a threatening voice and she raised the stone over her head. The moment was decisive, but a sudden inspiration saved me. "No, not I!" I answered in a loud and firm voice, completely without understanding the question. "Not you?" said the unknown woman, having lowered her voice, and slowly lowering the stone, she sat

down on a piece of debris and fastened her black, glittering eyes on me.[26]

This passage, with its "involuntary tremors," "congealed blood," and the labored comparison involving the suddenly awakened man is indicative of the conventional and trite nature of the exposition. It does not improve as the narrator goes on to present further details about the girl, related to him by his guide, Fernando: her love affair with a wounded foreign soldier whom her father had protected, the death of her beloved at the hands of drunken French deserters, and her subsequent madness, manifested by an obsessive desire to kill her fiancé's murderer. The story closes with a resumption of the frame details, supplemented by a bit of sententious rhetoric.

> In silence I returned to the detachment and for the whole journey I grieved, thinking about the unhappy girl. The ruins of Almodavar remained in my memory. "O people," thought I, "why do you torment one another, when, by doing good, you might be happy!"[27]

The same rather limited level of artistry is displayed by Bulgarin's historical tale of 1828, "The Fall of Venden," a fictionalized treatment of an episode from the times of Ivan the Terrible's Livonian campaigns. The work derives in large part from Volume IX of Karamzin's *History of the Russian State*,[28] although Bulgarin did not scruple to adapt Karamzin's material to suit the needs of his story. Karamzin reported that in 1577 Ivan and his troops, engaged in a systematic pacification of those Livonian towns which had abjured their allegiance to him, appeared at Venden, in whose castle Magnus, the King of Livonia and Ivan's sometime vassal, had taken refuge. The mere presence of The Terrible caused Magnus to have second thoughts about asserting his independence, and he immediately threw himself upon Ivan's mercy. But the German-Livonian soldiers and civilians, who had sworn allegiance to Magnus alone, were less sanguine about their chances for survival if they capitulated, particularly as Ivan had already sold whole Livonian towns into slavery and had decimated others. Therefore, when they refused to open the castle gates, Ivan's troops attacked. After three days all hope was lost, and, to avoid captivity and torture, the survivors by general consent blew themselves up by firing their powder supply. Henryk Boysman, who actually did the deed, somehow was not killed outright but died shortly thereafter—the enraged Ivan then empaled his corpse. The peaceful citizens of the town, who had not resisted the Russian troops or sided with the castle's defenders, were slaughtered. Magnus was unaccountably pardoned.

In the tradition of the historical romance, Bulgarin mixed his real figures with purely fictional ones, among whom were, as one might have expected, a beautiful Livonian girl, Eleonora, the beloved of Vladimir, a soldier of Ivan held hostage by the castle defenders. Belonging to hostile factions, these two seemed doomed to unhappiness or worse, but all came out well in the end. Another fictional figure, the wizard Marko, may well have derived from Mickiewicz's mysterious *wajdelota* of *Konrad Wallenrod*. The mysterious Marko is actually the last descendant of a family of Livonian pagan priests, and his secret mission is to avenge the earlier German usurpation of Livonia, as well as his mistreatment at the hands of his German masters. One might also note a "tower scene" involving Eleonora and Vladimir which is reminiscent of Mickiewicz's work.

Little need be said about the stylistic qualities of this tale, for they do not represent any noticeable improvement upon the previously discussed story by Bulgarin. Although the destruction of Venden took place in late summer, the author sets the time somewhat later so that he can use "autumn clouds" for atmospheric effects. The pair of lovers are conventionally virtuous and react in accordance with sentimental norms.

> For a whole week he [Vladimir] had languished within the cold walls of the Venden tower, and each night Eleonora came to sweeten his grief, to talk with him through the window, to convince him of her constant love and to quicken his hopes. Vladimir forgot the whole world during these sweet moments and considered himself happy.[29]

But one must give Bulgarin his due and note that his general style, his development of characters, and his handling of plot was actually no worse than that of, say, Zagoskin, whose historical romance *Yury Miloslavsky* was so well received by the reading public a year later.

"The Fall of Venden," like Bulgarin's putatively non-fictional "Peter the Great in the Naval Expedition from Petersburg to Vyborg," was a lavishly patriotic work and Bulgarin, in the face of the overwhelming historical evidence of Ivan's cruelty, enthusiastically assumed the task of rendering a positive picture of him against the background of the Venden massacre. In contrast to the gullible Magnus, Ivan is seen as one undeceived by the treacherous Marko. Following the destruction of the castle, Bulgarin has Ivan manifest a generous attitude toward his enemies; he pardons a German pastor and his daughter and admonishes the dying Boysman in a firm but kind manner. No mention is made of the drastic fate of the townspeople or the empaling of Boysman's corpse. Ivan's pardon of Magnus is emphasized, and, although at times Bulgarin virtually paraphrases Karamzin, he ignores the historian's summary remarks: "In one word, this *punishment of Venden* belongs to the most terrible exploits of Ivan's tyranny: it doubled the hatred of the Livonians for the Russians."[30]

A work belonging to the same genre as "The Fall of Venden" was Vladimir Titov's "The Monastery of Saint Bridget" ["Monastyr' Sv. Brigity"] (1831), which appeared over his pseudonym "Tit Kosmokratov." This piece was a factual-fictional historical tale set in early sixteenth-century Revel. In rather sober tones, which at times become almost pedantic (the story is equipped with footnotes regarding socio-politico-religious matters pertaining to the period), the author details the conflict in Revel between the Catholic knights, who occupy the castle dominating the town, and the bourgeois townsmen who have embraced the Reformation. A showdown develops when the local Catholic monastery refuses to release Aurora, the Burgermeister's daughter, who had taken vows when mistakenly informed that her betrothed,

Ernest, had perished at sea. However, the townspeople triumph and the girl is freed.

In this work the intrigue is simply a pretext for the author to provide, as it were, a picturesque sketch of Revel in
its heyday. One suspects, in fact, that the author himself was
inspired by a tour to the town, its Rathaus and museums. For
most of its length the tale wallows in background material,
and there is other evidence of the author's lack of narrative
facility. The characters are utterly conventional, both physi-
cally and emotionally, and, although there is some acceptable stylized dialogue in connection with the confrontation
of the opposing parties, the dramatic possibilities of the situations are not exploited. Withal, the work, despite its deficiencies, happily lacks the pretensions of Bulgarin's efforts in
the same genre.

Because it was written in 1810, Konstantin Batyushkov's
"Predslava and Dobrynya: An Ancient Tale" ["Predslava i
Dobrynja. Starinnaja povest' "] belongs to an earlier period
in the development of the historical tale than other works of
this genre found in *Northern Flowers*. It was published in the
final issue of the almanac, where it was accompanied by a
slightly apologetic footnote,

> Maybe there will be found in this tale a lack of creativity
> and national identity [narodnost'], maybe it will be said
> that in it one does not see ancient Rus and Vladimir's
> court; nevertheless, the poetic soul of Batyushkov shines
> forth in it, as in his other works, and tender, noble feel-
> ings are expressed in beautiful, harmonious prose.[31]

If the editor of the almanac thought it necessary to justify
his choice of this work, particularly in view of the implication that evidence of creativity and *narodnost* is lacking, one
wonders why similar notes do not accompany the historical
tales of Titov and Bulgarin. Certainly from the point of view
of historical verisimilitude, Batyushkov does not seem to have
threatened Clio's virtue more vigorously than the other two,
especially when one considers that "Predslava and Dobrynya"
is manifestly a prose poem of legendary essence.

In hyperbolic tones Batyushkov "sings" of the tragic

love of the heroic knight Dobrynya and the comely Predslava, daughter of Prince Vladimir. Although the youth had
saved Vladimir himself from death at the hands of the
Pechenegs, his station was too modest to justify his marriage
to the princess, and, to the lovers' dismay, she is betrothed
to Radmir, a Bulgarian prince. Following a tournament at
which Dobrynya bests Radmir, the two lovers meet clan-
destinely, and Dobrynya, with the complete compliance of
Predslava, cuckolds Radmir *avant la lettre*. The jealous and
suspicious Bulgarian discovers the tryst, and in the battle
which follows kills Dobrynya, who is at a disadvantage since
he naturally does not enjoy the protection of his armor.
Predslava, "pressing her naked breast against her husband's
heart, fell lifeless upon his icy corpse . . . like a lily, plucked
by the breath of inclemency, like a sacrificial victim, conse-
crated to love and ineluctable fate."[32]

A sentimental tone, exemplified by the above quotation,
pervades this highly stylized work. To exploit further the
emotional potentials of his story, Batyushkov apostrophizes
both his hero and his readers, as, for example, in the following scene where Dobrynya, from the darkness outside Predslava's chambers, is indulging in a bit of Peeping Tomery.

> How thy heart beat, brave youth, when the beauty,
> having dismissed her companions, undid the knots of her
> secret garments! How thy heart beat, unhappy and at
> the same time happiest of mortals, when her hand bared
> her bosom, like two mounds of purest snow; when her
> hair was carelessly strewn over her high forehead and
> alabaster shoulders! No, the human tongue has not the
> power to describe the passions burning in the breast of
> our knight! But you, flaming lovers, transport yourselves
> by thought to those times of passion and blissfulness,
> when accident or love, the ruler of the world (for even
> accident is submissive to it), when love revealed its se-
> crets to you; you, happy ones, may feel the blissfulness
> of Dobrynya![33]

It need hardly be stressed that this style, notwithstanding
the mellifluous phrases and tender sentiments, was something

of an anachronism in an almanac of 1832. Not that similar stylistic elements did not appear in the prose literature of that time, but they were on the way out. Some authors, for want of better means, particularly in seeking to express emotions, still did draw from the well of Sentimentalism, but virtually no one by the beginning of the fourth decade of the century was writing entire stories in this tone. One supposes that this work's presence in the almanac's last issue is evidence of the difficulties encountered by the editors in finding sufficient prose contributions.

Certainly the numerous genres and subgenres represented by the foregoing examples in *Northern Flowers* testify to the eclectic nature of the almanac's prose sections, and perhaps also to Delvig's confidence in the eclectic interests of his prospective clientele. But despite their sheer numbers, very many of the works previously discussed were quite short—commendably so, in some instances—and it was in fact fiction which dominated the prose sections. Taking into account all issues, roughly one-third of the prose was purely fiction, one-fourth was devoted to literary criticism, one-fifth was represented by nonfictional travel accounts, and one-fifth involved lettres of various sorts.[34] One must also note some interesting developments in the proportions devoted to each of these categories in the course of the almanac's history. Travel accounts, as has been seen, were very popular only in the earlier issues, whereas in the first edition there was no fiction at all— only in 1828 did the almanac begin to feature imaginative prose. From that point on, fiction asserted its rights and, although in some years criticism actually occupied more pages, thanks to the long essays of Orest Somov, in the long run fiction embraced more total pages than other categories.[35]

Some of the fiction found in *Northern Flowers* is so lacking in dominant characteristics or common identifying features that its classification is difficult. One might, of course, simply lump this sort of contribution under the heading of short story, but that would create the impression that there is some essential similarity between these characterless works and other more easily categorized pieces of short fiction found in the same classification, when, in fact, none exists.

Such a characterless piece of fiction is "The Light Brown Tress" ["Rusaja kosa"] (1827), signed Z——y.[36] The first half consists almost exclusively of a dialogue between two devotees of literature, a certain D. and a friend named Minsky. D., having pressed his friend to explain why he has recently been avoiding their literary circle, learns that Minsky has been singularly affected by the sight of some countess' light brown hair. On D.'s subsequent visit, Minsky, who has somewhat recovered from his enchantment, tells him

> In our life, Alexander, there are certain privileged minutes in which an insignificant but wonderful accident discloses to us our moral existence, indicates the capabilities hidden in us, and decides the fate of our entire life. . . . From this current adventure I have become convinced, I repeat, that I must sometime complement myself with another half, that I have an intended, and I consider the light brown tress as a pledge for my future happiness.[37]

In the second part of the story are related details of Minsky's later betrothal and marriage. In conclusion, the author admonishes his readers: "Young people! Fire is dangerous, water is dangerous, but a light brown tress is the most dangerous of all."[38]

Interwoven into this fabric of frivolous inanity are some remarks relating to literature, and it is evident from the tastes of Minsky and D. that the author admires Rousseau, Schiller, Herder, Byron, Karamzin, Zhukovsky, and Pushkin—as well he might. In this company Mr. Z——y is a stunted pygmy. But one thing must be said in his favor: despite the ludicrousness of his general conception and Minsky's bizarre psychological progress, the expository passages are simple, succinct, and lucid. This author knew *how* to express himself better than a number of his fellow contributors to *Northern Flowers;* his trouble was that he didn't know *what* to say.[39]

"An Isolated Little House on Vasiliev Island" ["Uedinennyj domik na vasil'evskom"], which appeared over the name Tit Kosmokratov (pseudonym of Vladimir Titov) in the 1829 issue of *Northern Flowers*, is a Hoffmannesque tale of the supernatural; more specifically, it concerns a devil's ultimately fatal interference in the lives of ordinary people. The story is presented by a narrator who, at the conclusion of his tale, informs the reader that his story originated in the Petersburg middle class, where it was somewhat of an oral legend.

The remote house on Vasiliev Island is the home of Vera, a young woman, and her widowed mother, who, it is darkly hinted, was guilty of her husband's death. They live a life of seclusion and genteel poverty, occasionally visited by their distant relation Paul, a would-be bon vivant. Paul, who is unaware that Vera loves him, introduces his enigmatic friend, Bartholomew, to the girl and her mother. The latter encourages Bartholomew's visits, the more so that he seems well-to-do and quite infatuated with her daughter. Meanwhile, Bartholomew involves Paul with a mysterious princess, who distracts his attention from the family on Vasiliev Island. By the time Paul breaks with the princess, Bartholomew has almost conquered Vera's heart, primarily because of his apparent solicitude for her dying mother. However, Bartholomew's demonic intentions become clear when he not only prevents the mother from receiving last rites but in the presence of her corpse proposes to Vera a future life together without the blessings of the church. When Vera rejects this blasphemous proposal, the house bursts into flames and she barely escapes with her life. Vera soon dies, and Paul, overcome with remorse and semi-insane, spends the rest of the short period alloted him in complete seclusion.

Only at the end of the tale does the narrator suggest that the story might not be true; in general the supernatural elements are introduced in the same straightforward manner as the more credible material. Of course, the diabolical essence of Bartholomew is soon evident to the reader, and this heightens the interest with which one watches him spin his fatal web. Yet, it must be admitted that there is very little to recommend this tale of intrigue. The characters are conventional and are given only those qualities which enable them logically to serve the plot. Their emotions are stereotyped and their reactions predictable. Bartholomew, despite his prodigious incendiary talent, is a rather banal demon, and one wonders, since he possesses supernatural power, why it takes him so long to dominate the action. The story is overly long (about eight thousand words) owing to considerable irrelevant material, and, although the narrative style is for the most part simple and direct, it is marked by occasional paraphrastic, tumid passages which make one suspect that the author had parodistic intentions. The description of Vera's death is a typical example: "Spring had not yet succeeded in decorating the meadow with new green when this flower, which had promised a luxuriant development, concealed itself irrevocably in the bosom of all-embracing nature."[40] There are some humorous elements on the level of author-reader relations, as, for example, when the reader, having been prepared for the scene of Paul's assignation with the princess, is told: "But here I shall interrupt my picture and, in imitation of the best Classical and Romantic writers of ancient, medieval, and modern times, leave it to you to complete it from your own source of imagination."[41] Yet, notwithstanding some modest virtues, this work is obviously the product of a relatively inexperienced author, who, though deserving praise for his (usually) simple style, nonetheless talks far too long for the story he has to tell.

Perhaps the most interesting aspect of "An Isolated Little House on Vasiliev Island" is that the plot and certain of the details originated with Pushkin. According to A. I. Delvig, Pushkin told this story at the Karamzins' to a group of eager listeners which included Titov-Kosmokratov, who later wrote down the tale. Pushkin apparently was shown the manuscript and made certain corrections (but not enough!); at Baron Delvig's insistence the work was given to *Northern Flowers*.[42] Pushkin's role is confirmed by the outline for a story found in one of his notebooks. The title of this projected work was "The Infatuated Devil," and the characters and plot are closely paralleled by Titov's story.[43] It would, however, be incorrect to assume that Titov's rendition was in any direct way a product of Pushkin's art, for there are far more essential differences between the prose styles of these two authors than similarities.

"The Bedouin Girl: An Eastern Tale" ["Beduinka. Vostočnaja povest' "], which appeared in the 1828 issue of *Northern Flowers*, was the first of two translations from Arabian originals contributed to the almanac by Osip Senkovsky (Polish form is Józef Sękowski), writer, critic, journalist, and professor of Oriental languages at the University of St. Petersburg. Without knowing the original, it is difficult to assess the success of this piece as a translation or to know the extent to which it may be merely an adaptation or imitation of an Arabian work. In *Polar Star* Senkovsky had previously published a number of brief prose tales translated primarily from Arabian, one of which, "The Knight of the Dun-Colored Horse: An Arabian Qasidah," was termed "charming" by Pushkin, who urged Alexander Bestuzhev "to hold this Senkovsky by the collar."[44] An interest in literature of the Near East was quite common at this time in circles of Russian and Polish Romantic poets, and the appearance of Senkovsky's apparent translations in *Polar Star* and *Northern Flowers* further indicates that their editors also thought readers would find such exotic fare enticing.

"The Bedouin Girl," whatever its reception by Delvig's subscribers, is hardly likely to enthuse twentieth-century readers. The plot itself is simple: when an impoverished Bedouin protests to the Caliph that a provincial governor has taken his wife Soada, from him, the sympathetic Caliph orders the woman sent to him, whereupon her beauty inspires his own infatuation. The Caliph offers her a choice between his luxurious life or destitution with her husband. The ever virtuous Soada chooses the latter, which so impresses the Caliph that he richly rewards the Bedouin. This story of virtue's reward is heavily laden with local color details which one suspects were supplied by the translator to enhance the exotic atmosphere. The characters express themselves in a very formal, dramatic style, and in making his complaint to the Caliph the exhausted, abused, and half-dead Bedouin actually breaks into verse. Even the exposition is stylized

> When Soada arrived in Damascus, she was presented to the Caliph. He was astonished at her beauty, with which the charms of all the wives in his harem could not compare. Lofty, like a palm from the banks of the Nile, in

her walk she lightly bowed, like the shaft of a desert
horseman's spear made of Bagdad cane. Her body had
the charming color of silver with a light mixture of
gold, and the eyes glittering with sparks expressed that
ravishing charm of love and tenderness which so marvelously shines in the eyes of a young doe when she,
having turned her supple neck to one side, looks with a
mother's love on two tiny fawns joined to her paps.[45]

And so on in this manner.

In 1830 Senkovsky again appeared with a translation,
"The Thief: An Arabian Tale" ["Vor. Arabskaja povest' "],
which went much further than his previous contribution in
emphasizing peculiarly Eastern elements. There are over two
dozen Arabic terms and expressions transcribed directly into
Russian, some translated parenthetically and others explained
in the sixteen footnotes which accompany the story. In order to illuminate the foreign content still more, Senkovsky
put into italics that part of the dialogue which represented
"original and generally used Arabian expressions, preserved
here by the translator in order to acquaint the reader with
the real tone of Arabian conversation."[46]

Despite the encumbrance of this apparatus, "The Thief"
is a pleasing tale. Presented as the narration of "the well-
known Arabian writer Abu-Said-Asmai," the story begins
with Abu's arrival at the reception hall of Khaled, the Governor of Bassora. Khaled chides Abu with having satirized his
manner of justice and proposes that the poet sit in judgment
on a young man, Zeid, who had recently been caught stealing
from a garden. Zeid, obviously too wealthy to have deliberately engaged in such a mean crime, obdurately refuses
to disclose his motivation. Khaled proposes to Abu that they
get the young man drunk and learn the truth from him, and
so a private banquet takes place that night. But all efforts are
in vain, and the angered Khaled announces that the traditional
punishment, dismemberment of one arm at the elbow, will
take place the following day. As the fatal moment approaches
the next morning, Zeid remains calm but silent. Just as the
sword is about to fall, a young woman runs forward and in-
terferes. Questioned by Khaled, she reveals that Zeid is her

lover and that his apparent crime was simply an act to pro-
tect her name when he had been discovered in her father's
garden. Khaled, touched by her tale and Zeid's resolute defense of her honor, successfully intercedes with her father
and richly rewards Zeid. The narrator concludes by identifying Zeid as Abu Nuwas, subsequently a renowned poet.

A tour de force of saturated local color, the story contains much detail calculated to interest its Russian audience:
descriptions of the governor's court, the lavish banquet, ju-
diciary customs, formulae for social relations, examples of ex-
temporized poetry, elements of Islamic religious tradition, not
to mention information of a sociological nature. The characters, of course, are flat and designed simply to serve the plot
and function as mouthpieces for the presentation of florid and
exotic Arabic expressions.

It is clear that there are limitations to the proliferation
of this type of exotic tale, since to a considerable extent the
interest that it arouses is dependent upon the reader's lack of
information about the subject matter. One can imagine that
an inquisitive person previously uninformed about Arabian
life and customs would eagerly read the first example he encountered of this type of story; but, after a few more, the
novelty of the information would be lost—and with it the
reader's attention. Of greater importance is the fact that since
Senkovsky's contributions to *Northern Flowers* did not, in
fact, add anything new to the supply of devices available to
prose writers of his times, we must look upon these two tales
simply as somewhat unusual variations upon existing prose
norms, rather than as truly original contributions to the development of Russian prose literature.

The two works of Prince Vladimir Odoevsky, one of
which appeared in each of the last two issues of the almanac,
represent a somewhat unusual type of prose narrative for that
period. These rather brief stories are fictionalized episodes
from the lives of Ludwig van Beethoven and Giambatista
Piranesi. But even the episodes themselves are mere frame-
works serving to bear Odoevsky's ideas about art and the
artist. One might consider these two contributions a form of
popularized philosophy, the attractiveness of which is en-

hanced by combining it with intimate glimpses of the personalities—albeit theoretical—of these illustrious men.

"Beethoven's Last Quartet" ["Poslednij kvartet Beetgovena"] (1831) is prefaced with a quotation from E.T.A.
Hoffmann's *Serapion Brothers* emphasizing, in connection
with the apparent madness of Hoffmann's Krespel, the com-
pulsion of certain persons to manifest ideas which for more
prosaic people would always remain in the realm of secretive
thoughts. Odoevsky's indebtedness to Hoffmann need not be
detailed here; suffice it to say that the former was one of the
most active and convinced disciples of the German author,
whose influence on Russian literature was particularly strong
in the thirties, when he inspired many tales with supernatural content and a number of *Kunstnovellen*—stories about
men of artistic inclinations and accomplishments.[47]

The story is set in Vienna in 1827, the year Beethoven
died, and it opens with a scene in which musicians are attempting to perform the master's latest quartet. They find the
work totally uncongenial, almost a parody of his earlier
achievements, and ascribe its failure to the composer's deafness or insanity. Suddenly Beethoven himself enters, followed
by a young woman. Luisa. He struggles unsuccessfully to
listen to the music until suddenly he catches the sound of one
wild harmony; in childish exaltation he is led away by the
young woman. The scene then shifts to his garret, where
Luisa, his last faithful student, somehow has managed to
keep him alive through his poverty. There he plays a new
composition on a dilapidated, stringless pianoforte and ha-
rangues Luisa about his aspirations, the pedantry of his critics,
the essential difference between the ecstacy that accompanies
his creation of music and the cold rapture of other composers.
Then, from a neighboring house, he hears strains of *Egmont,*
throws open the window and falls to his knees. The story ends
with a sardonic epilogue: at a brilliant ball someone mentions
that Kapellmeister Beethoven has died penniless, but the remark passes unnoticed, since everyone is paying attention to
an account of a petty quarrel at the court of some German
prince.

The philosophical views expressed through the medium

of this story are of little concern to this discussion. What is important is that "Beethoven's Last Quartet" was immediately recognized as an outstanding example of Russian artistic prose, and as such was reprinted in Galakhov's *Russian Chrestomathy* through eight editions.[48] It is true that the style of this work, particularly when viewed in the context of so many of the other prose contributions to *Northern Flowers,* does manifest unusual clarity and control. The exposition is direct, uncluttered, and perfectly lucid, quite in contrast to the painfully labored efforts of, for example, Bulgarin with his forced emotion, his hyperbolic epithets, the outworn metaphors and similes, and the frenetic dialogue. In fact, Odoevsky's work is almost entirely devoid of metaphorical language and presents no example of any kind of simile. Adjectives are usually employed for purely qualitative distinctions. In other words, the ornamental features common to so many works of the period, utilized owing to the mistaken view that quality was connected with floridity, are absent. The story could potentially have been pathetic, particularly where the author touched upon Beethoven's poverty, the lack of appreciation for his work, his deafness, but Odoevsky was content primarily just to report, letting the reader provide the emotional response.

> At the end of town on the fourth story of an old stone house is a small, stuffy room divided by a partition. A bed with a torn quilt, several bunches of music paper, the remains of a pianoforte—these are its entire ornamentation. This was the habitation, this was the world of the immortal Beethoven.[49]

The scene of the deaf composer vigorously demonstrating his new composition to Luisa, unaware that the old piano is no longer functioning as an instrument, is the more effective for its avoidance of deliberate emotional coloration.

> With these words Beethoven went to the pianoforte, which had not one sound string, and with a significant look, hit the empty keys. Monotonously he knocked on the dry wood of the broken instrument, but at the same time the most difficult fugues in five or six voices passed through all the secrets of counterpoint and became sub-

missive to the fingers of *Egmont's* creator, while he strove to lend to his music as much expression as possible.[50]

One should note, as do the editors of Odoevsky's 1959 Moscow edition, that his broad and detailed knowledge of music and composers may have been the source of the musical information needed by Pushkin to write his famous little tragedy, *Mozart and Salieri*.[51] To this one might also add the hypothesis that Pushkin's opposition of the natural-born composer, Mozart, for whom success comes easily, and the studious but essentially talentless drudge, Salieri, may reflect Odoevsky's story, in which Beethoven sees his own creative rapture as something quite different from the cold rapture of his pedantic critics, for whom reasons and rules are demanded to explain all aspects of new and daring compositions.

In 1832 appeared the second of Odoevsky's unusual stories, "Opere del Cavaliere Giambattista Piranesi," which the author provided with a footnote confirming that its similarity to "Beethoven's Last Quartet" was not accidental, since they were fragments of one and the same composition, only somewhat rounded out."[52] Both, in fact, did appear as parts of this author's *Russian Nights*, a collection of thematically unified stories published in 1844.[53]

This second tale reveals an imagination and originality on the part of Odoevsky which is unusual for the period, and it further presents a pleasing humorous quality. As the title suggests, the central figure of this story is Giambattista Piranesi, the eighteenth-century Venetian engraver of Roman monuments and would-be architect. However, it is never clear if the hero of the tale, who identifies himself as Piranesi, is in fact Piranesi or simply some deluded eccentric who claims his name; it depends on whether the reader accepts or rejects certain supernatural conditions. The story proper is prefaced by the narrator's enthusiastic description of the pleasures of bibliophilia, a mania which one day led him to an antiquarian bookstore in a remote corner of Petersburg. There he encountered a bizarre old foreigner inspecting a book of poorly done architectural engravings. The narrator, fascinated by a collection of Piranesi's sketches, recommended them to the eccentric, who withdrew in horror and begged that the book be closed. Undaunted, the narrator proposed to buy it, and at the sight of his purse the old man cried out, "Money!" The narrator asked if the man were in need and received the astounding reply that at first only the modest sum of one hundred million was required, to be expended on building an arch between Mt. Etna and Vesuvius to frame triumphal gates for a park leading to a projected castle. The eccentric then declared himself to be Piranesi, notwithstanding official notification of his death in 1778. He went on to explain (the rest of the story is his monologue, except for the conclusion) that as a youth he had studied with Michelangelo (died 1564), who encouraged him to an independent career. Since that time he had led a wandering life, pleasing all with his projected works but unable to begin them due to lack of sufficient financial support. As old age approached he determined to publish his plans, which he did after engraving them himself, but, as he subsequently discovered to his misery, each artistic creation, each picture, became the habitation of evil spirits. These spirits, displeased with their constricted existence, have since tortured him, preventing his death (he is, he adds, the Eternal Jew).

> In vain I wander from land to land, vainly searching to find if somewhere some magnificent building, constructed by my rivals to mock me, has collapsed. Often in Rome at night I approach the walls built by that happy Michelangelo, and with a weak hand I strike that damned cupola, which doesn't even think to tremble, or in Pisa I hang by both hands on that worthless tower, which in the course of seven centuries bends towards the earth but refuses to stretch out on it."[54]

The putative Piranesi's complaints continue, and he concludes with a plea for "only a hundred million." The narrator gives him a bill, which the eccentric declares will be added to the sum he is saving to have Mt. Blanc completely removed so that it won't interfere with the view of his castle. They part.

Odoevsky has here combined, as Hoffmann did before him, the themes of genius and insanity, presenting in a humorous form some significant reflections on the plight of an artist tormented by an ideal he cannot hope to achieve. As Beethoven, burdened by his deafness, was driven to insanity by his own inability to capture on paper the divine melodies he had mentally conceived, Piranesi also becomes insane because his vast projects are unrealizable. Odoevsky, of course, was aware of the preposterousness of his Piranesi's projects, but at no time does he mock the old crank's delusions of grandeur. The fate of Odoevsky's ridiculous Piranesi is symbolic of the fate of all men of genius, whose unfettered imaginations can conceive of perfection but whose ideals are frustrated by reality. Piranesi is moreover a pathetic figure, a victim of his own vast creative powers and of an unceasing will to accomplish his impossible dreams, a will which even defeats the powers of death. He is ludicrous, but he is sublime.

Particularly notable among the contributors of prose to *Northern Flowers* was Orest Somov, the almanac's most active supplier of fiction. His four stories display qualities quite unusual for the period. With these works Somov significantly anticipates certain of Nikolay Gogol's themes and techniques, not to mention Somov's use of devices which later became stock ingredients for Russian literature, such as the interior monologue or skaz. In fact, the importance of Somov to the development of Russian prose still is generally unrecognized, because no collected edition of his tales ever appeared and his works have remained in the relative obscurity of various journals and almanacs of the twenties and early thirties. But he was, in fact, a writer of imagination and sophistication, whose talent qualifies him for as much eminence as Alexander Bestuzhev and whose weakest works are no worse than the best of Bulgarin.

Like the young Gogol, who followed him closely, Somov was a local color Romanticist, and many of his stories concern Ukranian history, traditions, legends, and way of life. His titles reflect this concern: "The Water Spirit" (1829), "The Werewolf" (1829), "Tales of Buried Treasure" (1830), "Kupalov Evening" (1831), "Kiev Witches" (1833). Three of his four pieces in *Northern Flowers* have Ukrainian settings.

Somov's first piece of fiction for *Northern Flowers* was

"The Holy Fool: A Little Russian Tale" ["Jurodivyj. Malorossijskaja byl' "] (1827) and appeared over the pseudonym "Porfiry Baisky." "Holy fool" is not a particularly felicitous translation of the Russian *yurodivy*, but there is no good equivalent in English. For that matter, the socio-psychological type to which it refers does not have a counterpart in the non-Orthodox world. The term refers to apparently demented beggar pilgrims who wandered about Russia entrusting their rather uncertain existence to God and charitable persons. Pious, or credulous, Russians believed these people to be "chosen" or even holy, and they took pains to be generous to these mendicant zealots, whose self-mortification and enigmatic prophecies excited superstitious admiration or fear. Tolstoy treated this type in *Childhood,* and it will be remembered that the compassionate Princess Mary in *War and Peace* was particularly solicitous of these people.

Despite the subtitle's emphasis on the Ukrainian character of this story, there is nothing about it which necessarily demands a Little Russian setting. And unlike many of Somov's stories set in the Ukraine, there is no special emphasis upon local color. Yet the tale is undeniably Romantic according to Somov's prescription presented in his essay of 1823, "On Romantic Poetry," an application to Russian circumstances of Madame de Stael's ideas on national literatures, since the tale's central theme derives from native sources. The story concerns a fated tragedy involving a *yurodivy*, called Vasily the Half-Wit, and an insouciant young officer named Melsky. Melsky is a rather superficial youth, and it is owing to shortcomings in his personality that events move toward a tragic conclusion. He thus serves as the dynamic element for shaping the plot; Vasily's reactions to Melsky's activities provide the author an opportunity to illuminate the unusual features of his title character. The events are treated from Melsky's point of view, and, since we see Vasily through the youth's puzzled gaze, the fool remains an enigmatic figure to the end.

The two first meet on a night-darkened highroad after Melsky's carriage upsets, his horses having shied at the fool, who was sleeping at the edge of the road. The furious coachman and the curious officer interrogate the man, whose appearance and subsequent uncanny knowledge of apparent secrets combine to create an ominous presentiment in Melsky. This note of mysterious foreboding is struck very heavily in the early part of the story.

> Melsky also went to his bedroom and lay down on the bed. He thought that fatigue from his suburban diversions and dances and from his involuntary promenade [his horses had run away after the accident] would give him a heavy and calm sleep, but he was wrong. The strange image of his strange guest, his words, in which he partly had revealed what had happened and what would happen in the future, did not leave the mind of the young officer. In different ways he tried to convince himself that the words of the half-wit were the usual product of a disordered mind and that where the fool apparently had hinted at matters which he could not have known, he had spoken at random, knowing the usual habits of servants, and what he had said to the soldier might have been heard from one of his comrades. Nonetheless the *yurodivy* constantly appeared in his mind's eye. Several times Melsky closed his eyes and tried to force himself to sleep, but it was so stuffy, his room constrained him, the walls seemed to press around the bed, and the ceiling seemed to lean over it toward the floor. Chagrined, Melsky turned over, cursed himself for this hitherto unknown weakness, again closed his eyes. But if at times he was on the point of sleep, then the image of the *yurodivy*, his pale sunken cheeks, his morose gaze and wandering eyes, his tall figure, which grew higher and higher and finally became gigantic, all this persisted in the reveries of the young officer and tormented him like the delirium of a burning fever.[55]

The suspense increases when Melsky is accosted by the fool several days later as he is setting off to a soiree. Vasily urges him to turn back, citing the proverb: "Our tongue is our enemy." Melsky pays no heed, and, once at the party, indulges his wit at the expense of the other guests. An artillery officer takes offense and a challenge ensues. The combatants meet the next morning, and as the duel begins the *yurodivy* rushes between them, crying for them to desist. He is dragged off but breaks away again and interposes himself between the antagonists just as they fire—he is felled by the artillery officer's bullet. The duelists are reconciled while assisting the mortally wounded man. Taken to a peasant's house, Vasily lingers four days and then disappears. Melsky traces him to the graveyard, where he finds the fool's body next to the grave of his benefactress, Melsky's aunt. Thus the *yurodivy* fulfills the final prophecy: that he would lead Melsky to the grave of his aunt.

Admittedly, this story is no masterpiece. Nonetheless, it is artistically on a considerably higher level than most contemporary narratives. Its worth, however, is not attributable simply to its relative superiority to most of the fiction written at that time. Perhaps its appeal derives from the general aura of realism, for once one accepts the inexplicable powers of the fool to foretell the future and the fated outcome of his relationship with the officer—a not too difficult concession—then the story becomes entirely possible, if not probable. Somov develops the mystery element well, each of several dramatic encounters between Melsky and the fool concluding with some ominous prophecy. The *yurodivy* is intrinsically interesting as a peculiar social type, and it is not necessary for the reader's curiosity to be satisfied regarding the fool's background, the source of his powers, his real psychological condition. What Somov does expose of Melsky's inner state is quite in keeping with the general idea of his character derived from his actions.

For the most part the exposition is unencumbered by the ornamental paraphrasis so typical of the so-called Romantic period in the development of Russian prose. But there are exceptions: "The moon, the faithful companion of Ukrainian summer nights, sprinkled its silver light."[56] Occasionally emotional reactions are described in accordance with Romantic formulae: "a chill spread along all his limbs."[57] And though Somov was an avowed enemy of literary Sentimentalism, his story does have some lachrymose moments: learning of his master's forthcoming duel, Melsky's faithful servant "went into the vestibule and cried bitter tears."[58] As the fool lies wounded, Melsky bends over him and "sheds tears into his face—a gift of gratitude and humanity of which he was not ashamed."[59] And there is an unequivocally sentimental reconciliation between the two duelists: "kneeling and not taking his hand from the compress, the artillery officer leaned forward toward Melsky. They kissed one another."[60]

Notwithstanding the above quotations, the pervading style is direct and objective, with only a slight coloration of authorial attitude. The following passage is typical.

For a long time Melsky remained in this state. A light tap on the shoulder aroused him from his obliviousness. Starting, he looked around. Before him stood Svidov, his second; further away were both witnesses of the duel on his behalf, officers of their regiment.

"Enough meditating on the vanity of this world," said Svidov to him cheerily. "It's now half-past five; we have an hour and a half left. Order some vodka for us and a bite to eat. We won't give you anything, brother —don't get peeved: wait a while. Such games are played on an empty stomach."

In decisive situations the calmness and cheerful disposition of a comrade's spirits act strongly on others; and so it was now. The three officers cheerfully occupied themselves with the proffered breakfast. Melsky sat with them, although he ate nothing. Svidov enlivened the conversation. He joked, made his companions laugh at Melsky, saying that he had purposely tried to cut out a lachrymose mask for himself because he was planning to read his adversary's funeral service, and so forth. Infected by the laughter, Melsky himself became quite cheerful, especially toward the end of the breakfast when Svidov, followed by the other two officers, poured full glasses of wine, raised them and loudly cried, "To your health, Melsky."

"I shall thank you, gentlemen, in two hours, and not before," Melsky replied unconstrainedly.

Svidov looked at his watch. "Oho, friends, we've feasted for some time. It's half-past six. Melsky, order your pistols and charges. I, as the organizer of your life or death—don't get pale, dear friend—want to ascertain if the ammunition is in proper condition."

The pistols were inspected, the horses brought up, and in ten minutes the four comrades were already outside town.[61]

One should also call attention to the dynamic *in medias res* opening of the story, a quality which Pushkin's prose also possessed and which Tolstoy felt was the proper way to initiate a narrative.

A young officer was happily traveling from a certain suburban village where he had passed the day in a most pleasant circle—a circle of hospitable landowners, their sweet daughters, and five or six of his young comrades. He was hastening to town for the night, because on the next day he had guard duty.[62]

During the thirties such brisk introductory statements were a common feature of prose narratives. Two other stories published by Somov in *Northern Flowers* also begin without any introductory preamble.[63]

One should not conclude a discussion of "The Holy Fool" without referring to certain elements which became, as it were, standard ingredients in Russian fiction. The duel itself subsequently became a major theme in Russian literature, and the actual combat was often preceded, as it was in this story, by a description of nature which heightens the awareness of the evil shortly to be committed. On the fateful morning nature shows her best face: "The early birds were chirruping in the little garden. The morning was charming, dew sparkled on the grass." Similar mornings are ruefully noted by Lermontov's Pechorin, Turgenev's Chulkaturin and Bazarov, Dostoevsky's Zosima, and Chekhov's Laevsky. Svidov, the dueling enthusiast, ever ready to urge a comrade into a duel (and into the next world), heads a union of cold-blooded experts to which also belong Pushkin's Zaretsky, Lermontov's Captain of Dragoons, and many others, including Kuprin's garrison officers.

There is a possibility, perhaps remote, that Somov's story

grew from a seed planted by Pushkin's *Boris Godunov*, although the drama was not published until 1831, Pushkin finished the work at Mikhailovskoe in 1825, and Somov might have had access to it through Prince Vyazemsky, Baron Delvig, or even directly, since he was acquainted with Pushkin. *Boris Godunov* would certainly have interested and attracted Somov, because it could almost have been written to exemplify the kind of national Romanticism he had called for in his essay of 1823.[64] But the important thing here is that in Pushkin's drama a *yurodivy* plays a significant role. In reading or hearing Pushkin's play, Somov could well have been struck by the possibility of further exploiting such a peculiarly national type by a prose narrative. It is known, incidentally, that Pushkin made use of Somov's "Kiev Witches" when composing his ballad of 1833, "The Hussar."[65]

"The Holy Fool" was followed in 1828 by "The Rebel (An Excerpt from a Little Russian Tale)" ["Gajdamak (Otryvok iz malorossijskoj povesti)"], again signed with the pseudonym "Porfiry Baisky." In this story the narrative elements form a loose warp almost hidden under the woof of local color, and it is manifest that the author was in fact more interested in presenting details of Ukrainian traditions, apparel, food, entertainment, and temperament than in telling a story. Technically, "The Rebel" is a historical tale; it concerns the exploits of the famous Garkusha, an eighteenth-century Ukrainian Robin Hood. Somov had previously dealt with this figure in another story bearing the same title which had appeared in the *Neva Almanac* in 1827.[66] That earlier tale concerned Garkusha's almost miraculous escape after his betrayal to the Cossacks. A brief version of it is interpolated into "The Rebel" to provide background for the characterization of the hero.

The plot involves a conventional situation. A young officer, Kwietczyński, in love with Prisya, the daughter of the wealthy Pan Gritsenko, has been rejected by her haughty father on the grounds of his poverty. At her name-day celebration, which accompanies the closing of the fair at Korolewicz, a wealthy Pole appears at Gritsenko's home and requests lodgings for himself and his retinue. The hospitable Ukrainian is pleased with his illustrious guest, but he is not so happy to find Kwietczyński among the latter's party. However, the Pole charms his host and all those attending the name day by regaling them with amusing stories and liberal quantities of his own Hungarian wine. The next morning the Pole tells Gritsenko that he intends to give Kwietczyński a large sum, and thus he gains Gritsenko's consent to his daughter's marriage. Prisya and Kwietczyński are wed the following day, and during the subsequent festivities the Polish benefactor and his servants slip away unnoticed. Gritsenko later receives a letter from his mysterious guest admonishing him to respect his daughter and son-in-law and to treat his servants more humanely. The writer of this missive closes by identifying himself as Garkusha, whose name alone is sufficient to ensure compliance with the admonition.

Somov prefaces the story with a lengthy description of life in the remote Ukraine in the eighties of the previous century. The simplicity, rusticity and self-sufficiency of both the peasants and the petty gentry are stressed, but the author somewhat wistfully notes that although the old traditions have remained rooted in the simple folk, who still drink home-brewed spirits, play traditional instruments, and amuse themselves with tales of water spirits, witches, and ghosts, the gentry have adopted foreign customs. This introduction is peppered with Ukrainian terms, some explained parenthetically and others clarified by numerous footnotes. Direct address to the reader and transitional phrases, such as "to note in passing" and "now the question concerns" convey an impression of informal narration.

The story itself is initiated by a rather static description of Prisya's name-day party. Here the slow pace and wealth of detail suggest a typical opening of a historical novel rather than a short story, and this impression is superficially strengthened by the division of the work into chapters, each with its motto from Ukrainian folk traditions. In fact one of the major weaknesses of this story is just this imbalance between the deliberate beginning, where so much detail is provided in proportion to the action, and the ending, where the author seems in a hurry to wind up his plot, even to the point of ignoring the dramatic potential of his denouement.[67] A disproportionate emphasis is also reflected in the area of characterization, where considerable attention is focused upon the comic servant Stetsko, whose role in the tale is peripheral, while the pair of lovers are treated very sketchily. However, it must be admitted that they are sufficiently developed to satisfy the demands of the intrigue, and from what little we do see of them we can conclude that Somov did us a favor by ignoring this sentimental twosome.

The story is legendary and the characters are the types one would expect of a fairy tale: the greedy and intransigent father, the comic servant, the poor but honest suitor, the virtuous maiden who has sworn eternal love, and the "good fairy" who appears *deus ex machina* to resolve the woes of the frustrated lovers. There is a heavy stylization or conventionalization of the characters to make their behavior conform to certain dominant tones: the coarseness and avarice of Gritsenko, the audacity and munificence of Garkusha (even the most naïve reader must realize that the mysterious Pole is the Rebel), the cowardice and reluctance of the servant, Stetsko. None of this is very engrossing, at least for an adult. There is little development of suspense, first because we know that we are dealing with a fairy tale and that fairy-tale lovers, however vapid, somehow overcome all obstacles. Our real interest arises from the local color elements, which combine to create a rich and impressive (and, one suspects, hyperbolic and idealized) picture of life in the eighteenth-century Ukraine.

This story, like most of Somov's, shows its author to be an innovator and experimenter with respect to form. In delineating Stetsko, Somov employed "interior monologue," a device which at the time of his writing certainly had no tradition in Russian prose narratives and of which European literature had not yet presented examples.[68] Perhaps it would be too drastic to call this "interior monologue," but it presents some of that device's typical features: direct report in the first person of a character's thoughts as they are actually generated by internal and external stimuli: Stetsko's monologue is not "interior," since he articulates it, but, be that as it may, it is obviously intended to reveal his thoughts at the moment they emerge on the conscious level.

There was nothing for it: poor Stetsko had to set off on his unpleasant mission. On the other hand, puddling the mud of the street with his feet, he gave vent to his chagrin in bitter complaints and did not spare his master in the following speech, which burst forth disjointedly.

"The proverb is right: 'Jump, you devil, as the master orders! . . .' It's all very well for him to sit in a warm and bright room and drink his berry wine with guests. Would he go in my place in such weather, on such a night, and to such a place? O, Saintly Mother of God! . . . What! . . . Who's here? Who's making that noise? Who's whispering? . . . No, it only seems so: it's the dried leaves in the master's garden which rustle from the rain. . . . I'm no coward and will stand up for myself. I can handle the living. Only a ghost or werewolf—that's no brother of mine. But then, what will be, will be! In any case, I have my defense on me. Against a ghost, the cross, and against the living, a club. You think and think, why aren't I myself a master! I would eat rich things to my heart's content, I'd hoard up trunks full of money and sleep on the stove, and for amusement I'd make Pan Gritsenko jump over this club or I'd send him in the middle of the night to call all the blind singers and bandalore players in the vicinity. . . , Not a star in the sky, not a light in the huts. Everyone's gone to bed. That's a fine time to wander about the streets! A good man wouldn't even chase a dog out now. God will judge you, Pan Gritsenko!"[69]

The presentation of these rambling and fragmentary thoughts, which give the reader the impression of being privy to the flux and flow of ideas as they take form in the mind of the character, admittedly represents a rudimentary stage in the development of the interior monologue. Yet if the critic Chernyskevsky could see portions of "Pechorin's Journal" in *A Hero of Our Times* as an antecedent to Tolstoy's fully developed interior monologues in *Sevastopol Tales,* we are also justified in calling attention to Somov's experimentation with the device.[70]

In 1830 Somov again appeared in *Northern Flowers* as a contributor of fiction, and once again his work manifested those elements of originality which place him in the vanguard of those author-experimenters responsible for the rapid maturation of Russian fiction during the twenties and thirties. "Kikimora (A Tale of a Russian Peasant on the Highroad)" ["Kikimora (Rasskaz russkogo krest'janina na bol'šoj doroge)"] is presented almost entirely in the words of Faddey, an ingenuous and superstitious peasant driver. This garrulous soul recounts to his gentry passenger the tribulations of a family in his village which was bedeviled by kikimora, a variety of house spirit similar to a Poltergeist. They had first become aware of kikimora's visitations when they noticed that little Varya, who usually was put to bed dirty and unkempt, appeared each morning to have been unaccountably cleaned and combed. Though kikimora was obviously benign, still they distrusted its dark powers and so appealed to the priest for an exorcism; he upbraided them for their superstitions and declared that such spirits did not exist. The German bailiff was not so scrupulous and agreed to perform the exorcism, for which he needed considerable money and copious quantities of rum. These the family gratefully provided, but after the bailiff's efforts kikimora still persisted, playing malicious tricks on everyone except Varya. A mendicant crone was then appealed to, and she did provide an exorcism, but before it could be performed Varya fell into a trance, climbed to the rooftree of the hut, and threw herself to the ground with apparently fatal results. The grief-stricken family carried out the crone's ritual and prepared to bury Varya; however, the crone opportunely reappeared and Varya mysteriously returned to life, evidently unaffected by her experience.

One is immediately struck (particularly if one considers the date of composition) by the unusual manner in which the story is presented. It begins as a pure, unmarked dialogue between Faddey and his passenger, the latter chiding the peasant, who had promised a story about kikimora, for his digressiveness. Faddey then begins his anecdote, which is narrated by him in the past tense. Occasionally the passenger interrupts with comments or questions, which reestablish the dialogue. We are well into the story before we encounter the first indication that the passenger-peasant dialogue is not being presented omnisciently but is enclosed within the first-person narration of Faddey's one-time passenger, who treats his encounter with the driver retrospectively. This frame is extremely tenuous; only two brief comments within the story qualify Faddey's remarks: "grumbled Faddey and silently began to shake the reins" and "said Faddey, more cheerfully and confidently than before." These comments are supplemented by the principal narrator's (the one-time passenger's) concluding paragraph regarding his unsuccessful efforts to loosen the driver's tongue once he had finished the tale about the kikimora

> Here Faddey crossed himself and after that yelled at the horses, waved his whip and rushed along at full speed. Try as I might, I couldn't get another word from him. And in that stubborn silence he conveyed me to the last station, where he also taciturnly thanked me with a bow when I gave him the stipulated additional fare.[71]

Somov, of course, might have dispensed with this frame. Certainly the first two indications of its existence are quite unnecessary; the last paragraph is of more importance, since it serves to terminate the relationship between the passenger and the driver and adds a rather amusing postscript to what the reader had already deduced regarding Faddey's personality. But probably the real reason for its presence was simply that at the period of the story's composition there was no precedent for the presentation of a story within the structure of free, or unframed, dialogue. Somov may have felt that a justification for the dialogue was expected, and so he provided the linking sequence: passenger-principal narrator (author). Thus the existence or preservation of the dialogue was legitimized.

The essential content of "Kikimora" is connected with

Faddey's tale, whose narrative gains its interest perhaps less from the unusual theme than from his racy, picturesque language. Indeed, the reader's attention is deliberately focused upon the highly unliterary but intriguingly colorful idiom of the driver, which manifests both class and individual peculiarities,

> We had a bailiff then in our settlement, I don't know, a German or a Frenchman, from Mitava. By name and patronymic he was called *Vot-on Ivanovich* [*Vot-on* literally means "There he is." As a foreigner, the bailiff probably used *vot-on* incorrectly to initiate his sentences, somewhat like "Well, now."], but I don't know how to say his last name at all. Our constable, Elisey, what was then in the counting house up at the manor, called him Mr. *Von-Baron*. This *Von-Baron* was a great joker. When, like it happened, that we take a rest after working for the master, well then he gives out with stories about foreign folk no bigger than an ell with goat's feet, about bewitched castles, about corpses that wander about there at night without heads. . . . He used to tell us more than a little: you couldn't get it all in three baskets. He spoke Russian not awfully well; sometimes in his talk you could crack your skull and still get no sense. . . . The peasants were of the view that Vot-on Ivanovich had *plenty in his nose*. As for me, I never noticed anything except snuf. . . . True enough, in the master's yard he thought up some sort of machines for sowing and threshing grain. Only his thresher almost threshed his own head, and no matter how much a dozen men worked on it, they still couldn't thresh a single sheaf.[72]

By presenting the major portion of his tale in this manner, Somov achieved here a technique later to be termed skaz—the artistic utilization of a surrogate narrator who presents a story in his own individualized and racy idiom. "Kikimora" is probably the first extended use of skaz in Russian literature, and thus Somov stands at the head of a distinguished fraternity of writers known for their use of the technique, a group which includes Gogol, Dostoevsky, Leskov, Remizov, Zoshchenko, and others.

"Matchmaking" ["Svatovstvo"], which appeared in 1832, was considerably longer than Somov's other pieces of fiction for the almanac—almost nine thousand words. In a brief afterword, Somov disclaimed credit for the story itself, stating that he only provided the sixteen footnotes: "These fragments from the memoirs of Demid Kalistratovich Slastyona were conveyed to me by one of his countrymen. As their editor, I had only to add notes to explain certain Little Russian words, customs, etc."[73] For the actual author to pose as editor, or collector, of a story or stories was a common practice in the thirties, utilized presumably to lend more verisimilitude to works of fiction. Pushkin's *Belkin* and Gogol's *Red Panko* are better known examples of such authorial masks.

Subtitled "From the Memoirs of an Old Man about his Youth" ["Iz vospominanij starika o ego molodosti"], "Matchmaking" is a rambling account of the tribulations faced by the narrator in his unsuccessful quest for the hand of his first love. The story further serves as a vehicle for the presentation of all sorts of information regarding the Ukrainian petty gentry, village life, gentry diversions, dress, education, and includes a detailed account of the formalities connected with the traditional means of becoming engaged. Demid Kalistratovich presents his tale in an informal, personal manner which gives the impression of oral narration. In fact, the opening of the story has the form of a one-sided dialogue, the narrator asking questions on behalf of his readers and then providing the answers.

> Maybe, gentlemen, you are surprised, you are looking at one another and whispering among yourselves: "Who," you say, "is talking to us? And what's the use of one stranger irritating other strangers, and why should the inhabitant of a provincial hamlet speak to those who live in the capital and torment our ears, which are accustomed to choice expressions and involved greetings?" Permit me, gentlemen, to report everything about myself that is necessary. I remind you only that I myself was a learned person, and if it had not been for the damned

school holidays, then it might have been that I would never have lost my knowledge of Latin.[74]

Although the narrative here gives the impression of direct speech, we cannot consider this an example of skaz, since it is not Demid Kalistratovich's speech mannerisms that are reproduced here but rather his supposed literary style. But the peculiarly personal tone persists through most of the story, with an alternation of didactic, sentimental, sardonic, and ironic overtones, depending upon whether the narrator is concerned with information about Ukrainian customs, is treating his relationship to his beloved, is describing his almost catastrophic social debut, or is talking about his intended mother-in-law. But poor Demid Kalistratovich is not much more successful as a memoirist than as a would-be bridegroom, and his story is filled with as many disgressions as his personal affairs were fraught with frustrating obstacles. But, of course, it is just this rambling style which constitutes a large part of the tale's charm.

Demid Kalistratovich is one of the first of the long line of pathetic civil servants who populate Russian literature. The tragi-comic treatment of his fortunes, or misfortunes, was echoed by later generations of similarly misunderstood, frustrated, and browbeaten quill drivers. There is a real pathos about this simple, well-meaning man whose good intentions and innate generosity were not reciprocated by fate. His story ends on a plaintive note which stresses his loneliness and sadness.

> As for me, I no longer think of marriage. My first dreams of happiness have vanished like smoke, and now I while away my time as an old, kinless bachelor. I go to work, I strictly observe my oath of office, and I bear indifferently the complaints of my fellow workers, whose opinions differ from mine. In the evening I read whatever God provides and write my memoirs from boredom. I don't know whether they will interest you, dear sirs, as much as me. In any case, I wish you happiness.[75]

Notwithstanding the rather plaintive tone of this conclusion, the general atmosphere of the narrative is lighthearted and humorous. Somov creates both situational and verbal humor, often blending the two. Thus, we smile at the young Demid's abortive efforts to show himself to his fellow villagers as the sophisticated fashion plate from the capital. Dressed in a garish manner, he appeared before the local society at a wedding reception.

> The local worthies, some in black or dark blue dress coats, bared their teeth at my appearance. I was scared stiff. However, remembering the words of my mommy and quite conscious of my own dandified raiment, I said to myself, "It's envy, envy!" Probably some of them lacked the things which I had in my wardrobe. Others were arrayed in little dress coats which were dock-tailed in order to use less cloth. This thought gave me new confidence. I bowed to all sides and set about looking for the hostess. At that moment she herself carried in vodka for her guests. I thrust forward to kiss her hand, knocked my elbow against the tray—the decanter and glasses clashed together and were thrown to one side, the vodka spilled onto the floor and the hostess' dress. By good fortune she held on to the tray with her strong hands. However, the laughter of all the guests—a demonic, heartrending laughter—resounded around me. Having kissed the hostess' hand, I drew back quickly at the same time as she bent forward in order to respond to my kiss with one of the forehead. A new misfortune! My head knocked her in the face so hard that sparks flew from her eyes and she almost had a nosebleed. The hostess cried out involuntarily and pressed her left hand to her face, while a solicitous worthy supported her tray and thus prevented the potable supplies from complete destruction. I admit that at this point I became confounded from fright. I couldn't see where I stood and almost rushed headlong from the house.[76]

There is certain evidence in this work of Somov's familiarity with the work of Vasily Narezhny, A *Russian Gil Blas,* written almost two decades earlier. Both are comic memoirs of natural-born bunglers whose series of misfortunes are initiated by the inconstancy of women. But Narezhny's picaresque novel bears a Classical stamp—indeed, the influence of *Candide* is quite manifest—whereas in Somov's work the emphasis on local color, the almost didactic focusing upon details of the engagement ritual, the typical Ukrainian figures (such as the pettifogging matchmaker), and the individualization of the central character, who emerges as a flesh and blood human rather than simply as a complex of humors—all this indicates a Romantic orientation.

Somov died in 1833, still a relatively young man. It is useless to speculate what he might have done had his literary career been extended, but from what evidence we have of his actual accomplishments as a prose writer, it is clear that he was an important innovator both in the area of stylistics and themes. In this he is quite atypical for a writer of the second rank, since for the most part secondary authors simply provide variations of elements introduced by their more imaginative or daring colleagues. In opposition to the general rule, therefore, Somov seems to have provided the rough sketches for new means of literary expression, which more gifted writers subsequently exploited to their full potentials. In *Northern Flowers* alone he presented early, if not the first, examples in Russian literature of the interior monologue, skaz, and the individualized memoir. He was one of the first Romantics to perceive and exploit the potentials of Ukrainian local color, and he recognized also the literary possibilities of Russian national types, such as the *yurodivy* or the tragi-comic petty clerk. And for his period he displayed an unusual ability for lucid, objective exposition. His shortcomings, which were probably the result of too rapid composition and insufficient editing, were principally connected with the structures of his works, which at times became rather shapeless through the incorporation of unimportant or peripheral elements. But all things considered, he significantly raised the general artistic level of the prose in Delvig's almanac, and, owing to that almanac's wide circulation and popularity, he had an important influence upon the development of more sophisticated literary tastes.

Two more works of short fiction, both of which appeared in the final issue, should be mentioned, although they lack the quality of the selections from Odoevsky or Somov. Alexander Nikitenko's "An Excerpt from the Novel: *Leon or Idealism*" ["Otryvok iz romana: Leon ili Idealizm"] opens with the author's note explaining that the inner life of the spirit is a vast and varied subject, and that this particular work is but a prologue to an entire novel which is nearing completion. The story itself is Leon's retrospective confession to one of the *persona* of the novel in which he describes the circumstances of his education and moral development. This is presented in a florid, metaphoric language which conveys little definite idea of the narrator's personality. We learn simply that he was a sensitive child, a dreamer who shut himself off from the unspiritual interests which governed his parents' world. But there are no episodes to give substance to his generalizations about himself or his behavior.

> In a word, I was a riddle to my parents and my tutor. The latter, with all his French enthusiasm, more than once proclaimed me a genius, but a minute later he tearfully complained to my father that I was the most stupid creature among all the children he knew both in Russia and France. Sometimes he was ready to admit that I was an angel of meekness, but suddenly some unexpected prank bridled his tongue or loosed it to promise me nothing more nor less than a future as a leader of a band of cutthroats on the order of Schiller's Moor.[77]

This personal history continues to the time Leon is a university student, but our impressions of him are never clarified. As an analysis of the development of a personality the work is not successful. The interest which the story does stimulate is in connection with its implicit criticism of contemporary society, directed primarily at the education of gentry youth by foreign masters-of-all-arts, an education which is concerned with appearances rather than intellectual achievement. There is also an implied criticism of the urban gentry, which is occupied with banal social activities and mundane business affairs, and allusions to the primitive habits and behavior of the rural gentry. The work strongly conveys the impression that the development and practice of idealism is impossible under such conditions.[78]

Nikitenko in no way advances the capabilities of the Russian literary language. His style, for the most part, is early Karamzinian—sentimental, paraphrastic, metaphoric, and indefinite. One example will suffice. Speaking of his mother's fatalistic acceptance of the necessity of marriage, Leon says,

> Still at times her heart sank in anguish, sensing the decisive, imminent hour of parting with its most pure dreams and hopes. Finally it submitted to the law of necessity, and the bright days of her youth, which had bloomed in the radiance of moral beauty, darkened in her memory, as the heavenly azure with its effulgent stars grows dim in the stormy clouds of autumn nights. Not by desire, not by constraint, but drawn by the force of circumstances, with a heart extinguished without love, she finally gave her hand to the man who became my father.[79]

"An Excerpt from the Chinese Novel: *Hau-Tsu-Dzhuan*, that is, A Matchless Marriage, a Translation from the Chinese" ["Otryvok iz kitajskogo romana: *Xau-Cju-Džuan'*, t. e. bezprimernyj brak. Perevod s Kitajskogo"] is an anonymous contribution (1832). Apparently one of the episodes from a picaresque novel, it concerns the protagonist's tribulations after he thwarts another Chinese gentleman's attempt to seduce a young lady. To accomplish his revenge, the would-be seducer makes use of certain obligatory social conventions: thus, he calls upon the protagonist, who must, according to the code, return the visit. When the hero is under the villain's roof, he is presented with a series of visitors, with each of whom he is obligated to drink. Finally the well-intoxicated hero demurs, insults are exchanged, and the host orders his servants to attack the hero. However, the latter escapes.

Though the characters are flat, the situation is amusing, and the story gains interest from the description of the exotic social conventions and the involved formulae for address which characterize the dialogue.

The popularity of the historical tale [istoričeskaja povest'] in the first quarter of the nineteenth century is attested by the several examples of that genre in the almanac. By the end of the twenties this type of story, thanks to the indispensable influence of Walter Scott, had developed into a more ambitious form, the historical novel [istoričeskij roman]. In the year 1829 Mikhail Zagoskin's *Yury Miloslavsky, or the Russians in 1612* was published, and within the next three years Pushkin, Gogol, Bulgarin, Shevyrev, and Lazhechnikov all tried their hand at the genre.[80] Pushkin, Gogol and Lazhechnikov all contributed parts of historical novels to *Northern Flowers*, beginning in 1829 with Pushkin's "Chapter IV from a Historical Novel" ["IV Glava iz istoričeskogo romana"], published anonymously. This is an almost complete version of the fourth chapter of his unfinished "The Moor of Peter the Great," a fictionalized biography of the author's famous ancestor, Abraham Hannibal. This excerpt concerns the unexpected appearance of Peter the Great at the home of the boyar Rzhevsky, where he requests the hand of the boyar's daughter for his Abyssinian favorite. In the tradition of the historical novel, there is a wealth of detail regarding food, apparel, furnishings, customs, and the speech is stylized to suggest the historical period. Little more need be said here about this work, which has been discussed by many commentators, except that its presence in the almanac contributed significantly to the general quality of the prose section.

In the 1831 *Northern Flowers* appeared a quite different example of the historical novel, a work entitled simply "A Chapter from a Historical Novel" ["Glava iz istoričeskogo romana"], signed "o o o o," the work of the twenty-year-old Nikolay Gogol. This fragment was one of several connected with his unfinished novel "The Hetman."[81] It concerns the mission of a certain Lapczyński to contact a secret ally of the Poles known as the Mirgorod Colonel. In the virtually trackless wastes of the Ukraine, he encounters a peasant returning from a fair, who offers him the hospitality of his home. On the way the peasant recounts a tale about a solitary pine tree, unusual in that region, which stands by the path. Lapczyński and his garrulous companion arrive at the latter's hut, which is swarming with children and animals, and after some preliminaries, the peasant reveals to the astonished Lapczyński that he is the Mirgorod Colonel.

Much more than the excerpt from Pushkin's novel, this piece reveals the influence of Walter Scott: a central figure travels on a dangerous mission; he encounters an enigmatic person who later is revealed to be someone of importance; the countryside is described through the eyes of the protagonist; there are auctorial digressions commenting on the changes between the past and present; a local legend is interpolated; the apparel of the people is detailed, the habitations fully described, with emphasis on furnishings, decorations, utensils, weapons, arrangement. Further, the speech of the characters, particularly the secondary ones, is stylized to conform to type, class, occupation, time, and place. There is also the probable influence here of l'école frénétique and its master, Charles Robert Maturin, author of *Melmoth the Wanderer*: the fiery eyes of the mysterious peasant, the malevolent pine tree which drips blood, the ominous nocturnal setting with stage illumination for atmosphere and effect. But there is some typical Gogol as well.

> Wide and narrow limewood benches encircled the entire room; by the doors hulked a stove with an opening below partly screened by a grating from behind which peeped out chickens, geese, turkeys, and domestic rabbits. Each of these dumb lodgers fussed in his own way: cheeped, cackled, gaggled, and, it seemed, made known that his voice too was taking part in the general dissonance.[82]

The final issue of *Northern Flowers* contained a selection from Ivan Lazhechnikov's *The Last Novik*, a novel which, unlike the aforementioned early ventures of Pushkin and Gogol, was ultimately completed (in 1833). Entitled "Doomsday (An Excerpt from the Novel: *The Last Novik*)" ["Strašnyj sud (Otryvok iz romana: *Poslednij Novik*)"], the piece describes the protagonist's arrival at a village of Old Believers, where he finds that the inhabitants have shrouded themselves and lain down in coffins to await the imminent hour of judgement. The attention to landscape and the local color details are typical for the genre, but the work gains interest from the quite unusual subject matter. Further, the author exploits the possibilities of humor afforded by the example of human folly with which his piece deals: the scene of several hundred deceived "corpses" rising from their coffins and stumbling over their shrouds is quite amusing. The one drawback to this episode is the excessive use of the specialized terms employed by the Old Believers; unlike regionalisms or dialectal variants, this sort of jargon does not reinforce the local color, and, further, the footnotes which accompany these words intrude upon the illusion of reality.

Chapter VII

Afterword

In Russia literary almanacs had an effect far greater than one might expect from publications which appeared only annually and often had a very limited span of existence. Much more than simply casual anthologies of verse and prose to be perused with nominal attention, they were for the most part *the* place in which leading poets and prose writers chose to expose their works to the public for the first time. Of course, important original works also appeared on the pages of weeklies and monthlies, and others were published separately, but, irrespective of these other means of publication, almanacs themselves played a vital role in presenting to the public the most recent compositions of many authors.[1] New poets continually made their debuts in almanacs, and in many cases the best works of established authors were published initially on their pages.

The Russian literary world of the twenties and thirties was very conscious of the significance of these annual collections, and they were awaited with impatience and anticipation. It was a literary event when a quality almanac appeared, and its contents were carefully reviewed and discussed by the critics. In 1829 the *Moscow Telegraph* summarized the situation as follows: "In Russia almanacs . . . are important books; they are representative of the year's endeavors of almost all our poets."[2]

There can be little doubt about the real importance of *Northern Flowers,* since for almost a decade it was a major medium of publication for the Pushkin Pleiad. There was, of course, baser metal mixed with the gold, since the works of mediocre talents also found a place on the almanac's pages, but the general impression provided by the tables of contents of the poetry sections of the eight issues is one of brilliance.

The situation with respect to prose in *Northern Flowers* was not so favorable. At the time the almanac first appeared Russian literature did not yet have a dynamic prose tradition, and the early issues reveal this weakness. Prose writers seemed capable of little more than travel notes, short sketches, historical tales, or exotic legends (often translated or adapted from foreign sources), and the preponderant style was what might be called neo-Karamzin. But with each new issue there is additional evidence that prose was coming of age—or of adolescence. The almanac's last issues display new forms, devices, themes, and types; and in some cases there is evidence of a new prose style quite suitable for objective narration.

The role of *Northern Flowers* in the area of literary criticism was most productive. The almanac correctly supported authors whose reputations have since become firmly established, and it did this not only by publishing their works but by evaluating them in its critical sections. Somov's annual surveys of the preceding year's literary production were, despite a lack of specificity, important guides for public appraisal of current works, and his constant insistence upon the need for an adequate prose language—and his admonitions to careless stylists—must certainly have influenced aspiring prose writers. The example of his own imaginative prose confirmed his assertions about the possibility of an independent domestic prose literature based on national themes and types.

The critical stance of *Northern Flowers,* which was reflected in its choice of authors and works, demonstrated also that new trends in literature did not necessarily have to imply the abandonment of older ones, that Romanticism might develop without denying Classicism, that innovation did not necessitate rejection of established forms and norms. In this respect by its example the almanac exerted a moderating influence upon the unnecessarily vehement and raucous conflict between the extremes of the conservative and modernist camps.

The one area of literature where *Northern Flowers* was particularly weak was in drama, but this was due to the generally weak development of Russian drama itself rather than to the indifference of the almanac's editors. The few dramatic selections which did appear in Delvig's almanac were limited to translated excerpts from Shakespeare, Schiller, and two minor playwrights. The only original drama was a scene from Pushkin's *Boris Godunov*, but this was less than three pages in length and, though not without significance, it could hardly be said to compensate for the almost total absence of dramatic selections.

The period in which this almanac was published was one of the most generative in the history of Russian literature. It not only witnessed the high point of the so-called Golden Age of Russian poetry but also saw the emergence of prose as poetry's vigorous competitor. At the same time Romanticism established its legitimacy,[3] and the banner of *narodnost* was planted on the Russian Parnassus; the eight issues of *Northern Flowers* clearly reflect these developments.

APPENDICES / NOTES / INDEX

Contributors and Works

Immediately below in Russian alphabetical order are all the works appearing in the eight issues of *Northern Flowers*. Authors identified only by initials, letters, or numerals are included here. Prose works have an indication [P] preceding the title. At the end of this appendix is a supplementary list of works appearing over asterisks or otherwise completely anonymous. Standard transliteration has been used to render names and titles.

Ballë, I.
1827: Nesčastnomu.

Baratynskij, Evgenyj
1825: [P] Istorija Koketstva.
       Opravdanie.
       Sonet.
       Čerep.
       Zvezdočka.
1826: K Annete.
       L. S. P——nu.
       Nadpis'.
1827: A. A. V——nu.
       Pesnja.
       Telema i Makar.
       Najada.
       Ėpigramma.
       Bogdanoviču.

1828: Otryvok iz poèmy: *Bal'nyj večer*.
Poslednjaja smert'.
1829: Pereselenie duš (Skazka).
Smert' (Podražanie A. Šen'e).
Derevnja.
Starik.
Antologičeskie stixotvorenija.
Besenok.
1830: Èpigramma.
Scena iz poèmy Vera i neverie.
Muza.
1831: Novinskoe (Otryvok iz 2 glavy romana: *Naložnica*).
Sara (Otryvok iz romana: *Naložnica*) Glava V.
1832: Moj Èlizij.

Batjuškov, Konstantin
1826: K N. N.
Podražanie Ariostu.
1827: [P] Pis'mo k S. iz Gotenburga. Ijunja 19, 1814 goda.
1828: Èlegija.
1832: [P] Predslava i Dobrynja. Starinnaja povest'.

Bestužev, Nikolaj
1826: [P] Traktirnaja lestnica.

Bičurin, Nikita
1832: [P] Bajkal (Pis'mo k O. M. S——).

Bulgarin, Faddej
1827: [P] Razvaliny Al'modavarskie.
1828: [P] Padenie Vendena. Istoričeskaja povest' (Dejstvie v
XVI-m veke (Posvjaščeno M. A. Lon —— voj).
1829: [P] Petr Velikij v morskom poxode iz Peterburga k
Vyborgu (1710 goda) (Istoričeskij otryvok).

V —— [See *Grigorovič, Vasilij*]

Velikopol'skij, Ivan
1826: K podarennomu lokonu.
1827: Vospominanie (Iz Lamartina).

Venevitinov, Dmitrij
1827: Tri rozy.
Pesn' Greka.
1829: [P] Tri èpoxi ljubvi (Otryvok iz nekončennogo romana).
Zaveščanie.

Verderevskij, Vasilij
1828: Dve ody iz Goracija (Oda 5, Kn. II, Oda 25, Kn. I).
1829: Proricanie Nereja (Gorac. Oda 15, Kn. I).
1831: K Fidile (Gorac. Oda 23, Kn. III) (Posvjašč. A. P.
V——oj).
K Mel'pomene (Gorac. Oda 3, Kn. IV).

Voejkov, Aleksandr
1825: [P] Progulka v sele Kuskove.

Volkov, Platon
1831: Mečta.

Volkov, T.
1831: Rusalki (Fantazija).

Volkonskaja, Knjaginja Zinaida
1830: [P] Otryvki iz putevyx zapisok.
1831: [P] Otryvki iz putevyx zapisok.
1832: Nadgrobnaja pesn' slavjanskogo gusljara.
Moej zvezde.

Vostokov, Aleksandr
1825: Serbskie pesni: I, II, III.
1826: K druz'jam.
Stroenie Skadra (Iz Serbskix narodyx pesen', Kn. II, No. 5).
1827: Serbskie pesni: Janja Mizinica (V sobranii Vuka Stefano-
viča, Kn. I, No. 394).
Sestra devjati brat'ev (Kn. I, No. 404).
Devica i solnce (Kn. I, No. 200).
Žalobnaja pesnja blagorodnoj Asan-Aginicy (Iz pervogo
izdanija Serbskix pesen': mala prostonarondn'a Slaveno-
Serbska pesnarica, u Vieni. 1814, str. 113).

Vrončenko, Mixail
1829: Irlandskie melodii (Iz Mura).

Vjazemskij, Knjaz' Petr
1825: Mladyj pevec.
Nedovol'nyj (S francuzskogo).
K žurnalnym bliznecam.
Prostoserdečnyj otvet.
Čerta mestnosti.
K Knjazne ***, pri posylke ej moix pesen'.
1826: O. S. Puškinoj.
Xarakteristika.
Al'bom.
Narvskij vodopad.
Sem' pjatnic na nedele.
K mnimoj sčastlivice.
1827: [P] Vyderžki iz zapisnoj knižki.
Netlennyj cvetok.
Slezy proščanija.
1828: More.
Russkij romantik russkomu klassiku.
1829: [P] Vyderžki iz zapisnoj knižki.
Poslanie k A. A. B. pri posylke portreta.
Predosteréženie.
Stansy (Anne Ivanovne Gotovcovoj).
Èpigrammy.
Prostovolosaja golovka.
Irlandskaja melodija (Iz Mura).
1830: Sleza.
1831: Osen' 1830 goda
Svjatočnaja šutka.
Èpigramma.
Lesa.
Roditel'skij dom.
K žurnal'nym blagoprijateljam.
K A. O. P***.
1832: Xandra. Pesnja.
Toska (V. I. Buxarinoj).
D. A. Okulovoj.
Volodin'ke Karamzinu.
Do svidanija.
Predopredelenie.

Glebov, Aleksandr
1827: Volšebnyj sad (Stixotvornaja fantazija).
       Avgust mesjac (1826 g.)

Glebov, Dmitrij
1827: Son (Iz Bajrona.)

Glinka, Fedor
1825: [P] Drevnie zamki (Pis'mo VI, k drugu).
       [P] Neuznánnaja.
       Psalom (Podražanie).
       Želanie Boga (Iz Ps. 41).
       Videnie v lune.
1826: [P] Neponjatnyj sojuz.
       [P] Nerazlučnye.
       [P] Vožatyj.
       Smert' Fignera (Opyt narodnoj poèzii).
       Čerty oseni.
       Stepnaja žizn'. Vospominanija. Poxod.
1827: [P] Čudesnaja soputnica.
       [P] Osennie dni (Kartina).
       Netlennye Glaza. Vostočnyj Apolog (Iz Xafisa).
       Priključenie.
1828: [P] Dve sestry, ili: kotoroj otdat' preimuščestvo?
       [P] Vosxoždenie solnca v burnoe osennee utro (Kartina s
       natury).
       Psalom LXII.
       Peregovory v Beloj Cerkvi (Čerta iz žizni Bogdana Xmel'-
       nickogo).
1830: [P] Vstuplenie bol'šoj dejstvujuščej armii na poziciju pri
       S. Tarutine (Otryvok iz Istorii 1812 goda).
       Ne naša storona.
       Psalom LXVII.
       Deva i videnie.
       Car' i mudrec.
1831: [P] Novaja probirnaja palatka.
       Neponjatnaja vešč'.
       Otradnoe čuvstvo.
       Toska o nem.
       K sinemu nebu.
       Bednost' i utešenie.

       Osen' i sel'skoe žit'e.
       Primety.
1832: [P] Važnyj spor (Allegorija).
       Lesnye vojny (Iz poèmy: *Deva Karel'skix lesov*).
       Otryvok iz poèmy: Bez"imjannye ili *Deva Karel'skix lesov*.
       Psalom 103-j.
       Sozercanie.

Gnedič, Nikolaj
1825: Na smert' N. N.
       Grečeskie prostonarodnye pesni.
1826: Pojas Kipridy. Otryvok iz xiv pesni Iliady.
1827: Rybaki: Idillija.
1828: K P. A. Pl——vu, otvet na ego poslanie (Otryvok).
1831: K P. A. Pletnevu, otvet na ego poslanie.

Gogol', Nikolaj
1831: [P] Glava iz istoričeskogo romana.

Gotovcova, Anna
1829: K Ju. N. Bartenevu.
       A. S. P.

Greč, Nikolaj
1828: [P] O žizni i sočinenijax Karamzina.

Grigorovič, Vasilij
1826: [P] O sostojanii xudožestv v Rossii.
1827: [P] O sostojanii xudožestv v Rossii.

Grigor'ev, Vasilij
1825: K nevernoj.
1827: Beštau.
1828: Setovanie (Izail'skaja pesn').
       Poslanie k N. F——u.
1829: Gruzinka.

      D—— a—— [See *Rostopčina*.]

Dargomyžskaja, Mar'ja
1825: Dva červjaka (Basnja).

Daškov, Dmitrij
1825: [P] Izvestie o Grečeskix i Latinskix rukopisjax v seral'skoj
          biblioteke.
1826: [P] Ešče neskol'ko slov o seral'skoj biblioteke.

Delarju, Mixail
1830: Poèt (Sonet).
          K Neve.
          Angelu-Xranitelju.
          Sleza ljubvi (B. S. M. Del'vig).
1831: Son i smert'.
          Vyzdorovlenie.
          Glicere.
          Mogila poèta (Posvjaščaetsja pamjati V——va).
1832: Uvjadajuščaja roza.
          Zamužnej Elene.
          Psalom.
          Mirra (Poèma Ovidija Nazona).
          Èlegija.
          Anfologičeskoe četverostišie.
          K***, pri posylke tetradi stixov.
          Lizan'ke Del'vig.

Del'vig, Baron Anton
1825: Pesnja.
          Russkie pesni.
          Romans.
          Kupal'nicy (Idillija).
1826: V al'bom S. G. K——oj.
          My.
          Èpitafija.
          Russkaja pesnja.
          Dve zvezdočki.
          N. I. Gnediču.
          Luna.
1827: Difiramb (Na priezd trex druzej).
          Druz'ja (E. A. Baratynskomu).
          V al'bom A. N. V——f.
          Genij-Xranitel' (Snovidenie).
1828: [P] [Notes regarding forthcoming works].
          Na smert' V——va.
          Na smert' sobački: Amiki.

Zastol'naja pesnja.
Otvet.
Utešenie.
Idillija.
Èpigramma.
Smert'.

1829: Son.
Xor. Dlja vypuska vospitannic Imperatorskogo Xar'kovskogo Instituta.
Romans.

1830: Četyre vozrasta fantazii.
Otstavnoj soldat (Russkaja idillija).
Grust'.
Slezy ljubvi.
Russkaja pesnja.
Malorossijskaja melodija.
Udel poèta.
Izobretenie vajanija. Idillija (Posvjaščaetsja V. I. Grigoroviču).

1832: Pjat' stixotvorenij Barona Del'viga: K Morfeju; Sonet; Russkie pesni: 1, 2; Otryvok.

Dmitriev, Ivan

1832: Vasiliju Andreeviču Žukovskomu. po slučaju polučenija otnego dvux stixotvorenij na vzjatie Varšavy.

Žukovskij, Vasilij

1825: Prividenie.
Tainstvennyj posetitel'.
Noč'.
Motylek i cvety.

1829: Toržestvo pobeditelej (Iz Šillera).
Videnie.
Otryvki iz *Iliady*.
More.

1832: Otvet Ivanu Ivanoviču Dmitrievu.
Sraženie s zmeem.

Zagorskij, Mixail

1825: Perčatka (Iz Šillera).
[?] Car' Fuleskij (Iz Gete)

Zajcevskij, Efim
1828:   Učan-su (Posvjaščaetsja Anne Evstaf'evne Udom).
1829:   B. F. R——oj.

Z——ij
1827:   [P] Rusaja kosa. Proizšestvie iz žizni M.

Izmajlov, Aleksandr
1825:   Ej že (V den' ee roždenija).
        S. D. P. (V den' ee Angela).
1826:   Strelki. Basnja.
1829:   Skupoj i okulist. Skazka.
1830:   Skotskoe pravosudie. Basnja.
        Obmančivaja naružnost'. Basnja.

Izmajlov, Vladimir
1828:   Kon' i žerebenok. Basnja (Iz Florijana).
1829:   [P] O novoj žurnal'noj kritike.

Illičevskij, Aleksej
1826:   [P] Putešestvie iz Sent-Bernard.
        Tri slepca.
        Nadpis' k istočniku.
        N. N., podnosja ej jabloko.
        Ėpitafija.
        Madrigal.
1827:   [P] Primečatel'nyj slepoj.
        Sel'skaja sirota. Ėlegija Sume.
        Na drevnjuju vazu.
        Orel i čelovek.
        K bratu.
1828:   Tri soneta (Iz Mickeviča).
        K portretu Lomonosova.
        K časam, pri otsylke ix sestre.
        Oproveržennaja poslovica.
        Žaloba na sčastie.
        Sila nadeždy.
        Sočinitelju poslanij.
1829:   K statue Ariadny.
        K fantazii (Podražanie anglijskomu).

Kazanskij, D. [See *Delarju, Mixail*]

Katenin, Pavel
1829:   Staraja byl'.
1830:   Èlegija.

Kozlov, Ivan
1825:   *Good Night.* Dobraja noč' (Iz Bajrona).
        Son nevesty. Ballada.
        Kiev.
        Irlandskaja pesja (Iz Mura).
        K Kn. M. A. G., uroždennoj K. S.
1826:   Javlenie Klorindy Tankredu (Iz *Osvoboždennogo Ierusa-
        lima*).
        Stansy k Nikolaju Ivanoviču Gnediču (Na Kavkaz i
        Krym).
        Knjažne S. R——l' [with Pletnev].
        Evrejskaja melodija. Iz Bajrona.
        Na pogrebenie anglijskogo generala Sira Džona Mura.
1827:   Podražanie Šatobrianu o razzorenii Rima i o vosstanovlenii
        Xristianstva (Otryvok, posvjaščennyj Aleksandru Ivanoviču
        Turgenevu).
        Lunnaja noč' v Kremle (Iz poèmy: Natal'ja Dolgorukaja,
        posvjaščennoj V. A. Zukovskomu).
1828:   Večernij zvon. T. S. Vdmrv——oj.
1829:   Stancy (Vol'noe podražanie Adamu Mickeviču).
        Zarja pogasla.
1830:   K teni ee. *Hast thou prayed?*
        Iz bajronova *Don-Žuana* (Vol'noe podražanie).
1831:   Pesnja Desdemony (S Anglij.).

Komarov, Aleksandr
1832:   Noč'.
        Otryvok iz sel'skoj poèmy: Maša.

Korostylev, Aleksej [See *Bestužev, Nikolaj*]

Kosmokratov, T. T. [See *Titov, Vladimir*]

Kotljarevskij, Ivan
1830:   Malorossijskaja pesnja.

Krylov, Aleksandr
1825: V Al'bom N. N. V——oj.
1829: K Klenu (Podražanie Parni).
A. A. K——oj.

Krylov, Ivan
1825: Muxa i pčela. Basnja.
Bogač i poèt. Basnja.
Prixožanin. Basnja.
Lev sostarevšijsja.
Tri poceluja.
Lisica i osel.
1828: Alekseju Nikolaeviču Oleninu, pri dostavlenii poslednego izdanija Basen'.
1829: Èpitafija.
Britvy. Basnja.
Bednyj bogač.
Puški i parusa. Basnja.

Krjukov, Aleksandr
1829: 1. Noč'. 2. Luna. 3. Smert'.
Nečajannaja vstreča.
1830: [P] Kirgizskij nabeg (Druz'jam moim).

Lažečnikov, Ivan
1832: [P] Strašnyj sud (Otryvok iz romana: *Poslednij Novik*).

M.
1828: Pčela i motylek.

Maksimovič, Mixail
1832: [P] O žizni rastenij (Posvjaščaetsja M. P. V.).

Masal'skij, Konstantin
1825: More i zemlja (S Grečeskogo, 1820).
1826: Razvaliny.
1829: K ruč'ju. S Ispanskogo (Iz Vil'egasa).

Meščerskij, Knjaz' Aleksandr
1832: Stancy.

Nikitenko, Aleksandr
1832:   [P] Otryvok iz romana: *Leon ili Idealizm.*

Obodovskij, Platon
1825:   Vesennij gimn Vsederžitelju (Vo vremja pervogo groma).
1826:   Persidskij romans (Iz povesti: *Orsan i Leila*).
            Otryvki iz Persidskoj povesti: *Orsan i Leila.*
1827:   Otryvok iz Mjul'nerovoj tragedii: *Die Schuld.*
            Veličie mira (Podražanie Šilleru).
1828:   Končina Blagotvoritelja.
            Proročestvo o Messii.
1829:   Otryvok iz Šillerovoj tragedii: *Don Karlos.*
            Scena iz tragedii Šekspira: *Romeo i Julija.*
1830:   Èrminija (Sel'skaja èlegija).
            [?] Scena iz tragedii Šekspira *Romeo i Julija.*

Og——v, A.
1826:   Moja èpitafija (Podražanie Skarronu).

Odoevskij, Knjaz' Vladimir
1831:   [P] Poslednij kvartet Beetgovena.
1832:   [P] Opere del Cavaliere Giambattista Piranesi.

Oznobišin, Dmitrij
1826:   Mir fantazii.
1827:   Fialka (Podražanie Ibn-Rumi).

Ostolopov, Nikolaj
1825:   Kot i belka (Basnja).

P——ij
1825:   [P] Otryvki pisem iz Italii.

Pletnev, Petr
1825:   [P] Pis'mo k Grafine S. I. S. o russkix poètax.
            Izmena.
            Al'bom.
            A. N. S——voj.
            K I. I. Kozlovu.
            Razluka.

1826: Stansky k D***.
       S. M. S——oj (Sonet).
       Ideal.
       Ob"jasnenie.
       P. S., Knjažne S. R——l' [with Kozlov].
1827: Sadovnik.
       Rassudok i strast'.
       Vospominanie.
       Noč'.
1828: [P] O stixotvorenijax Baratynskogo.
       Bezvestnost'.
       Solovej.
1831: K N. I. Gnediču.
       Otryvok.

Pogodin, Mixail
1832: [P] Nečto o nauke (Otryvok iz pis'ma k Grafine N).

Podolinskij, Andrej
1828: Firdousi.
       Stansy.
1829: Sirota.
       Dva strannika.
1830: Protivopoložnosti.
       Gurija.

Puškin, Aleksandr
1825: Pesn' o veščem Olege.
       Demon.
       Otryvki iz *Evgenija Onegina*, poèmy A. Puškina.
       Prozerpina.
1826: [P] Otryvok iz pis'ma A. S. Puškina k D.
       Podražanija Koranu.
       Baratynskomu. Iz Bessarabii.
       Emu že.
       Otryvki iz vtoroj pesni *Evgenija Onegina*, poèmy A. Puškina.
       Otryvok iz poèmy: *Cygany*.
1827: Pis'mo Tat'jany. (Iz 3-ej Pesni *Evgenija Onegina*).
       Otryvok iz III glavy *Evgenija Onegina*.
       K***.
       19 Oktjabrja.

1828:   [P] Otryvki iz pisem. mysli i zamečanija.
        Graf Nulin.
        Otryvok iz Borisa Godunova. 1604. 16 Oktjabrja. Granica
        Litovskaja.
        Èlegija.
        Angel.
        Čerep (Poslanie k D.).
1829:   [P] IV Glava iz istoričeskogo romana.
        Vospominanie.
        Ty i vy.
        Dva vorona.
        Ljubopytnyj.
        To Dawe, Esqr.
        Podražanie Anakreonu.
        Otvet Kateninu.
        K I. V. S.
        Napersnik.
        Predčuvstvie.
        Gorod pyšnyj.
        Ne poj, krasavica, pri mne.
        Otvet.
        K Ja.
        Portret.
        V Al'bom P. A. O.
1830:   [P] Otryvok iz literaturnyx letopisej.
        Otryvok iz VII glavy *Evgenija Onegina.*
        Zimnij večer.
        Èpigramma.
        Olegov ščit.
        2-go Nojabrja.
        K**.
        Ja vas ljubil.
        K N. N.
        Èpigramma.
        26 Maija 1828.
1831:   Poètu (Sonet).
        Otvet anonimu.
        Monastyr' na Kazbeke.
        Otryvok.
        Obval.
1832:   *Mocart i Sal'eri.*
        Anfologičeskie èpigrammy.

Dorožnye žaloby.
Èxo.
Delibaš.
Ančar, drevo jada.
Besy.

Puškin, Vasilij
1829:   Otryvok iz povesti: Kapitan Xrabrov.

R——a, Z——ja
1831:   Ljubila ja.

Raič, Semen
1826:   K Lide. Podražanie K. Gallu.

Rozen, Baron Egor
1829:   Tajna rozy (Podražanie arabskomu).
1830:   Put' ljubvi.
          Venčal'nyj obrjad.
          Mogil'naja roza.
1832:   Pastušij rog v Peterburge.
          Prokljatie.
          Grečanke.

Rostopčina, Evdokija
1831:   Talisman

Rotčev, Aleksandr
1827:   Podražanie arabskomu.
1829:   Mnimomu klassiku.
          T'ma (Iz Lorda Bajrona).
1830:   V al'bom K. N. U——voj.

Senkovskij, Osip
1828:   [P] Beduinka. Vostočnaja povest'.
1830:   [P] Vor. Arabskaja povest'.

Skljarevskij, P.
1827:   Pljaska (Iz Šillera).

Somov, Orest

1827: [P] Jurodivyj. Malorossijskaja byl'.
1828: [P] Obzor rossijskoj slovesnosti za 1827 god.
[P] Gajdamak (Otryvok iz malorossijskoj povesti).
1829: [P] Obzor rossijskoj slovesnosti za 1828 god.
1830: [P] Obozrenie Rossijskoj Slovesnosti za pervuju polovinu 1829 goda.
[P] Kikimora (Rasskaz russkogo krest'janina na bol'soj doroge).
1831: [P] Obozrenie Rossijskoj Slovesnosti za vtoruju polovinu 1829 i pervuju 1830 goda.
1832: [P] Svatovstvo (Iz vospominanij starika o ego molodosti).
[P] Živoj v obiteli blaženstva večnogo (Mečta).

Stavelov, N.

1832: Strannik.

Stankevič, Nikolaj

1831: Filin (Perevod).
1832: Pesn' duxov nad vodami (Iz Gete).
Boj časov na Spasskoj bašne.

Strujskij, Dmitrij

1831: [P] Vyderžki iz zapisnoj knižki.
Al'pijskie sosny.
Slezy.
1832: [P] Duma. Posvjaščena pamjati Grafa Kapodistria (Otr.).
T'ma (Podražanie Bajronu).
Vozroždenie.

Suxanov, Mixail

1828: Cvetok i ternovnik. Basnja.

Teplova, Nadežda

1832: Jazyk očej.
K nej.
Ljubov'.

Teplova, Serafima

1832: Sestre v al'bom.

Tepljakov, Viktor
1830: Stranniki.
1831: [P] Pis'mo III iz Turcii. Varna, 14 Aprelja 1829 goda.
Pervaja Frakijskaja èlegija. Otplytie.
Sovremennoe blagopolučie.
Rumilijskaja pesnja.
1832: Žestokij prizrak.
The Blue Stockings.

Timaševa, Ekaterina
1831: Otvet.
1832: K zastenčivomu.
K nezabvennomu.

Titov, Vladimir
1829: [P] Uedinennyj domik na vasil'evskom. Povest'.
1831: [P] Monastyr' Sv. Brigity (Povest').

Trilunnyj [See Strujskij, Dmitrij]

Tumanskij, Vasilij
1825: Moja ljubov'.
Èlegija.
1828: Prekrasnym glazam.
1830: Spasi menja.
Pensée (Posv. Gr. E. P. P.).
1831: Mysl' o juge.
Gondol'er i poèt (Perevod neizdannyx stixov A. šen'e).
Romans (Na golos val'sa Beetgovena).
Sud'ba.
Ideal.

Tumanskij, Fedor
1825: K——.
1826: Èlegija.
K uvjadajuščej krasavice.
Molitva.
Èlegija.
1827: 18 Aprelja.
Ptička.
1830: Rodina.

Xomjakov, Aleksej
1830:   Proščanie s Adrianopolem.

——*č*
1832:   Polnoč'.

Šaxovskoj, Knjaz' Aleksandr
1832:   Svodnye deti. Basnja.
        Nadpisi k dvum gruppam tvorenija I. P. Martosa.

Šibaev, N. I.
1831:   Neapol'.
        Èlegija.
1832:   Utešenie (Iz A. Šen'e).

Ševyrev, Stepan
1826:   Večer (Iz Sillera).
        Lilija i roza (V al'bom T. E. E——oj).
1831:   Čtenie Danta.
        Dve pesni. Ljubov' do sčastija i posle.
        Širokko.
        Oda Goracija poslednjaja (IV, k. 16).
        K Febu.
        Trojstvo.

Šemiot, Valentin
1827:   Èlegija (Iz Parni) 1825.
1830:   Druz'jam.

Šiškov, Aleksandr Ardal'onovič
1830:   Èl'fa.

Sčastnyj, Vasilij
1829:   Beseda miloj devy.
        Kto pripodnjal neskromnoju rukoj.
1831:   Otryvok iz dramatičeskoj poèmy Iosifa Korženevskogo:
        Otšel'nik.
1832:   Tureckaja pesnja.
        Otryvok iz dramatičeskoj poèmy: *Otšel'nik.*
        Kamin.
        Dva želanija.

Jazykov, Nikolaj
1826:   Otryvok iz povesti Ala.
         Dve kartimy.
         Slava Bogu.
1828:   K njane.
1829:   A. N. V——fu.
         Baronu A. A. Del'vigu.
1831:   Èlegija.
1832:   Pesnja.
         Im.
         Bessonnica.
         K——e K——e Ja——'.
         I. V. K. (Ob I. V.).
         A. A. Del'vigu.

Jakovlev, Mixail [*Luk'janovič* or *Alekseevič?*]
1826:   Èlegija.
1827:   Èpigramma.

Jakubovič, Luk'jan
1832:   Iran (Iz Gafiza).
         Muzyka.
         Mol'ba.
         Ukrainskie melodii 1 & 2.
         Lešij.
         Zima.

l—— 8——
1827:   Son Zlodeja (Iz Sadija).
         Odinočestvo (Iz Lamartina).

Works appearing over asterisks and those completely un-identified. The first lines of poetic works have been given to assist those who seek to identify these pieces.

1825
   [P] Afonskaja gora.   Otryvok iz putešestvija po Grecii v 1820 godu.
Cvety, vybrannye iz Grečeskoj Anfologii.

Car' Fuleskij (Iz Gete)   [Byl v Fule car'; emu drug milyj] [Perhaps Zagorskij].

1826

[P] Firdausi.

[P] Russkie poklonniki v Ierusalime   (Otryvok iz putešestvija po Grecii i Palestine v 1820 godu).

Podražanie 136 Psalmu   (Na čužyx beregax, gde vlastvuet tiran).

17 Sentjabrja 1824 [Blažen, komu s privetlivoj ulybkoj].

Poščada pevca   [Zevs, naxmurjas', gljadel na drevnjuju grexnicu zemlju].

Nadpis' k Portretu Lirika   [Potomstvo! vot Petrov].

1827

[P] Otryvki pisem iz Italii.   20 Nojabrja 1824 goda, Neapol'.

1828

Xarakteristika   [Obrityj, blednyj i xudoj].

Nadpisi k izobraženijam nekotoryx Ital'janskix Poètov. 1. Dante, 2. Petrarka. 3. Grob Ariosta, 4. Tasso.

Nadeždy   (S Nemeckogo) [Nežnym vesennim cvetam nadeždy smertnyx podobny].

Padajuščie zvezdy   (Podraž. Beranžeru) [Ty, deduška, po zvezdam znaeš'].

Partizany. Otryvok [V lesu dremučem, na poljane].

1829

[P] O novoustroennoj cerkvi pri obuxovskoj gradskoj bol'nice.

1830

Èlegija [Dovol'no! vižu: ot menja].

1831

Trizna   [Utixnul boj Gafurskij].

Luna   [Vstal veter s zapada].

Bal   [Otkrylsja bal. Kružas', leteli].

1832

[P] Otryvok iz kitajskogo romana: *Xau-Cju-Džuan'*, t. e. bezprimernyj brak.   Perevod s Kitajskogo.

Ubegajuščej krasavice   [O! ne begi tak skoro ot menja].

Contents by Years

These tables of contents are based on the authors' names and titles as they appear in the various issues, not as they appear in the tables of contents found in the almanacs themselves. The latter, when provided, sometimes list only titles or list titles by author; often they are incomplete. Standard transliteration has been used to render authors' names and titles. Information within brackets was supplied by myself.

I. *Severnye Cvety na 1825 god*

PROZA

POÈZIJA

II. *Severnye Cvety na 1826 god*

P R O Z A

POÈZIJA

III. *Severnye Cvety na 1827 god*

PROZA

IV. *Severnye Cvety na 1828 god*

PROZA

V. *Severnye Cvety na 1829 god*

PROZA

POÈZIJA

VI. *Severnye Cvety na 1830 god*

PROZA

VII. *Severnye Cvety na 1831 god*

PROZA

POÈZIJA

VIII. *Severnye Cvety na 1832 god*

PROZA

NOTES

I. Introduction to the Period: 1825 - 1832

1. Ivan Goncharov and Mikhail Lermontov both attended the University of Moscow wiith Belinsky and Stankevich but took little or no part in their philosophico-literary circles.
2. There is no good English translation of *narodnost* [narodnost']. Roughly, it means "national identity" or "national essence." *Narod* itself means "people" or "nation," and the *-nost* ending is a common suffix for abstract nouns.

II. History of *Northern Flowers*

1. "Zametka o Poljarnoj Zvezde i Severnyx Cvetax," *Russkij Arxiv*, II (1873), xcviii.
2. A. I. Del'vig, *Moi vospominanija* (Moskva, 1912–13), I, p. 76.
3. *Russkaja Starina*, LXIV (1889), 376.
4. See Ryleev's letter of 7 September, 1823, K. F. Ryleev, *Polnoe sobranie sočinenij* (Moskva-Leningrad, 1934), pp. 469–70.
5. Bulgarin coined the word "Voyeykovism" to describe this activity. See *Poljarnaja Zvezda* (Moskva-Leningrad, 1960), p. 889.
6. *Literaturnyj Arxiv* (Moskva-Leningrad, 1938), I, p. 422. It is unlikely that an earlier protest against unauthorized reprinting which Ryleev and Bestuzhev drafted in the summer of 1823 was specifically intended for Voyeykov, as is theorized in the comments to this draft in *Literaturnoe Nasledstvo 59,* (Moskva, 1954), 140. On the first of July, Ryleev wrote a very friendly letter to Voyeykov, and his subsequent patron-

age of Voyeykov in September in the affair with Bulgarin would indicate that his relations with Voyeykov were amiable at that time. This would hardly have been the case if he had envisaged Voyeykov as the principal addressee of the following protest: "The editors of *Polar Star* request all collectors of so-called literary news, exemplary compositions and similar literary mosaics to spare their publication and not arbitrarily reprint from it either prose or verse. Otherwise, if anyone henceforth intends to make use of the barbaric right of corsairs, then we in turn will not fail to use the European right of embargo" (*ibid.*). Of course, it was one thing to reprint without permission, which many did, but quite another to pirate a hitherto unpublished work intended for another journal. The latter action by Voyeykow in connection with *The Robber Brothers* was really unprecedented and unconscionable.

7. *Literaturnoe Nasledstvo 60* (Moskva, 1956), č. 1, 224.

8. *Ibid.*, 226.

9. See Comments to "The Unpublished Correspondence of Ryleev," *Literaturnoe Nasledstvo 59*, 150; Puškin, *Polnoe sobranie sočinenij v desjati tomax* (Moskva-Leningrad, 1949), I, p. 432.

10. Puškin, *Polnoe sobranie sočinenij v desjati tomax*, II, p. 245.

11. He apparently read final proof. See "Poljarnaja Zvezda i Nevskij Al'manax," *Russkaja Starina*, XVIII (1901), 267.

12. *Sočinenija i perepiski Ryleeva* (Sanktpeterburg, 1874), p. 308.

13. *Literaturnoe Nasledstvo 60*, č 1, 228.

14. *Ibid.*

15. *Moskovskij Telegraf*, 1825, č 1. 330. Quoted in V. Maslov, *Literaturnaja dejatel'nost Ryleeva* (Kiev, 1911–12), pp. 371–72.

16. *Literaturnoe Nasledstvo 59*, 148.

17. Ryleev, *Polnoe sobranie sočinenij*, p. 494.

18. *Ibid.*

19. In view of these exterior indications of a continuing amity between Ryleev and Delvig, the commentaries and footnotes to Letter No. 8 (Ryleev to Bulgarin) published in *Literaturnoe Nasledstvo 59*, which suggest that relations between the two were increasingly strained in 1825, seem hardly justified.

20. Ryleev, *Polnoe sobranie, sočinenij*, p. 497.

21. Ryleev, an official of the Russian-American Company, was

head of the Northern Society, a secret revolutionary group. Bestuzhev, a military officer, became a member of the Northern Society's Supreme Council in April, 1825. For their roles in the December Uprising Ryleev was executed and Bestuzhev sentenced to penal servitude. After imprisonment in Finland and exile in Siberia, Bestuzhev was allowed to join the Russian army as a soldier. He served with distinction in the campaigns against the Caucasian tribesmen and was made an officer in 1836. The following year he was killed during a landing near Adler on the coast of the Black Sea.

22. In his letters to Pushkin of March 25 and May 12, Ryleev had already referred to his forthcoming almanac as *Little Star*. However, this probably reflected a sort of facetious modesty rather than indicating that already in the spring of 1825 he had determined to limit the scope of the following issue. Note that in November, 1825, Ryleev used the term *Polar* [*Star*] in referring to the almanac then in press.

23. See *Poljarnaja Zvezda*, pp. 885–86. This volume contains the reconstructed work.

24. "Pis'ma, soxranivšiesja v bumagax VI. Vas. Izmajlova (Pis'ma Oresta Somova)," *Moskovskoe Obozrenie*, 1877, No. 23, 290.

25. *Ibid.*

26. *Snowdrop* also appeared in 1830, but Delvig was apparently not directly involved. It was published by Aladin; possibly Somov served as managing editor.

27. The record was shared by Aladin's *Neva Almanac* [*Nevskij Almanax*], which was published continuously from 1825 to 1833.

28. Puškin, *Pis'ma*, pod red. V. L. Modzalevskogo (Moskva-Leningrad, 1926–35), II, pp. 398–400.

29. Puškin, *Polnoe sobranie sočinenij v desjati tomax*, VII, p. 149.

30. *Ibid.*, III, p. 168.

31. Puškin, *Pis'ma*, II, pp. 421–22.

32. *Ibid.*, p. 428.

33. Karlovo was the name of Bulgarin's estate near Dorpat.

34. Puškin, *Pis'ma*, II, p. 421.

35. A. I. Del'vig, *Moi vospominanija*, I, 111–12.

36. Puškin, *Pis'ma*, III, p. 492.

37. See N. K. Zamkov, "K istorii 'Literaturnoj Gazety' barona A. A. Del'viga," *Russkaja Starina*, CLXVI (1916). 272. Delvig was even prepared to complain to the Tsar, but he was dis-

suaded by Count Dmitry Bludov, who explained that one
might complain to the Tsar about anything but not about
Benckendorff. Bludov did extract from Benckendorff a grudg-
ing apology to Delvig, but the *Literary Gazette* was only allowed to continue with Orest Somov as editor. It struggled
on until mid-1831.

38. The sentence repeats the first lines of a poem by Glinka in
    Northern Flowers for 1831.
39. Puškin, *Pis'ma*, III, p. 5.
40. Puškin, *Pis'ma*, II, pp. 428–29.
41. Puškin, *Pis'ma*, III, p. 10.
42. *Ibid.*, p. 187.
43. *Ibid.*, p. 16.
44. *Ibid.*, p. 34.
45. *Ibid.*, p. 343.
46. *Ibid.*, p. 35.
47. *Ibid.*, p. 379.
48. *Ibid.*, p. 41.
49. *Ibid.*, p. 47. Pushkin's reference to Delvig's widow having
    lost the major part of her small estate alludes to the theft
    of a large sum of cash from the Delvigs' house at the time of
    the Baron's death.
50. *Ibid.*, p. 54.
51. *Ibid.*, p. 55.
52. *Ibid.*, p. 405.
53. *Ibid.*, p. 55.
54. *Ibid.*, p. 439. Pushkin did not use all the material which Glinka
    sent.
55. *Ibid.*, p. 405.
56. Two of Somov's letters to Pushkin relating to the publica-
    tion of *Northern Flowers for 1832* are to be found in "Neiz-
    dannye pis'ma k Puškinu," *Literaturnoe Nasledstvo 16–18*
    (Moskva, 1934), 588–92. The commentary of Yu. Oksman
    accompanying these letters is most interesting.

III.   Appearance and General Contents of the Eight Issues

1. The author was Vasily Ivanovich Grigorovich (1792–1865),
   Secretary of the Academy of Arts.

IV.   Literary Criticism in *Northern Flowers*

1. *Severnye Cvety na 1825 god.* 3–80.
2. Puškin, *Pis'ma,* pod red. V. L. Modzalevskogo (Moska-Leningrad, 1926–35), III, p. 114.
3. *Ibid.,* p. 122.
4. *Poljarnaja Zvezda* (Moska-Leningrad, 1960), p. 877.
5. See "Literaturno-èstetičeskie pozicii 'Poljarnoj zvezdy,' " *Ibid.,* pp. 838 ff.
6. Confirmation can be found in Pushkin's letter to Zhukovsky of late May or early June, 1825. "You ask what the purpose of *The Gypsies* is? That's one for you. The purpose of poetry is poetry as Delvig says (if he didn't steal it)" (Puškin, *Pis'ma,* I p. 134).
7. *Severnye Cvety na 1829 god,* 23. The *Observer* died with its first issue.
8. V. Orlov links "To the Journalistic Twins" with the conflict centering around Griboedov's *Woe From Wit,* a portion of which was published in 1825 in Bulgarin's *Russian Thalia.* This is hardly likely, since Vyazemsky's epigram appeared before the onset of the polemics around Griboedov's play. See V. Orlov, *Èpigramma i satira istorii literaturnoj bor'by XIX-go veka* (Moskva-Leningrad, 1931), p. 204.
9. Note that Pletnyev in his "Letter" included both Pisarev and Mikhail Dmitriev among his preferred poets. Though Pisarev was openly antagonistic to the misty melancholy of Zhukovsky, he was respected by most of the younger generation of writers for his accomplishments as a playwright; Mikhail Dmitriev was opposed to the extremes of both the Classicist and Romantic camps.
10. The wit does not lend itself to translation: "Ty govoriš', čto ja raskol'nik,/Ja govorju: ty starover." *Raskolnik* implies breaking away from tradition, *starover* implies holding conservative ideas. Both terms are applied to those who broke with the official Orthodox Church in the seventeenth century.
11. *Severnye Cvety na 1828 god,* 151–52.
12. *Severnye Cvety na 1831 god,* 7.
13. See my "Pushkin's Concept of Romanticism," *Studies in Romanticism,* III (Autumn, 1963), 38–9.
14. *Severnye Cvety na 1829 god,* 27.

15. *Severnye Cvety na 1828 god,* 17.

16. *Ibid.,* 21.

17. *Ibid.,* 78–79.

18. *Severnye Cvety na 1829 god,* 83–84.

19. *Severnye Cvety na 1831 god,* 74.

20. *Ibid.,* 56–57.

21. *Severnye Cvety na 1828 god,* 9.

22. *Severnye Cvety na 1830 god,* 48.

23. Three later volumes of Bulgarin's *Works* were also pointedly ignored, except for Pogodin's *Moscow Herald* which, as an answer to Somov, justified the general silence on the grounds that these volumes did not represent "literary news."

24. *Sevrnye Cvety na 1828 god.* 51–52.

25. *Ibid.,* 54.

26. *Severnye Cvety na 1830 god,* 92–93.

27. V. V. Danilov, "O. M. Somov, sotrudnik Del'viga i Puškina," *Russkij Filologičeskij Vestnik,* LX (1908), 197.

28. *Severnye Cvety na 1831 god,* 14.

29. Educated in the cadet corps school, Bulgarin served with the Uhlans in the wars of 1805–7. Dismissed from the service for disciplinary reasons, he later entered a French Uhlan regiment and subsequently fought the Russians. After his capture in 1814 he was tried for treason and acquitted (Puškin, *Pis'ma,* I, p. 305).

30. *Severnye Cvety na 1831 god* 69–70. In an article entitled "What was said in praise of the works of F. Bulgarin when the honorable O. M. Somov collaborated with the periodical publications of N. I. Grech and F. Bulgarin and what Mr. Somov said against the works of F. Bulgarin when the honorable O. M. Somov ceased collaborating with the periodicals of N. I. Grech and F. Bulgarin," Bulgarin called attention to the change in Somov's evaluation of his works after Somov had been dismissed from *Northern Bee.* See N. Zamkov, "K istorii 'Literaturnoj Gazety' barona A. A. Del'viga," *Russkaja Starina,* CLXVI (1916), 280. Of course, Bulgarin's appraisal of Somov's talent underwent an equally extensive change (Danilov, "O. M. Somov," 146).

31. Puškin, *Pis'ma,* III, p. 34.

32. This was in an unfinished "Rebuttal Against Criticism" begun in Boldino in 1830. Puškin, *Polnoe sobranie sočinenij v desjati tomax* (Moskva-Leningrad, 1949). VII, p. 167.

33. *Severnye Cvety na 1828 god*, 223–25.
34. *Ibid.*, 198–99.
35. *Severnye Cvety na 1831 god*, 15.
36. *Ibid.*, 25.
37. *Ibid.*, 94–95.
38. *Puškin-Kritik* (Moskva-Leningrad, 1934), p. 166.
39. *Ibid.*, pp. 163 ff. The version in *Northern Flowers* does not contain direct references to Glinka, Izmailov, and the Moscow Censorship Board. Otherwise, however, it is as complete as the draft composed in 1829, in which Pushkin did detail their roles.
40. *Severnye Cvety na 1828 god*, 25.
41. *Severnye Cvety na 1829 god*, 10.
42. He asked Pogodin to collaborate with him on a history of Peter the Great.
43. *Severnye Cvety na 1830 god*, 55–56.
44. *Severnye Cvety na 1827 god*, 56–57.
45. *Severnye Cvety na 1830 god*, 36.
46. *Ibid.*, 37.
47. Among others, Prince Vyazemsky. In a letter dated April 7, 1829, to I. I. Dmitriev, he wrote: "I can't understand how Raich could lower himself to such a degree. His *Galatea* reminds me of those old women in Moscow who trade in rotten apples on street corners: the same kind of goods and the same abusive language." See Puškin, *Pis'ma*, II, p. 378.
48. *Ibid.*, pp. 37–38.
49. *Ibid.*
50. *Severnye Cvety na 1828 god*, 304.
51. *Ibid.*, 308.
52. Baratynsky's reputation as a poet diminished in the course of his lifetime.
53. *Severnye Cvety na 1828 god*, 80.
54. *Severnye Cvety na 1829 god*, 17.
55. *Severnye Cvety na 1831 god*, 46.
56. *Severnye Cvety na 1830 god*, 77–78.
57. Gogol's "The Fearful Wild Boar" appeared in the *Literary Gazette*, III (January 1, 1831) under the title "The Teacher." However, the issue of the *Literary Gazette* was delayed and thus came out somewhat later than *Northern Flowers for 1831*.

V. Poetry and Poets

1. Dates in parentheses indicate the issue of *Northern Flowers* in which the particular work appeared.
2. The piece was inspired by an anonymous poem, identified as the work of the Egyptologist I. A. Gulyanov, which expressed the conviction that Pushkin's marriage would give new inspiration to his poetry.
3. The complete list of authors and titles is in Appendix A.
4. This was written at the end of his career. See P. A. Vjazemskij, *Polnoe sobranie sočinenij* (S.-Peterburg, 1878–96), X, p. 43.
5. Puškin, *Pis'ma*, pod red. V. L. Modzalevskogo (Moska-Leningrad, 1926–35), II, p. 11.
6. This epigram was composed in 1821 or earlier.
7. Many similar works appeared during the same period in other almanacs and journals.
8. Pushkin provided comments and suggestions on textual revisions, some of which Vyazemsky incorporated in the published version.
9. *Severnye Cvety na 1831 god*, 112.
10. This matter is discussed in Chapter II.
11. *A History of Russian Literature* (New York, 1949), p. 79.
12. *Severnye Cvety na 1830 god*, 32.
13. Baratynsky's comments are fully presented and discussed in Tomashevsky's notes to A. A. Del'vig, *Polnoe sobranie stixotvorenij* (Leningrad, 1959), pp. 329–31.
14. *Severnye Cvety na 1828 god*, 96.
15. A. A. Del'vig, *Polnoe sobranie stixotvorenij*. p. 325.
16. *Severnye Cvety na 1830 god*, 94.
17. In July, 1831, Pushkin wrote to Pletnyev in connection with the memorial issue of the almanac: "Write Baratynsky—he'll send us a treasure" (Puškin, *Pis'ma*, III, p. 34). But Baratynsky didn't respond, probably because he had nothing to send. In a letter to Kireevsky he declared: "I am answering all compilers of almanacs that I have no verses, and in a few days I'll answer the same to Pushkin" (*ibid.*, p. 344). Baratynsky's deep affection for Delvig, coupled with Pushkin's insistence on a contribution, apparently brought forth "My Elision."
18. Italics mine. Baratynsky here repeats the locutions which are

typical of Zhukovsky's imitators. *Severnye Cvety na 1827 god*, 336.

19. Lines 485–533 of *The Ball* (1828) and fragments from Chapters II and V of *The Concubine* (1831).
20. *Polnoe sobranie sočinenij E. A. Boratynskago*, pod red. M. L. Gofmana (Petrograd, 1915), II, p. 247.
21. *Ibid.*, 257–63. Bulgarin, who openly kept a mistress, pretended to be scandalized by the appearance of *The Concubine* and even reluctant to review the almanac containing it. Puškin, *Pis'ma*, III, p. 170.
22. Wolfe would be completely forgotten but for this one poem.
23. "Javlenie Klorindy Tankredu (Iz Osvoboždennogo Ierusalima)."
24. *Severnye Cvety na 1829 god*, 126.
25. *Literaturnoe Nasledstvo* 19–21 (Moska, 1935), 51.
26. Further evidence of this interest is shown by Bulgarin's "The Fall of Venden" and Titov's "The Monastery of Saint Bridget."
27. "Two Pictures" was originally to be published in *Little Star*; it was given to *Northern Flowers* after *Little Star* was suppressed.
28. A. A. Del'vig, *Polnoe sobranie stixotvorenij*, p. 163.
29. *Severnye Cvety na 1832 god*, 185.
30. *Ibid.*, 186.
31. Another fable with a similar title, "The Bee and the Fly," concerns the preference of indolent Russians for life abroad.
32. *Severnye Cvety na 1825 god*, 291.
33. *Severnye Cvety na 1829 god*, 68.
34. *Severnye Cvety na 1825 god*, 285.
35. *Ibid.*, 260. Italics his.
36. In the course of his career, Zhukovsky translated ballads of Uhland, Goethe, Southey, and Walter Scott, but his best efforts, according to Belinsky, were represented by three of the nine or so ballads he translated from Schiller.
37. *Severnye Cvety na 1829 god*, 76.
38. *Severnye Cvety na 1828 god*, 23. Italics mine.
39. A number of the members of this society were employed in the Moscow archives of the Ministry of Foreign Affairs. and thus they are also identified as Archive Youths [Arxivnye junoši]. Odoevsky, with Wilhelm Küchelbecker, edited the almanac *Mnemosyne*, which served unofficially as the organ of this group. It appeared in four parts in 1824 and 1825. Both

the almanac and the society were discontinued as an act of prudence following the Decembrist Uprising.

40. D. V. Venevitinov, *Polnoe sobranie sočinenij* (Moskva-Leningrad, 1934), p. 442.

41. Puškin, *Polnoe sobranie sočinenij* (n.p. 1937–50), XI, p. 220.

42. An original tragedy, *Andromache*, was finished in 1818, after nine years of effort.

43. *Severnye Cvety na 1829 god*, 120.

44. *Severnye Cvety na 1830 god*. 15.

45. Puškin, *Polnoe sobranie sočinenij v desjati tomax*, (Moskva-Leningrad, 1949), VII, p. 125.

46. *Puškin, Pis'ma*, III, p. 5.

47. *Severnye Cvety na 1826 god*, 122.

48. *Severnye Cvety na 1828 god*, 67.

49. Probably Alexandre Soumet, 1788–1845, whom Illichevsky may have met while in France.

50. Prince Vyazemsky in 1827 translated the *Crimean Sonnets* into prose, and poetic translations by Kozlov, Poznansky, Shchastny, and Illichevsky of various individual sonnets shortly appeared.

51. Puškin, *Pis'ma*, I, p. 243.

52. This fact itself makes even more dubious the idea put forth in "The Literary-Aesthetic Position of *Polar Star*" (see *Poljarnaja Zvezda*, [Moskva-Leningrad, 1960], pp. 803 ff.) which would have it that Pletnyev broke with Bestuzhev as a result of the latter's criticism of him and Delvig in "A Look at the Old and the New Literature in Russia," the lead article in *Polar Star for 1823*. Presumably, this incited Pletnyev to the negative review of *Polar Star* in the *Emulator of Enlightenment*, for which he was censured by members of the Free Society. According to this interpretation, this conflict led Delvig and Pletnyev to plan a competitive almanac, i.e., *Northern Flowers*. All this is highly questionable. That Pletnyev maintained good relations with the editors of *Polar Star* is evident from Ryleev's letter to Pushkin in April of 1825, where he mentions having been at Pletnyev's house. Further, in *Polar Star for 1824* Bestuzhev complimented Pletnyev's poetry in his critical survey, "A Look at Russian Literature During 1823." While one cannot ignore a few minor tensions between those involved in the editorial work for *Polar Star* and *Northern Flowers*, particularly after the latter's initial success, it is quite incorrect to imply that the

establishment of *Northern Flowers* was a sort of anti-Decembrist conspiracy.

53. *Severnye Cvety na 1826 god*, 83.

54. See Puškin, *Pis'ma*, I, p. 36. The letter was written in 1822.

55. N. V. Gerbel'. *Russkie Poèty* (Sanktpeterburg, 1873), p. 247.

56. *Severnye Cvety na 1831 god*, 58. Pletnyev's poem had been published previously, but only fragments of Gnedich's reply had appeared theretofore. See editor's note to "K. N. I. Gnediču" (*ibid.*, 57).

57. *Severnye Cvety na 1832 god*, 181.

58. Puškin, *Pis'ma*, III, p. 18.

59. Perhaps the most interesting aspect of this translation is Pushkin's footnote, which begins: "Many of the tragedies ascribed to Shakespeare do not belong to him but were simply edited by him. The tragedy *Romeo and Juliet*, which by its style completely differs from his known methods, so clearly enters into his dramatic system and bears so many traces of his free and expansive brush that one must consider it Shakespeare's composition." See *Severnye Cvety na 1830 god*, 108–10.

60. Many of the Romantics considered Shakespeare, along with Calderón, Lope de Vega. and Corneille, as their precursor.

61. See Ryleev's letter to Tumansky of 3 October, 1823. K. F. Ryleev, *Polnoe sobranie sočinenij* (Moskva-Leningrad, 1934), p. 472.

62. Puškin, *Pis'ma*, I, p. 70. See also Pushkin's earlier letter to his brother of August, 1823 (*ibid.*, p. 53).

63. *Ibid.*, p. 152.

64. *Severnye Cvety na 1831 god*, 6.

65. Puškin, *Polnoe sobranie sočinenij v desjati tomax*, V, p. 204.

66. Gerbel states that only eight of his poems appeared in print (*Russkie Poèty*, p. 333). This is obviously incorrect.

67. See note 39 for this chapter.

68. Anyone daring to criticize Bulgarin did so at the risk of personal abuse and negative reviews. Pushkin referred to Shevyrev as "a hero." See Pushkin's letter to Pogodin of 19 February, 1828, Puškin, *Pis'ma*, II, p. 47.

69. *Ibid.*, p. 266.

70. His name was omitted from the index of contributors of poetry in the 1832 edition, despite his having four poems in that issue.

71. He and N. M. Konshin were coeditors of the almanac

Tsarskoe Selo in 1830. Rozen himself published the almanac *Alcyone* from 1831 to 1833.

72. Puškin, *Pis'ma*, III, p. 152. The translation was not published.

73. Count A. S. Stroganov and A. N. Olenin, directors of the Imperial Public Libraary, were responsible for this appointment.

74. A small volume containing twelve of these songs, published the same year, met with Pushkin's enthusiastic approval: "Your Greek songs are charming and a tour de force" (Puškin, *Pis'ma*, I, p. 118).

75. Gerbel', *Russkie Poèty*, p. 201.

76. *Severnye Cvety na 1831 god*, 65–66.

77. The title figure of the melodramatic novel by the Irish author, Charles Maturin.

78. His collected poems were published in 1832.

79. Podolinsky was able to render a small service to Pushkin in Chernigov. Pushkin wished to send a letter with Podolinsky to General Raevsky, but lacked his personal seal; the youth was able to loan him his own, since their initials were the same—AP. Podolinsky, who had begun to write verses in school, regarded this coincidence of initials as a happy augury for his future success as a poet (Gerbel', *Russkie Poèty*, p. 374).

80. Gajdenkov, *Russkie poèty XIX veka* (Moskva, 1964), p. 404; Puškin, *Pis'ma*, III, p. 250.

81. Gerbel', *Russkie Poèty*, p. 375.

82. Eight line stanzas of trochaic tetrameter, with aBaBcDcD rhyme scheme.

83. There is some general information about Yakubovich in "Dlja biografii I. P. Saxarova," *Russkij Arxiv*, II (1873), 656–58. See also I. I. Panaev, *Literaturnye Vospominija* (Leningrad, 1950), pp. 65–66.

84. Yakubovich's collected poems appeared in 1837.

85. Two of his fables were printed in *Polar Star*, but then the list of that almanac's contributors included many persons less congenial to the political aims of the editors than Izmailov.

86. At least one of his works in *Polar Star* deserves attention: "Mamay's Attack (A Song of Boyan)" ["Našestvie Mamaja (Pesn' Bajana)"]. The poem begins with an introduction in imitation of *The Lay of the Host of Igor* [*Slovo o polku Igoreve*]; it lauds the heroism of those who defended Rus and

concludes on the theme that love of freedom is the supreme force. Its "civic" content was quite in keeping with Decembrist philosophy, elsewhere expressed in the poetry of Ryleev.

87. His birth date is incorrectly given in Brokgauz-Efron as 1813. The obituary in *Northern Bee* noted that he died at the age of thirty-one. See Peter Brang, *Puškin und Krjukov, zur Entstehungsgeschichte der "Kapitanskaja Dočka"* (Berlin, 1957), p. 21.

88. Peter Brang has established that Kryukov was also the author of "The Story of My Grandmother" ["Rasskaz moej babuški"], which appeared in the *Neva Almanac* [*Nevskij Almanax*] in 1832. The work had previously always been attributed to A. Kornilovich on the basis of its having been signed "A. K." Brang established the extensive influence of this work on Pushkin's *The Captain's Daughter* [*Kapitanskaja dočka*].

89. He first was published in 1827. *Hannibal on the Ruins of Carthage* [*Annibal na razvalinax Karfagena*] was given a poor review by Prince Vyazemsky (Puškin, *Pis'ma*, III, p. 298), and Orest Somov, in his debut as a critic for *Northern Flowers* in 1828, spoke of the monologues in the work as "long and boring" *Severnye Cvety na 1828 god*, 47). See the discussion of Pushkin's negative reaction to Struisky's "The Tomb of Kutuzov" ["Grobnica Kutuzova"] in *Pis'ma*, III, p. 298. Pushkin wrote to Madam Khitrovo that Struisky did not fulfill her commission to translate this work into French prose, because he didn't know how to spell French correctly, and, he added, "D'ailleurs les vers sont médiocres."

90. *Severnye Cvety na 1831 god*, 262.

91. *Ibid.*, 266–68.

92. *Severnye Cvety na 1832 god*, 39.

93. See below for a discussion of Alexander Rotchev's translation of this same work in *Northern Flowers for 1829*.

94. See the appendix of authors and contributions for the particular titles Verderevsky gave his works in *Northern Flowers*.

95. Fyodor Tyutchev (1803–73) did appear in various almanacs of the late twenties and early thirties, and Pushkin published a distinguished collection of his poems in the *Contemporary* in 1836 (signed only with the poet's initials), but it wasn't until 1850 that Nikolay Nekrasov's critical essay in the newly revived *Contemporary* established his permanent reputation.

96. See notes to *Polnoe sobranie sočinenij F. I. Tjutčeva, s kritiko-biografičeskim očerkom V. Ja. Brjusova* (S.-Peterburg, 1913), p. 428. Strangely, Briusov seems to have forgotten that Tyutchev's name appeared in *Northern Flowers* by error; in his introduction to this edition he notes Delvig's almanac among those periodicals in which Tyutchev's early works appeared (p. 12). Smirnov-Sokolsky, in *Russkie literaturnye al'manaxi i sborniki XVIII–XIX vv.* (Moskva, 1965), perpetuates the error in giving the contents of the 1827 almanac (p. 128).

97. *Severnye Cvety na 1829 god*, 141.

98. The group included Vissarion Belinsky and Konstantin Aksakov. At the University of Moscow Stankevich studied under several of those professors with whom Delvig's almanac was then engaged in literary polemics, including Mikhail Kachenovsky, Professor of Russian History and editor of the *Messenger of Europe*, Mikhail Pogodin, Professor of General History and editor of the *Moscow Herald*, and Stepan Shevyrev, Professor of Russian Literature (and contributor to *Northern Flowers*). Shevyrev, who had been associated with the Lovers of Wisdom society, may have influenced Stankevich's interest in German philosophy. For an interesting work in English which thoroughly reexamines Stankevich's presumed influence, see Edward J. Brown, *Stankevich and His Moscow Circle 1830–1840* (Stanford, 1966). The author states that Stankevich's poetry was "worthless" (p. 58).

99. Karolina Pavlova (1807–93) established her reputation at the end of the thirties.

100. *Severnye Cvety na 1829 god*, 181.

101. Puškin, *Pis'ma*, II, p. 58.

102. The fourth was Maria Lisitsyna, who was not a contributor to *Northern Flowers*.

103. *Severnye Cvety na 1831 god*, 90–91.

104. Puškin, *Pis'ma*, II, p. 206.

105. *Severnye Cvety na 1832 god*, 93. Smirnov-Sokolsky supports my contention that these works are indeed by Timasheva (pp. 169 and 170).

106. A number of this circle were active in the Lovers of Wisdom society.

107. See Chapter IV.

108. Pushkin's "An Epistle to V., Author of *A Satire on Gam-*

blers" ["Poslanie k V., sočinitelju satiry na igrokov"], which was published anonymously in *Northern Bee*, was accompanied by Bulgarin's malicious comment, *ex ungue leonem*. Velikopolsky took this epistle as a personal attack, but later the matter was cleared up. See Modzalevsky's notes for a full discussion of the controversy (Puškin, *Pis'ma*, II, pp. 283–86).

109. See A. P. Mogiljanskij, "Puškin i M. A. Jakovlev," *Puškin i ego vremja* (Lenigrad, 1962), pp. 270–73.

VI. The Prose in *Northern Flowers*

1. Pushkin's "An Excerpt from A. S. Pushkin's Letter to D." appeared even earlier, in the 1826 issue. This contribution belongs to the genre of travel notes and is presumably non-fiction.
2. *Severnye Cvety na 1827 god*, 97.
3. *Severnye Cvety na 1826 god*, 211.
4. *Ibid.*, 206.
5. *Ibid.*. 200.
6. *Severnye Cvety na 1830 god*, 116–17.
7. *Ibid.*, 150–52.
8. *Severnye Cvety na 1825 god*, 116.
9. *Ibid.*, 118.
10. *Severnye Cvety na 1829 god*, 233–34.
11. D. V. Venevitinov, *Polnoe sobranie sočinenij* (Moskva-Leningrad, 1934), p. 172.
12. The Academia edition reproduces this preface (73 ff.).
13. *Severnye Cvety na 1828 god*, 206–7.
14. See Chapter II for additional information.
15. *Severnye Cvety na 1825 god*, 100–103.
16. *Ibid.*, 104–8.
17. *Severnye Cvety na 1830 god*, 223.
18. *Severnye Cvety na 1826 god*, 225–26.
19. *Severnye Cvety na 1825 god*, 172.
20. *Severnye Cvety na 1827 god*, 118–19.
21. *Ibid.*, 40–41.
22. *Ibid.*, 36–37.
23. *Severnye Cvety na 1826 god*, 101–2.
24. *Ibid.*, 105.
25. See Puškin, *Pis'ma*, pod red. V. L. Modzalevskogo (Moskva-Leningrad, 1926–35), I, p. 381.

26. *Severnye Cvety na 1827 god,* 134–35.
27. *Ibid.,* 145.
28. *Istorija Gosudarstva Rossijskogo* (Sanktpeterburg, 1852), IX, pp. 258–65.
29. *Severnye Cvety na 1828 god,* 100.
30. *Istorija Gosudarstva Rossijskogo,* IX, p. 261.
31. *Severnye Cvety na 1832 god,* 1–2. The work, incidentally, had not previously been published.
32. *Ibid.,* 46.
33. *Ibid.,* 38–39.
34. Mathematicians will note that these fractions total only fifty-nine sixtieths, but the fractions are quite close enough for a rough estimate.
35. One may disagree with the gross categories on which these statements are based. If one lumps criticism, travel accounts, and lettres together, then obviously nonfiction occupies about two-thirds of the almanac's prose works. It is also true that that there were almost half again as many individual contributions here considered as lettres than individual fictional works. Be that as it may, it is not without significance that the almanac, which at first ignored fiction, gave it a substantial representation from 1828 on.
36. In transliteration: Z——ij
37. *Severnye Cvety na 1827 god,* 66–67.
38. *Ibid.,* 74.
39. This may have been the composition of Mikhail Pavlovich Zagorsky, a poet and translator whose Russian version of Schiller's "Der Handschuh" appeared in the first issue of *Northern Flowers.* Born in 1804, he died in 1824 just after completing his studies in the Historico-Philological Faculty of the University of Petersburg. He was a member of the Free Society of Lovers of Russian Iiterature, and a number of his works appeared in leading journals and almanacs of the twenties. The literary interests and tastes indicated by his translations and original works coincide with those expressed in "The Light Brown Tress." However, if he actually were the author of this work, it is strange that Delvig would have not indicated this by printing his full name at its conclusion, the more so that it was a posthumous publication. See Puškin, *Pis'ma,* I, pp. 534–35.
40. *Severnye Cvety na 1829 god,* 214.
41. *Ibid.,* 186.

42. A. I. Del'vig, *Moi vospominanija*, (Moska, 1912–13), I, p. 158.
43. Pisnaja, "Fabula 'Uedinennogo domika na Vasil'evskom,'" *Puškin i ego sovremenniki*, XXXI–XXXII (1927), 19–24.
44. *Poljarnaja Zvezda* (Moskva-Leningrad, 1960), p. 928.
45. *Severnye Cvetyr na 1828 god.* 178–79.
46. *Ibid.*, 275.
47. See my study, "Lermontov's *Shtoss: Hoax or Literary Credo?*" *Slavic Review* XXI (June, 1962), 282–83.
48. See V. F. Odoevskij, *Povesti i rasskazy* (Moskva, 1959), p. 456.
49. *Severnye Cvety na 1831 god*, 195.
50. *Ibid.*, 108–9.
51. V. F. Odoevskij, *Povesti i rasskazy*, p. 459.
52. *Severnye Cvety na 1832 god*, 48.
53. For *Russian Nights* Odoevsky reworked both stories. "Beethoven's Last Quartet" underwent merely some minor stylistic changes, but "Opere del Cavaliere Giambattista Piranesi" was extensively altered: the epigraph was removed, a new and considerably longer introduction was provided, and the setting changed from Petersburg to Naples. Compare *Northern Flowers'* versions with later texts in V. F. Odoevskij. *Povesti i rasskazy*.
54. *Severnye Cvety na 1832 god*, 62–63.
55. *Severnye Cvety na 1827 god*, 172–74.
56. *Ibid.*, 159.
57. *Ibid.*, 193.
58. *Ibid.*
59. *Ibid.*, 210.
60. *Ibid.*, 208.
61. *Ibid.*, 198–200.
62. *Ibid.*, 159.
63. Balzac may have been a source of this feature. See my "Lermontov and Balzac," *American Contributions to the Fifth International Congress of Slavists* (The Hague, 1964), 233–58.
64. Pushkin consistently referred to his drama as a "romantic tragedy." See my article, "Pushkin's Concept of Romanticism," *Studies in Romanticism, III* (Autumn, 1963), 24–41.
65. "D. N. Sadovnikov pišet: 'Vymyslom Gusara Puškin, po slovam V. D. Komovskogo, objazan Orestu Somovu. Smotrite ego kievskie ved'my v Novosel'e.' pišet Komovskij A. M. Jazykovu" (Puškin, *Pis'ma*, III, p. 649). See also V. V. Dani-

love, "Istočnik stixotvorenija A. A. Puškina 'Gusar'," *Russkij Filologičeskij Vestnik.* LXIV (1910), 243–52.

66. This story was originally destined for Bestuzhev's almanac *Little Star for 1826.* Somov gave it to the *Neva Almanac* after *Little Star* was suppressed.

67. For a period of several years Somov intended to create a novel dealing with the legendary Ukrainian hero Garkusha. In addition to the two stories already mentioned, he subsequently published episodes from the life of this personality in *Son of the Fatherland,* 1829, Nos. 23–25, and in the almanac *Dawn* in 1830. Although the present author has criticized the work which appeared in *Northern Flowers* from the point of view of its successfulness as a short story, he would have had to make many of the same negative evaluations had he treated the story as part of a longer work. Since Somov never realized his intention, and, in fact, did not really unify the episodes relating to Garkusha which he did publish, we are justified in treating the tale here considered as a short story.

68. The earliest example with which I am acquainted occurs in Balzac's *Grandeur et Décadence de César Birotteau,* first published in November, 1837.

69. *Severnye Cvety na 1828 god,* 246–47.

70. See Gleb Struve, "*Monologue intérieur:* The Origins of the Formula and the First Statement of Its Possibilities," *PMLA,* LXIX (December, 1954), 1101–11.

71. *Severnye Cvety na 1830 god,* 215.

72. *Ibid.,* 195–97.

73. *Severnye Cvety na 1832 god,* 238.

74. *Ibid.,* 153–54.

75. *Ibid.,* 238.

76. *Ibid.,* 173–75.

77. *Ibid.,* 262.

78. Alexander Nikitenko (1804–77) was born a serf, but owing to fortuitous circumstances he received an education. Through the patronage of Alexander Golitsyn he was able to attend the University of Petersburg, and subsequently he taught economics and literature at that institution. In addition, he lectured on literature at a number of Petersburg schools for advanced study and also served as a censor. His diary provides interesting information about personalities and cultural activities in Russia during the period of *Northern Flowers*' publication. Many of the remarks about the condi-

tion of contemporary society in this diary are reflected in "Leon, or Idealism." See A. V. Nikitenko, *Dnevnik v trex tomax* (n.p., 1955), I.

79. *Severnye Cvety na 1832 god*, 269–70.
80. Reference is made here to Gogol's and Pushkin's unfinished historical novels, "The Hetman" and "The Moor of Peter the Great," not *Taras Bulba* and *The Captain's Daughter*, published in 1835 and 1836 respectively.
81. See Vasilij Gippius, *Gogol'* (Leningrad, 1924). p. 71.
82. *Severnye Cvety na 1831 god*, 249.

VII. Afterword

1. In this connection it is interesting to note that even Delvig's and Somov's *Literary Gazette*, which appeared every five days and was exclusively devoted to literature, presented at most two short poems per issue.
2. Quoted in A. Myškovskaja, *Literaturnye problemy puškinskoj pory* (*Moskva*, 1934), p. 20.
3. I do not wholly accept A. Myshkovskaya's statement that the years 1823 (when *Polar Star* first appeared) to 1832 (when *Northern Flowers* ceased publication) "completely coincide with the moment of the dawn of romantic poetry and its sunset" (*ibid.*, p. 19). However, her generalization does further stress the significance of the period.

INDEX